# Choices in a Chaotic Campaign

In *Choices in a Chaotic Campaign*, Kim L. Fridkin and Patrick J. Kenney explore the dynamic nature of citizens' beliefs and behaviors in response to the historic 2020 US presidential campaign. In today's political environment where citizens can effortlessly gather information, it is important to move beyond standard political characteristics and consider the impact of preexisting psychological predispositions. Fridkin and Kenney argue that these predispositions influence assessments of campaign events and issues, and ultimately alter citizens' voting decisions. The book relies on data from an original three-wave panel study of over 4,000 people interviewed in September, October, and immediately after Election Day in November 2020. The timing of the surveys provides the analytical leverage to explore how views of the campaign alter citizens' impressions of the candidates. The book demonstrates that expanding the relevant citizen characteristics to include psychological predispositions increases our ability to understand how campaigns influence voters' decisions at the ballot box.

Kim L. Fridkin is Foundation Professor of Political Science at Arizona State University. With Patrick J. Kenney, she is the author of *Taking Aim at Attack Advertising* (2019) and *The Changing Face of Representation: The Gender of U.S. Senators and Constituent Communications* (2014).

Patrick J. Kenney is Foundation Professor of Political Science and Executive Vice Provost at Arizona State University. With Kim L. Fridkin, he is the author of *Taking Aim at Attack Advertising* (2019) and *The Changing Face of Representation: The Gender of U.S. Senators and Constituent Communications* (2014).

# Choices in a Chaotic Campaign

*Understanding Citizens' Decisions
in the 2020 Election*

### KIM L. FRIDKIN
*Arizona State University*

### PATRICK J. KENNEY
*Arizona State University*

Shaftesbury Road, Cambridge CB2 8EA, United Kingdom

One Liberty Plaza, 20th Floor, New York, NY 10006, USA

477 Williamstown Road, Port Melbourne, VIC 3207, Australia

314–321, 3rd Floor, Plot 3, Splendor Forum, Jasola District Centre, New Delhi – 110025, India

103 Penang Road, #05-06/07, Visioncrest Commercial, Singapore 238467

Cambridge University Press is part of Cambridge University Press & Assessment, a department of the University of Cambridge.

We share the University's mission to contribute to society through the pursuit of education, learning and research at the highest international levels of excellence.

www.cambridge.org
Information on this title: www.cambridge.org/9781009445917

DOI: 10.1017/9781009445863

© Kim L. Fridkin and Patrick J. Kenney 2024

This publication is in copyright. Subject to statutory exception and to the provisions of relevant collective licensing agreements, no reproduction of any part may take place without the written permission of Cambridge University Press & Assessment.

First published 2024

*A catalogue record for this publication is available from the British Library*

*A Cataloging-in-Publication data record for this book is available from the Library of Congress*

ISBN 978-1-009-44591-7 Hardback
ISBN 978-1-009-44587-0 Paperback

Cambridge University Press & Assessment has no responsibility for the persistence or accuracy of URLs for external or third-party internet websites referred to in this publication and does not guarantee that any content on such websites is, or will remain, accurate or appropriate.

*We dedicate this book to the memory of our parents*
*Barbara and Allan*
*Joe and Mary Jane*

# Contents

| | | |
|---|---|---|
| *List of Figures* | | *page* ix |
| *List of Tables* | | xi |
| *Preface* | | xiii |
| 1 | Understanding How Campaigns Matter | 1 |
| 2 | "A Hot Mess inside a Dumpster Fire inside a Train Wreck": Understanding the Impact of the First Presidential Debate | 37 |
| 3 | The Priming of COVID-19 during the Campaign: The Consequences of Trump's Coronavirus Diagnosis | 63 |
| 4 | Protests against Police Brutality: How Attitudes about Racial Injustice and Policing Affected Campaign 2020 | 92 |
| 5 | "A Rigged Election": How Views about Election Integrity Altered the Campaign | 122 |
| 6 | How the Campaign Shapes Voters' Decisions about the Candidates | 147 |
| 7 | The Impact of Campaign Messages on the Decision to Vote | 164 |
| 8 | How Campaign 2020 Matters | 193 |
| *Appendix* | | 211 |
| *References* | | 225 |
| *Index* | | 253 |

# Figures

| | | |
|---|---|---|
| 1.1 | How people's predispositions influence the consequences of campaigns | page 13 |
| 2.1 | Who won the debate by partisanship | 42 |
| 2.2 | Debate performance rating by partisanship | 43 |
| 2.3 | Debate performance rating by racial resentment | 51 |
| 2.4 | Impact of the first debate on October evaluations of the candidates | 59 |
| 3.1 | The most important issue facing the country | 72 |
| 3.2 | COVID-19 as the most important issue facing the country by partisanship | 73 |
| 3.3 | Impact of Trump's ability to handle COVID-19 on his feeling thermometer scores in September and October | 89 |
| 4.1 | Race relations as the most important problem in 2020 | 94 |
| 4.2 | Support for protests against police brutality during the 2020 campaign | 96 |
| 4.3 | Support for police during the 2020 campaign | 96 |
| 4.4 | Impact of support for social justice protests and support for police on feeling thermometer ratings of Trump and Biden in October | 117 |
| 5.1 | Weekly mentions of "rigged" election by Donald Trump | 124 |
| 5.2 | Partisan differences in confidence in the integrity of the 2020 election | 126 |
| 5.3 | Difference in confidence in the election by vote intention | 129 |
| 5.4 | How partisan news attention influences confidence in candidates' ability to ensure the integrity of US elections | 136 |

| | | |
|---|---|---|
| 6.1 | Impact of worries about COVID-19 on the feeling thermometer ratings of Trump and Biden in November | 154 |
| 6.2 | Impact of support for social justice protests on the feeling thermometer ratings of Trump and Biden in November | 155 |
| 7.1 | Turnout rates, 1920–2020 | 165 |

# Tables

1.1 Correlations between party identification and
 psychological predispositions                                    page 26
1.2 Comparison of 2020 panel survey with census data
 and Gallup survey data                                                28
1.3 Information about the panel survey design                          29
2.1 Ordinary least squares regression predicting assessments
 of the candidates' debate performance                                 48
2.2 OLS regression predicting "who won" the debate                     53
2.3 Impact of the first debate on overall evaluations of
 the presidential candidates                                           57
3.1 Explaining citizens' worries about COVID-19                        80
3.2 Impact of worries about COVID-19 on Trump's
 ability to deal with the pandemic                                     85
3.3 Impact of COVID-19 views on presidential approval
 of Donald Trump                                                       86
3.4 Impact of views about COVID-19 on overall
 evaluations of the presidential candidates                            88
4.1 Explaining support for social justice protests                    104
4.2 Explaining support for police                                     110
4.3 Impact of views of protests and police on overall
 evaluations of the presidential candidates                           115
5.1 Understanding people's confidence in the integrity
 of the election                                                      131
5.2 Explaining confidence in Biden's and Trump's ability
 to maintain the integrity of the election                            135

| | | |
|---|---|---|
| 5.3 | Impact of the integrity of the election on overall evaluations of the presidential candidates | 140 |
| 6.1 | Ordinary least squares regression predicting overall evaluations of the presidential candidates in November | 153 |
| 6.2 | MLM explaining changes in overall evaluations of the presidential candidates (September to November) | 158 |
| 6.3 | Multilevel logit modeling explaining changes in vote choice (September to November) | 161 |
| 7.1 | Multilevel logit model predicting turnout | 177 |
| 7.2 | Multilevel logit model predicting convenience voting | 184 |
| 8.1 | Impact of psychological predispositions on assessments of campaign events and issues | 197 |

# Preface

This book on the 2020 US presidential campaign represents a departure for us. Our collaboration to date, lasting more than thirty years, has been focused primarily on senate elections and negative campaigning. The current project began as an exploration into the impact of negative advertising during the 2020 presidential election. After launching a three-wave panel survey during the fall campaign, we began conducting some analyses and realized that psychological predispositions, like conspiracy thinking, authoritarianism, and conflict avoidance, played a powerful role in determining people's assessments of the central elements of the 2020 presidential campaign. Intrigued, we began to develop a theory to explore how psychological predispositions, along with partisan proclivities, influence people's views of campaign issues and events, ultimately influencing voting decisions. We develop our theory, *the citizen-centered theory of campaigns*, in our introductory chapter and present evidence supporting aspects of the theory in the following empirical chapters. We demonstrate that examining psychological predispositions, alongside traditional political factors, improves our ability to understand how campaigns influence voters' decisions not only at the ballot box but also regarding whether to go to the polls at all.

We relied on an original panel survey to test the citizen-centered theory of campaigns. The first wave occurred during the first three weeks of September; the second wave was conducted within a week of the first presidential debate and a couple of days after President Trump was diagnosed with COVID-19; and the final wave of the panel was completed between November 4 and November 6, 2020. In all, we collected survey data from 4,311 respondents, with 1,040 respondents completing each of the three waves of the panel survey.

Two talented graduate students improved this project along the way. First, Allie Williams did an excellent job helping with the construction and implementation of the panel survey. Second, Trudy Horsting's meticulous editing of our book manuscript was extremely valuable. We thank, too, Jan Box-Steffensmeier for her data analytical advice and for her friendship. We are also grateful for the generous financial support associated with our Arizona State University Foundation Professorships, allowing us to fund our panel survey.

We are pleased to have our book published at Cambridge University Press. Rachel Blaifeder, our editor, has been supportive of the project since our initial discussions at the American Political Science Association meeting in Seattle in 2021. We are especially grateful for Rachel's persistence in securing reviewers during the difficult post-COVID period and her guidance on how to improve the manuscript via the thoughtful reviewers.

We dedicate this book to our families. First and foremost, Kim is grateful to her husband, Bob, who patiently listened to her discussion of this book project over countless dinners, even offering fruitful ideas for additional analysis. Kim is also grateful to her daughters, Jennifer and Melissa, who inspire her every day. Pat, as always, is thankful to his wife, Sally, of forty-three years for her gracious and consistent support for all of his academic writing and administrative work. Pat's children, Jessica, Sean, Michael, Mary, as well as their spouses and our five grandchildren, Mason, Joseph, Ellie Grace, Juliette, Michael who are the joys of our lives.

# 1

# Understanding How Campaigns Matter

This book examines the time-honored yet unsettled question of whether campaigns ultimately shape citizens' assessments of the competing candidates. To be sure, the historic 2020 US presidential campaign is a fascinating setting to explore this question. This election captured the attention and interest of tens of millions of Americans and people across the globe. The number of citizens who voted in 2020 was a high-water mark for contemporary US presidential elections, with over 159 million ballots cast, representing over 66 percent of the voting-eligible population.[1] The 2020 presidential election was also the costliest election in US history, more than doubling the expenditures in the 2016 presidential election, with spending topping $5.7 billion.[2]

The political context of the election was dramatic. The entire presidential campaign was conducted during the COVID-19 pandemic. The incumbent president, Donald Trump, not only contracted the virus but was hospitalized on October 2, 2020, for three days, generating a national and international media frenzy. A *New York Times* article published on October 2 captured the intensity and anxiety of the moment:

President Trump was hospitalized on Friday evening after learning he had the coronavirus and experiencing what aides called coughing, congestion and fever, throwing the nation's leadership into uncertainty and destabilizing an already volatile campaign only 32 days before the election. Mr. Trump was flown to Walter Reed National Military Medical Center after being given an experimental antibody treatment as the White House rushed to cope with a commander-in-chief

[1] www.electproject.org/2020g
[2] www.opensecrets.org/news/2021/02/2020-cycle-cost-14p4-billion-doubling-16/

infected by a virus that has killed more than 208,000 people in the United States. (Baker and Haberman, 2020a)

President Trump was released on October 5, followed by a barrage of coverage focusing on his treatment and recovery. By the eve of the election, the United States led the world in cases and deaths due to COVID-19, with over 9 million Americans having contracted COVID-19 and more than 232,000 deaths from the illness.

The COVID-19 pandemic also plunged the nation and much of the globe into a recession. The Dow Jones Index, measuring the stock performance of the thirty largest companies on the US stock exchange, lost 37 percent of its value between February 12 and March 23. By April, the market began to recover, and by Election Day, stocks were trading in near record territory. The pandemic dramatically slowed economic growth by April 2020, halting a strong economic first quarter. But the economy began to improve during the summer and early fall. For instance, the percent change in the growth of the gross domestic product (GDP) from the first to second quarter of 2020 dropped by over 30 percent, representing the biggest contraction ever recorded, but the GDP rebounded in the third quarter. Finally, the unemployment rate increased from 3.5 percent in February to 14.8 percent in April, with over twenty million people out of work and wiping out a decade or more of employment gains. By October, the unemployment rate had dropped to 6.9 percent.[3] The COVID-19 pandemic produced an economic rollercoaster that Americans would ride from early spring through the fall of 2020.

The summer of 2020 saw the largest and most intense racial unrest in the nation since 1968 in the aftermath of the assassination of Martin Luther King. In 2020, the protests were ignited by the murder of George Floyd at the hands of the Minneapolis police over the Memorial Day weekend. Protests, demonstrations, marches, and gatherings took place across the nation, involving millions of people. The largest single day of protests may have occurred on June 6, 2020, with approximately 500,000 people in the streets in almost 550 cities and towns from coast to coast (Buchanan, Bui, and Patel, 2020). In total, as many as 26 million Americans participated in demonstrations and protests across the summer. While the vast majority of social justice marches were peaceful, property was vandalized and destroyed in multiple cities and thousands of protesters were arrested. The COVID-19 pandemic, a volatile economic recession, and racial unrest set the landscape for the 2020 general election contest. American citizens were

---

[3] www.bbc.com/news/world-45827430

intensely polarized around the two parties' nominees, holding strong preferences for their preferred candidates (French, 2020; Sides, Tausanovitch, and Vavreck, 2022). To heighten partisan anxieties further, tracking polls during the fall campaign suggested that Joe Biden was leading, but given the polling errors in the 2016 election predicting a comfortable Clinton victory, the status of the race was difficult to assess (NPR, 2020).

The highly polarized environment produced a set of unusual incidents. For example, the first presidential debate was intensely negative and unruly, with the moderator unable to keep order during the ninety-minute fracas. The behavior of the candidates led to unprecedented changes in the debate rules prior to the second debate, with the Commission on Presidential Debates deciding to mute the microphone of the candidate not speaking in order to minimize interruptions. Second, the incumbent president openly questioned the integrity of the election as the campaign moved toward Election Day. Sensing he was behind, Trump began to sow doubt regarding the security of the electoral process, repeatedly alleging that mail voting was fraught with fraud. While he had made allegations about voter fraud during the 2016 campaign, the frequency and intensity of claims was significantly greater in the 2020 campaign (Graham, 2020; Kessler and Rizzo, 2020). Interwoven with Trump's assertions about fraudulent ballots was his refusal to say he would accept the results of the election if he lost (Kapur, 2020).[4]

Electoral campaigns play a fundamental role in a representative democracy, helping citizens make decisions about their future leaders. Did events and issues during the 2020 presidential campaign influence people's views of the candidates, affecting their ultimate voting decisions? In *The Bitter End*, Sides, Tausanovitch, and Vavreck (2022: 245) show that the 2020 campaign did not sway voters but "intensified long-term trends toward greater polarization and calcification." In another ambitious examination of the 2020 campaign, Levendusky et al. (2023) show that different types of voters were exposed to different informational environments. Voters who were unwavering in their choice for president were often safely ensconced in echo chambers, reinforcing their preferences. In contrast, wavering voters often experienced a more complex and diverse media environment. By linking voters with their information environments, Levendusky et al. (2023) show how central issues of the campaign, like Trump's handling of the COVID-19 pandemic, affected voters' decisions.

---

[4] During the final presidential debate in 2016, Trump said he might not accept the results of the election if he felt it was rigged against him (Healy and Martin, 2016).

In our examination of the 2020 election, we are interested in exploring three key questions: How do citizens interpret salient issues and events during the months of the fall election? What are the different types of lenses utilized by citizens when they view and assess these events and issues? And do these assessments of events and issues shape how citizens evaluate the competing candidates and make choices between the candidates? We develop an original theory to help us answer these questions: the *citizen-centered theory of campaigns*.

We argue that the contemporary media landscape provides accessible, cheap, and numerous opportunities for citizens to follow the candidates and the campaign. This environment allows citizens to be more active in their search for information, increasing the importance of citizen characteristics, including psychological predispositions, when assessing the candidates, campaign events, and campaign issues. We hypothesize that psychological predispositions provide a lens for potential voters to understand and interpret the events and issues of the campaign. We will show that people's psychological predispositions consistently and powerfully influence views of the campaign and candidates, even taking into account people's partisan proclivities, their views of the economy, and their attention to partisan news sources. We turn first to review the state of the literature on "campaign effects" before elaborating on the theoretical framework guiding our investigation.

## HOW CAMPAIGNS MATTER: THE STATE OF THE LITERATURE

The first systematic study of campaign effects was conducted by Paul Lazarsfeld, Berelson, and Gaudet when they studied the 1940 US presidential election between President Franklin Roosevelt (Democrat) and Wendell Willkie (Republican). This election, too, was a historic presidential election as Franklin Roosevelt was the first president to seek a third term. After witnessing the rise of Hitler and the persuasiveness of propaganda in Nazi Germany during the 1930s, the researchers were interested in examining the impact of the mass media in presidential campaigns in the United States. Relying on an innovative and ambitious design, Lazarsfeld, Berelson, and Gaudet (1948) conducted a panel study of 600 people from Erie County, Ohio. These panel respondents were interviewed each month for the seven months leading up to the November presidential election.

The results of the study, reported in *The People's Choice*, found that newspapers and radio did not have a profound impact on voters' decisions.

## How Campaigns Matter: The State of the Literature 5

Instead, the news media largely reinforced preexisting predispositions. For example, Lazarsfeld, Berelson, and Gaudet report that over half of the panel respondents had decided on a candidate by June of the election year and only 8 percent of the sample switched their vote choice from one candidate to another during the course of the campaign.

While the findings of the study disconfirm the hypodermic needle theory of communication (i.e., people passively accept media messages), the authors maintain that campaigns do matter for the outcome of the election.[5] They argue that "political communication served the important purposes of preserving citizens' prior decisions instead of initiating new decisions. It kept the partisans 'in line' by reassuring them in their vote decision; it reduced defection from the ranks" (Lazarsfeld, Berelson, and Gaudet (1948: 87). In other words, the authors find that campaigns activate preexisting preferences.[6] For voters who are undecided or unsure of their voting decision, the campaign can activate predispositions.

The lack of persuasive effects described in the Columbia studies were later reinforced by research showing that presidential election outcomes can be predicted by factors in place well before the start of the general election campaign, such as the state of the economy and the popularity of the president (e.g., Hibbs, 2000; Lewis-Beck and Rice, 1992; Rosenstone, 1983; Tufte, 1978). For example, Gelman and King (1993) find that fundamental conditions (e.g., economic conditions) can predict the results of the election more accurately than polls taken during the campaign.

In addition, studies looking at contemporary elections have identified "minimal effects" of campaigns. For example, Coppock, Hill, and Vavreck (2020), examined the impact of nearly fifty political advertisements in a series of unique experiments over the course of the 2016 presidential election and find that these advertisements produce only small average effects on candidate favorability and vote choice.[7] Similarly, Kalla and Broockman (2018), conducted a meta-analysis of more than forty field experiments as well as designing and implementing their own field experiments prior to the 2016 election and find that, on average, campaign contact does not persuade voters. Aggarwal et al. (2023) utilized a massive field experiment involving two million people in five battleground states to examine whether an eight-month social media campaign altered turnout in the 2020 election. While the overall effect

---

[5] See Iyengar and Simon (2000) for a discussion of the hypodermic approach to persuasion.
[6] See also Berelson, Lazarsfeld, and McPhee's (1954) study of the 1948 presidential election.
[7] Also, see Coppock, Green, and Porter (2022) for similar small effects with digital advertising in the 2018 US midterm elections in Florida.

on turnout was effectively zero, the authors did find evidence for a small differential mobilization effect. That is, the advertising campaign had a small mobilizing effect among Biden leaners and a small demobilizing effect among Trump leaners.

Scholars, however, do not dispute that the influence of the fundamentals, such as the partisan distribution of the electorate and the economic health of the country, plays a key role in determining the outcome of elections. The fundamentals set the parameters for the presidential campaigns. More specifically, political campaigns are a mechanism where poorly informed voters learn about the contours of the election (e.g., how the state of the economy connects to their partisan predispositions). Vavreck (2009: 158) makes exactly this point when examining presidential elections from 1952 to 2008, saying, "The economy matters because the candidate who benefits from it talks about it a lot during the campaign and this makes voters more aware of the condition and this candidate's relationship to it." Precisely because campaigns send messages about key fundamentals, these factors become increasingly predictive of people's vote preferences as the campaign progresses (e.g., Campbell, 2008; Erikson and Wlezien, 2012; Gelman and King, 1993; Sides and Vavreck, 2014; Sides, Tausanovitch, and Vavreck, 2022).

In addition, a number of studies demonstrate that campaign events, like national nominating conventions and debates, can make a difference to voters (e.g., Hillygus and Shields, 2009; Holbrook, 1996; Panagopoulos, 2012; Shaw, 1999; Sides and Vavreck, 2014). For instance, Kenski, Hardy, and Jamieson (2010) and Johnston, Hagen, and Jamieson (2004), relying on large rolling cross sections of respondents over the length of the campaign, find voters respond in a systematic way to specific campaign events. Presidential debates, especially one-sided affairs, can alter the fundamentals of an electoral contest (Panagopoulos, 2012; Shaw, 1999; Weinschenk and Panagopoulos, 2016). For example, Hillygus and Shields (2009), when examining the dynamics of the 2000 presidential election, find that 16 percent of cross-pressured partisans (e.g., citizens who hold policy positions incongruent with their partisanship) and 20 percent of independents changed their vote preference after the presidential debates. Both presidential debates and national conventions can be consequential because citizens' attention is focused on the candidates and the campaign for a sustained period of time and citizens are likely to learn about the candidates' policy positions, personal characteristics, and issue priorities.

Political advertisements may also influence citizens' choices by providing information about the competing candidates (e.g., Brader, 2005;

Fridkin and Kenney, 2019; Huber and Arceneaux, 2007; Valentino, Hutchings, and Williams, 2004). For example, Huber and Arceneaux (2007), exploiting a natural experiment in the 2000 presidential election and matching records of locally broadcast presidential advertising with the opinions of National Annenberg Election Survey respondents, find that paid campaign advertising is successful in producing changes in vote preferences. More recently, Sides, Vavreck, and Warshaw (2022) look at the relationship between televised political advertisements and vote share between 2000 and 2018. They find that political advertising in presidential elections has a modest but significant impact on vote share, with advertising effects growing in strength in down-ballot contests. Some scholars also demonstrate that direct mail, personal canvassing, and phone calls can be persuasive (e.g., Arceneaux, 2007; Doherty and Adler, 2014).

More generally, the messages being sent by the candidates, political parties, and interest groups, as well as the coverage of these communications via traditional and online news, can inform voters about the competing candidates. For instance, numerous scholars demonstrate that voters learn about the issue stances of candidates during electoral campaigns, ultimately influencing voting decisions (e.g., Alvarez, 1998; Conover and Feldman, 1989; Dalager, 1996; Franklin, 1991; Holbrook, 1999). Alvarez and Glasgow (1997) use panel data from the 1976 and 1980 presidential elections as well as content analysis of campaign coverage and find that voters become better informed about the positions of candidates on a number of issues and these changes are related to the information flow of the campaigns. In addition, political campaigns can shape people's assessments of the candidates' character, leadership, empathy, and integrity, and these assessments influence overall evaluations of the candidates and eventual vote choice (e.g., Fridkin and Kenney, 2011; Popkin, 2012; Peterson, 2009).

Political campaigns are also influential in changing people's priorities among political issues. Candidates compete to set the public's agenda on specific issues that favor their candidacy. In the 1992 presidential election between President George H. W. Bush and his Democratic challenger, Bill Clinton, the Clinton campaign emphasized the country's economic woes during the general election campaign. In fact, in order to keep the campaign staff focused on the central issues of the campaign, Clinton's campaign manager, James Carville, posted a sign in the campaign headquarters saying "It's the economy, stupid" (Bennett, 2013).[8] By focusing

---

[8] The posted sign also included the phrases "Change versus more of the same" and "Don't forget about health care."

on the economy, an issue that would favor Clinton over Bush, the Clinton campaign sought to "prime" voters to think about the economy when evaluating the competing candidates. More generally, during campaigns, opposing candidates seek to adjust the importance voters attach to different considerations by emphasizing issues (or personal traits) that benefit their candidacy (Hillygus, 2010).

Several studies demonstrate the importance of priming specific considerations during political campaigns. For instance, researchers show that the impact of partisanship on candidate preferences increases as Election Day approaches (e.g., Erikson and Wlezien, 2012; Levendusky et al., 2023; Sides and Vavreck, 2014; Sides, Tausanovitch, and Vavreck, 2022). The campaign can also prime ideology (e.g., Hillygus and Shields, 2009), specific policy issues (e.g., Kenski, Hardy, and Jamieson, 2010), personal traits (e.g., Druckman, 2004), and affect (e.g., Kühne et al., 2011).

Thus far, we have considered how campaigns via political events, the news media, and campaign messages influence citizens' understanding of the candidates' issue positions, personal characteristics, and ideology. And we have discussed how campaigns influence the criteria voters think about when evaluating competing candidates. Campaigns, in addition, can influence voters by increasing (or decreasing) their likelihood of participating in the election. An extensive number of sophisticated field experiments examine how contacts by campaign organizations can prompt citizens to go to the polls on Election Day. A recent review of field experiments by Green and Gerber (2019) suggests that personal contact is most effective. For example, the authors estimate that door-to-door canvassing increases turnout by about 2.5 percentage points. Phone banking is less influential, but volunteer phone calls are more effective than commercial phone banking. Automated phone messages, in contrast, are ineffective.

Moving beyond traditional modes of mobilization, Malhotra et al. (2011) conducted two field experiments to explore whether text messages urging people to vote increase turnout. In both experiments, the authors find that text messages significantly increase mobilization, and these effects are most pronounced for habitual voters in low salient elections.[9] More recently, Mann (2021) conducted a field experiment where participants were randomly assigned to receive a mobilization treatment where they were reminded by a political chatbot (Resistbot) to vote.

---

[9] Similarly, Shaw, Dun, and Heise (2022), relying on a field experiment in three competitive congressional districts in California in 2018, also find text messages increase turnout.

These participants were also provided with information on polling locations. Mann finds that the experimental treatment increases turnout by nearly 2 percentage points.

The negativity of campaign messages, too, influences turnout in elections (e.g., Ansolabehere and Iyengar, 1999; Kahn and Kenney, 1999). A review of the literature suggests that negative messages including relevant information about the targeted candidate can increase participation in elections (e.g., Finkel and Geer, 1998) while negative messages packed with uncivil and irrelevant attacks may decrease turnout (e.g., Fridkin and Kenney, 2019).[10] Further, the important issues of the day may push people to the polls. For example, Burden and Wichowsky (2014), analyzing county-level data from 1976 to 2008, find that economic discontent mobilizes people to vote. In addition, polarization in people's views of the rival candidates increases people's likelihood of voting in an election (e.g., Abramowitz and Stone, 2006; Hetherington, 2008; Iyengar and Krupenkin, 2018).[11] Finally, research suggests that divisive primaries may affect participation in the general election (e.g., Fridkin et al., 2017). For example, Makse and Sokhey (2010), looking at voters in Ohio's Franklin County in 2008, find that Clinton primary voters participated less frequently in the fall campaign when compared to Obama primary voters.

In summary, the literature examining the impact of campaigns on voters indicates campaign communications and news media coverage are unlikely to persuade voters to switch from their existing preferences of one candidate to voting for another candidate. Further, fundamentals, such as the partisan distribution of the electorate, the state of the economy, and the popularity of the incumbent president, set the parameters for each electoral contest. However, events like presidential debates and national nominating conventions can influence views of the competing candidates and affect voting decisions. Further messages from the candidates, political parties, and the news media do inform voters about the candidates' policy positions, policy priorities, and personal characteristics. And campaign messages, via the candidates or the news media, can alter the criteria voters consider when evaluating the competing candidates. Finally, aspects of the campaign (e.g., mobilization messages, the

---

[10] Some scholars suggest that competitive campaigns will push people to the polls, but there is little evidence of a direct effect of the closeness of the race on turnout (e.g., Gerber et al., 2020). Instead, close contests lead campaign strategists to spend more money on mobilization efforts to encourage turnout (Cox and Munger, 1989).

[11] On the other hand, some research suggests that increases in polarization lead moderates to disengage from politics (e.g., Fiorina and Levendusky, 2006; Rogowski, 2014).

negativity of the campaign, salient issues, national crises) can encourage or discourage participation in the election. We turn next to articulating our theoretical expectations regarding how we expect campaigns to influence voters' decisions.

### CITIZEN-CENTERED THEORY OF CAMPAIGNS

With the literature as our anchor, we present a framework for understanding how people's predispositions influence interpretations of campaign events and issues, ultimately affecting evaluations of the competing candidates and vote choice. Citizens sit at the center of our theory. In today's media landscape, citizens take an active role in deciding what information they choose to acquire about candidates and campaigns (Arceneaux and Johnson, 2013). They can access a plethora of information widely and continuously via social media apps, internet sources, legacy news sources (e.g., newspapers, broadcast news), and partisan news outlets.[12] In a recent column in the *New York Times*, Frank Bruni makes precisely this point when he writes,

> Thanks to the sprawling real estate of cable television and the infinite expanse of the internet, we live in an age of so many information options, so many news purveyors, that we have an unprecedented ability to search out the one or ones that tell us precisely what we want to hear, for whatever reason we want to hear it. We needn't reckon with the truth. We can shop for it instead.[13]

Citizens' preexisting values and beliefs drive how they search and assimilate information during presidential elections. We have known for a long time that partisanship strongly influences how citizens view candidates during campaigns (e.g., Bartels, 2000, 2018; Campbell et al., 1960). The growth of partisan news outlets makes it easier for people to seek out partisan-congruent information, if they choose, thereby strengthening the impact of partisanship in contemporary campaigns (Levendusky et al., 2023; Sides, Tausanovitch, and Vavreck, 2022).

While people's political proclivities clearly influence the impact of campaigns, it is important to move beyond political predispositions and begin to systematically examine how psychological characteristics of

---

[12] More than nine in ten Americans have internet access, with 72 percent of adults using social media platforms, increasing the ease of acquiring information consistent with one's preexisting political attitudes. See the following PEW Research Center fact sheets for information about internet use and social media use. www.pewresearch.org/internet/fact-sheet/social-media/ www.pewresearch.org/internet/fact-sheet/internet-broadband/

[13] www.nytimes.com/2023/04/13/opinion/tucker-carlson-murdoch-fox.html

citizens influence their interpretation of electoral contests. There is widespread consensus among scholars that preexisting beliefs influence the assimilation of new information (e.g., Coppock, 2023; Gawronski, 2012; Jost, Baldassarri, and Druckman, 2022).[14] These preexisting beliefs may be driven by partisan proclivities as well as psychological predispositions. Further, these psychological and political characteristics influence people's receptiveness to different types of incoming information. In the end, people are a bundle of predispositions, and these predispositions will influence the acquisition and processing of new information.

To illustrate how psychological predispositions may influence the acquisition and interpretation of information, we consider people who believe in conspiracies. These individuals will be more likely to seek out information confirming their belief in conspiracies and will be more likely to dismiss reports that disconfirm their beliefs. For example, people suspicious about the safety of the COVID-19 vaccine may turn to YouTube to find out about possible side effects from the vaccine, including infertility and impotence. Similarly, these individuals may click on stories appearing on their Facebook feed reporting serious reactions to the COVID-19 vaccines and avoid other stories hailing the success of these vaccines. Further, since algorithms used by online platforms shower people with stories related to their initial searches (Barnhart, 2021; Finkel et al., 2020), concerns about the vaccines may be reinforced and accentuated by the plethora of stories disseminated to the screens of people who have previously searched for information on vaccine side effects. Finally, when confronted with information validating the safety of the COVID-19 vaccine, individuals may dismiss the evidence altogether, may be motivated to continue to search for confirmatory information, or may become more entrenched in their initial view about the vaccines (e.g., Glinitzer, Gummer, and Wagner, 2021; Ma, Dixon, and Hmielowski, 2019).

The idea that psychological predispositions may inform how citizens make decisions during campaigns is not new. More than sixty years ago, Lane (1955: 175) explained: "Each election, then, varies not only in the degree to which it evokes decisions determined by personality, but also with respect to the nature of the personality syndromes which are relevant." In fact, Lane found a relationship between authoritarian attitudes (versus equalitarian attitudes) and vote choice in the 1948 and 1952 presidential elections.

---

[14] While scholars disagree about the mechanism (i.e., motivated reasoning, Bayesian updating), they do not disagree that prior information influences the processing of incoming information (e.g., Coppock, 2023; Bullock, 2009; Druckman and McGrath, 2019; Gerber and Green, 1999; Redlawsk, 2002).

There are numerous examples exploring the link between psychological predispositions and vote choice. Kinder and Kam (2010) find that ethnocentrism, a deep-seated "psychological predisposition" rooted in tensions found in-group and out-group conflict, affected voters' assessments of McCain and Obama in the 2008 election. Uscinski et al. (2021), examining the 2020 election, identify an "antiestablishment dimension" of opinion (i.e., conspiracy thinking, populism, and Machiavellianism) that is orthogonal to the traditional left–right spectrum and associated with positive feelings toward Trump and Sanders but not related to views of Biden. Several scholars have examined the link between the Big Five Personality traits (i.e., extraversion, agreeableness, openness, conscientiousness, and neuroticism) and turnout in elections. For example, Mattila et al. (2011) find that extraversion and agreeableness increase participation, while Gerber et al. (2011) show that conscientiousness is negatively related to participation. Looking at vote choice in the 2004 presidential election, Barbaranelli et al. (2007) find that citizens with higher levels of agreeableness and openness are more likely to vote for the Democrat candidate, while conscientiousness and emotional stability are positively related to voting for the Republican candidate.[15]

In the context of the 2020 election, we identify a set of psychological predispositions we expect to be particularly salient given characteristics of the rival candidates and the important issues of the day. In particular, we theorize that five psychological predispositions are especially important for understanding people's assessment of the 2020 campaign: racial resentment, hostile sexism, authoritarianism, conspiratorial thinking, and conflict avoidance. Our key goal is to embrace Lane's (1955) observation and to systematically incorporate measures of psychological predispositions alongside political predispositions when exploring citizens' understanding and assessment of the campaign.[16]

In the next few pages, we dedicated a significant amount of time reviewing these concepts and explaining their relevance for the electoral

---

[15] These examples are illustrative. Not surprisingly, scholars have looked at the impact of additional personality characteristics on people's political attitudes and behaviors, such as the need for chaos, empathetic ability, and the need for cognition (e.g., Arceneaux et al., 2021; Feldman et al., 2019; DeZala, Golec, Cislak, and Wesolowska, 2010).

[16] To be sure, these five psychological predispositions do not represent an exhaustive list. However, if we can demonstrate these specific psychological characteristics affect how citizens perceive the events and issues of campaigns, then future scholarship can explore the importance of additional psychological predispositions. In the concluding chapter, we identify and discuss additional psychological characteristics and hypothesize how these characteristics may influence citizens in future campaigns.

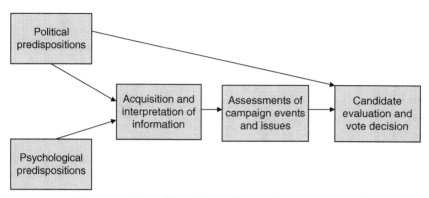

FIGURE 1.1 How people's predispositions influence the consequences of campaigns

contest between Trump and Biden. And, in the chapters to follow, we demonstrate that these psychological predispositions consistently and powerfully influence how people interpret campaign events and issues, even when people's political proclivities are taken into account.

To summarize, the citizen-centered theory of campaigns leads us to expect that people's predispositions (both political and psychological) will drive the procurement and assimilation of information, influencing how individuals evaluate campaign events and campaign issues, and ultimately how these evaluations influence their views of the competing candidates and their voting decisions. We describe this process in Figure 1.1. First, people's psychological and political predispositions are expected to affect the type of information accessed as well as the interpretation of this information. Second, acquired information will directly influence people's evaluations of major campaign events and issues. Third, people's assessments of these components of the campaign will shape evaluations of the candidates and decisions about voting. Political predispositions, such as partisanship, will indirectly and directly influence evaluations of the candidates as well as vote choice. In contrast, since psychological predispositions do not have a clear political direction, we do not expect psychological predispositions to directly influence views of the candidates and vote decisions.[17]

We turn next to discussing the five psychological predispositions we consider especially salient during the 2020 election. We discuss our reasoning for including each of these predispositions, offer our expectations

---

[17] Nevertheless, we will test for a direct link between psychological predispositions and overall evaluations of the candidates and vote preference.

about how each will influence assessments of the campaign, and present details about measurement.

## Racial Resentment

The first psychological predisposition we examine acknowledges the importance of racial attitudes in America. The issue of race predates the republic itself and is emblazoned into the nation's founding documents and history. The struggle with slavery and its tragic consequences, such as the Civil War, Reconstruction, and Jim Crow, have plagued the nation for more than two centuries. American citizens across generations have formed, altered, shared, and harbored views about race and many of its consequences (e.g., Du Bois, 1903; Kinder and Sanders, 1996; Myrdal, 1944; Sniderman and Piazza, 1993). There are trigger moments when views about race come to the fore such as the bombing of the 16th Street Baptist Church in Birmingham, Alabama, in the fall of 1963, a prelude to the Civil Rights Act of 1964; the murder of Martin Luther King in the spring of 1968, with subsequent protests across the country; and the epidemic of killings of Black men at the hands of police in 2014 (e.g., Eric Garner in New York City on July 17, 2014; Michael Brown in Ferguson, Missouri, on August 9, 2014), spurring the growth of the Black Lives Matter movement.

In the context of the 2020 campaign, views about race were inevitably going to be salient. The sitting president had a history of controversial behavior regarding race. In the 1970s, the US Department of Justice sued Trump and his father for violating the Fair Housing Act of 1968 by refusing to rent apartments to people "because of race and color" (Dunlap, 2015). Decades later, Trump became a political force when he embraced "birtherism" with the false charge that the nation's first Black president, Barack Obama, was not born in the United States (Abramson, 2016). And approximately six months into Trump's presidency, hundreds of neo-Nazis and white supremacists marched in Charlottesville to protest the removal of a statue of Robert E. Lee. On the day of these protests, August 12, 2017, a Black man named DeAndre Harris was beaten by at least four white supremacists. On the same day, a twenty-year-old white supremacist from Ohio drove his car into a crowd of counterprotesters, killing thirty-two-year-old Heather Heyer and injuring thirty-five others.[18]

---

[18] www.theguardian.com/us-news/2017/aug/18/charlottesville-mayor-opposes-robert-e-lee-statue-a-lightning-rod-for-terrorism

Speaking a few days later at a news conference, Trump said, "I think there's blame on both sides. If you look at both sides – I think there's blame on both sides...and you had some very bad people in that group, but you also had people that were very fine people, on both sides." Joe Biden said Trump's comments at the August press conference motivated him to challenge Trump in 2020: "With those words, the president of the United States assigned a moral equivalence between those spreading hate and those with the courage to stand against it" (Holan, 2019).

Based on the citizen-centered theory of campaigns, we expect people's views of race to influence their search for information and how they subsequently interpret and evaluate the candidates, campaign issues, and campaign events. As an illustration, Trump launched his successful presidential campaign in the summer of 2015 saying, "When Mexico sends its people, they're not sending the best. They're not sending you; they're sending people that have lots of problems and they're bringing those problems. They're bringing drugs, they're bringing crime. They're rapists and some, I assume, are good people" (Gamboa, 2015). Citizens who were sympathetic to Trump's message may have sought to acquire additional information confirming the link between immigration and crime and may have turned to news sites and social media platforms producing such content.[19] We argue that the easy availability of information supporting divergent viewpoints makes it possible for people to acquire communications consonant with their predilections, thereby affecting people's interpretation of racial messages during political campaigns.

We know that racial attitudes influence voting preferences (e.g., Valentino, Hutchings, and White, 2002), support for government policy (e.g., Gilens, 1995), and approval of the president (e.g., Tesler, 2013). While scholars have offered alternative measures of racism (for a review, see Huddy, Feldman and Sen, 2023), we utilize the racial resentment scale.[20] Kinder and Sanders (1996: 105–106) explain that racial resentment is a form of racism that rests on the view "that Blacks do not try hard enough to overcome the difficulties they face and they take what they have not earned." We rely on the following four items to measure

---

[19] For example, individuals sympathetic to Trump's message may have listened to a story appearing on Fox News that "shines light on the shocking crimes committed by illegal immigrants." www.youtube.com/watch?v=-MpAahd-Q6g

[20] According to Cramer (2020), the racial resentment scale has been the dominant measure of symbolic racism and strongly predicts political preferences and evaluations of political figures. Nevertheless, as Cramer discusses, alternative measures are available, including racial threat measures, implicit association tests of racism, and explicit racism measures.

racial resentment: (1) "Irish, Italians, Jewish, and many other minorities overcame prejudice and worked their way up. Blacks should do the same without any special favors." (2) "Over the past few years Blacks have gotten less than they deserve." (3) "It's really a matter of some people not trying hard enough; if Blacks would only try harder, they could be just as well off as whites." (4) "Generations of slavery and discrimination have created conditions that make it difficult for Blacks to work their way out of the lower class" (Henry and Sears, 2002: 260–261). Respondents are asked to agree or disagree with each of the statements on a five-point scale.[21]

## Hostile Sexism

The second psychological predisposition we examine recognizes the history of sexism in the United States. The dynamic nature of public opinion about women's rights and opportunities have formed the backbone of several large mass movements working to acquire greater equality for women in society, including the Women's Suffrage Movement as part of the Progressive Movement (1890s–1920s), the Second Wave Feminist Movement (1960s–1970s), and the #MeToo Movement (2006–present).[22]

While women's role in society has improved over the arc of US history, sexism remains a pernicious fact in contemporary society. For instance, women are still paid less than men, regardless of their level of education (Barroso and Brown, 2021). Further, women hold less than 30 percent of the seats in the US Congress and only 18 percent of the governorships (CAWP, 2021), and only 8 percent of the 500 largest corporations in the United States have women CEOs (Mazzoni, 2021). A poll conducted in the summer of 2020 showed that a majority (57 percent) of respondents believe "the U.S. hasn't gone far enough when it comes to giving women equal rights with men" (Barroso, 2020). Among respondents who think the country has work to do in achieving gender equality, 77 percent say sexual harassment is a major obstacle to women's equality; 67 percent say women do not have the same legal rights as men; 66 percent say

---

[21] Items 1 and 3 are scored such that high agreement indicates high levels of racial resentment while items 2 and 4 are scored such that high disagreement indicates high levels of racial resentment. With our survey data, Cronbach's alpha for the racial resentment scale is .82. The mean (and standard deviation) of the racial resentment scale for our sample is 12.23 (4.42). The scale ranges from a low of 4 to a high of 20.

[22] See Grady (2018) for a discussion of the different waves of feminism.

societal expectations are different for men and women; and 64 percent say women are less likely to be in positions of power compared to men.

With this backdrop, the candidacy and election of Donald Trump in 2016 was seen by some as an assault on women, spurring the Women's March on the day after Trump's inauguration in January 2017. Hundreds of thousands gathered in Washington and thousands more protested in cities across the country (Hartocolli and Alcindor, 2017). Trump has a long history of misogyny, sexual harassment, sexism, and unwanted sexual advances (Nelson, 2016). A total of eighteen women publicly accused him of sexual misconduct (Keneally, 2020). Further, he repeatedly disparaged women's looks, such as calling comedian Rosie O'Donnell "a big fat pig," "disgusting," "a slob," and "a very unattractive person."

Biden's history with women was not unblemished. For instance, he faced sharp criticism for his treatment of Anita Hill during the Clarence Thomas hearings in 1991. However, since those hearings more than thirty years ago, Biden worked to "redeem himself with women" by advocating for women, such as introducing the Violence against Women Act in 1994 (Kranish and Viser, 2020). In March 2020, he committed to picking a woman to be the vice president if he secured the Democratic nomination. A few months later, he made good on his promise by picking Kamala Harris as his running mate (Schwartz, 2020). Harris was a historic choice: the first Black woman and the first person of Indian descent to be nominated for national office by a major party (Burns and Glueck, 2020).

A growing literature suggests that people's attitudes toward women influence their views of politics, including assessments of presidential candidates (e.g., Filindra, Kaplan, and Buyuker, 2021; Glick, 2019; Ratliff et al., 2019; Schaffner, MacWilliams, and Nteta, 2018). While sexist attitudes have been measured in a number of ways (e.g., Larsen and Long, 1988; Spence and Hahn, 1997), we turn to Glick and Fiske's (2001: 116) ambivalence sexism theory that highlights the "coexistence of power difference and intimate interdependence between the sexes." This conceptualization produces two dimensions of sexism: hostile sexism and benevolent sexism. Hostile sexism justifies men's power through sexist antipathy and predicts hostility toward women who are seen as challenging men's power. Benevolent sexism legitimizes men's power by promising women that men will take care of them, predicting benevolence toward women who behave in a way consistent with conventional gender norms.

We focus on hostile sexism, characterized by negative attitudes that demean women, including viewing women as untrustworthy, power-seeking, and manipulative (Glick and Fiske, 1996). Glick (2019: 715) explains that given Trump's "misogynistic behavior and heteronormative masculinity, hostile sexists would likely view Trump as holding similar attitudes to themselves." We rely on the following four items developed by Glick and Fiske to assess hostile sexism: (1) Many women are actually seeking special favors, such as hiring policies that favor them over men, under the guise of asking for "equality." (2) Feminists are not seeking for women to have more power than men. (3) Most women interpret innocent remarks or acts as being sexist. (4) Feminists are making entirely reasonable demands of men.[23]

According to the citizen-centered theory of campaigns, people's level of hostile sexism will influence their search for campaign information, thereby reinforcing their views of women's role in politics and society. We expect hostile sexists to accumulate information supporting their stereotypical views of women, potentially altering how they view the political candidates and the campaign. For example, we hypothesize that hostile sexists will agree with Trump's characterization of Kamala Harris, the Democratic vice-presidential nominee, as "nasty," "mad," "angry," and "a monster" (Clifton, 2020; Summers, 2020). Further, these individuals may pursue sources and stories portraying Harris in a negative light, leading to the development of even more critical views of Harris over the course of the campaign.

### Authoritarianism

The United States was founded on rebellion against the actions of a remote and unaccountable king. Charles Edel (2021) explains that the Declaration of Independence articulates "American opposition to the closed, authoritarian models of governance that they knew from abroad and feared would develop in their own country." Nevertheless, the country has dealt with authoritarian figures throughout its history, including Joseph McCarthy who stoked national fears during the Cold War and presented himself as the arbitrator of truth surrounded by deceitful enemies.

Authoritarianism among the public, too, is not new to US politics. The study of the authoritarian personality began with Adorno et al. (1950),

---

[23] Respondents are asked to indicate (on a four-point scale) their level of agreement with each statement from "strongly disagree" to "strongly agree." For items 1 and 3, strongly agree indicates high levels of hostile sexism, and for items 2 and 4, "strongly disagree" indicates high levels of hostile sexism. With our survey data, Cronbach's alpha for the hostile sexism scale is .53. The mean (and standard deviation) of the hostile sexism scale for our sample is 9.42 (2.59); the scale ranges from 4 to 16.

who described an authoritarian as someone who admires figures of strength, disdains those who are weak, prefers conventionalism, rigidity, and stereotypical thinking, and exhibits aggression toward out-groups. More recent scholars confirm that conformity, obedience to authority, and out-group aggression are central to understanding authoritarianism (e.g., Altemeyer, 1981; Feldman and Stenner, 1997; Stenner, 2005). Finally, Butler shows (2013) that authoritarians, compared to nonauthoritarians, are more fearful of both social threats (e.g., social disorder) and personal threats (e.g., confronting a dangerous situation).

Trump, during his campaigns and while governing, showed signs of authoritarianism by embracing autocratic rulers abroad, stoking fears about immigrants (e.g., calling Latinos "animals" and "invaders"),[24] and damaging democratic norms at home, including interfering with judicial independence, attacking the news media, and questioning the integrity of the election. Also, he flattered authoritarian strongmen like Vladimir Putin of Russia, Rodrigo Duterte of the Philippines, and North Korean dictator Kim Jong Un. According to senior aides, in a phone call with Putin in the early days of the administration, Trump was "obsequious" and "fawning," even apologizing to the dictator for not calling him sooner (Leonnig, Harris, and Dawsey, 2019).

Research on authoritarianism and politics has consistently demonstrated a strong relationship between level of authoritarian thinking and generalized prejudice, nationalism, opposition to civil liberties, and support for aggressive foreign policy (for a review, see Caprara and Vecchione, 2013). In addition, some researchers find that authoritarians are more likely to support prejudicial and restrictive government policies in response to threat (e.g., Feldman, 2003; Feldman and Stenner, 1997; Lavine, Lodge, and Freitas, 2005, but also see Hetherington and Suhay, 2011). Finally, in the 2016 election, a number of studies demonstrate a positive correlation between support for Donald Trump and level of authoritarian thinking (e.g., Choma and Hanoch, 2017; Knuckey and Hassan, 2020; Womick et al., 2019).

When Lane (1955: 173) explored the impact of the "authoritarian personality" in the 1952 presidential election, he argued that "in an electoral situation, as in any other situation, personality factors play a double role: (1) they affect the perceptions of the individual, screening

---

[24] www.washingtonpost.com/news/the-fix/wp/2018/05/16/trumps-animals-comment-on-undocumented-immigrants-earn-backlash-historical-comparisons/

www.washingtonpost.com/outlook/2019/03/17/trump-sees-immigrants-invaders-white-nationalist-terrorists-do-too/

out some stimuli, distorting others, and leaving others intact; and (2) they shape the responses of a person, selecting among the various possible responses those which are more serviceable to basic personality needs." His argument is entirely consistent with the citizen-centered theory of campaigns.

During Trump's 2016 campaign, his presidency, and his reelection campaign, he presented himself as the strong leader who was needed at this moment in US history to protect Americans from dangerous elements inside and outside their borders. We expect that Trump's rhetoric will resonate differently depending on people's level of authoritarianism, thereby influencing how they obtain and process campaign news and altering assessments of the competing candidates.

To measure authoritarianism, we rely on Feldman and Stenner's (1997) measure that likens hierarchical thinking in child-rearing with hierarchical thinking in society.[25] Respondents are given the following instructions: "Although there are a number of qualities that people feel that children should have, every person thinks that some are more important than others. Read the following pairs of desirable qualities. Please indicate which one is more important for a child to have: (1) Respect for Elders or Independence; (2) Obedience or Self-Reliance; (3) Curiosity or Good Manners: (4) Being Considerate or Well-Behaved."[26] In a recent examination, Engelhardt, Feldman, and Hetherington (2021) show that the child-rearing measure of authoritarianism is related to Right-Wing Authoritarianism (RWA), suggesting both measures are tapping the same underlying concept. Second, the authors demonstrate that the child-rearing measure assesses authoritarianism equally well for whites and nonwhites. Third, the authors find no evidence that the child-rearing measure of authoritarianism is endogenous to political and social attitudes, a critique leveled against the RWA measure. Finally, the child-rearing measure is temporally stable as one would expect from a measure tapping a "personality adaptation."

---

[25] Engelhardt, Feldman, and Hetherington (2021) argue that the widely used RWA scale is problematic because of endogeneity between the dependent and explanatory variables. For example, the authors point out that some of the RWA items closely mimic the rhetoric of right-wing politicians and right-leaning media sources, making it difficult to sort out causal claims.

[26] The authoritarian response is "Respect for Elders," "Obedience," "Good Manners," and "Being Well-Behaved." The Cronbach's alpha for the authoritarian index is .48 with our survey data. The mean (and standard deviation) of the authoritarian scale for our sample is 2.22 (1.20). The scale ranges from a low of 0 to a high of 4.

## Conflict Avoidance

We turn next to discussing the psychological predisposition of conflict avoidance. E. E. Schattschneider (1960: 3), in his classic book *The Semi-Sovereign People: A Realist's View of Democracy in America*, suggests politics is about conflict: "At the nub of all politics are: first, the way in which the public participates in the spread of the conflict and, second, the processes by which the unstable relation of the public to the conflict is controlled." It is no secret that conflict is baked into electoral campaigns with competition around the development of public policies, representation, and resources. Further, the conflictual nature of politics is highlighted in news coverage. In particular, news media organizations embrace the "conflict frame" by emphasizing "conflict between individuals, groups, or institutions as a means of capturing audience interest" (Semetko and Valkenburg, 2000: 95). For example, clashes between political elites of opposing parties in Congress, intraparty disagreements over policy, or news descriptions of elections often employ metaphors like "battle," "fight," and "brawl."

It is also not surprising that people vary in their comfort with conflict, with some people hoping to avoid confrontation altogether while others may actually seek it out (Ulbig and Funk, 1999). People's tolerance of conflict is important in family relationships, in the workplace, and in educational settings (e.g., Barsky and Wood, 2005; Koerner and Fitzpatrick, 1997; Weider-Hatfield and Hatfield, 1995). Tolerance toward conflict has been conceptualized as a stable disposition resulting from early childhood socialization (e.g., Bresnahan et al., 2009; Mutz, 2002; Testa, Hibbing, and Ritchie, 2014).

A number of scholars have examined the impact of conflict avoidance on a range of political attitudes and behaviors. For example, Mutz and Reeves (2005) show that exposure to incivility lowers political trust among people high in conflict avoidance. Sydnor (2019) finds that conflict-avoidant individuals are more likely to experience negative affect (e.g., disgust, anger) when exposed to incivility. And several studies have examined the link between level of conflict avoidance and political participation (e.g., Bjarnøe, de Vreese, and Albæk, 2020; Mutz, 2002; Sydnor, 2019; Ulbig and Funk, 1999; Wolak, 2020).

The 2020 presidential campaign was rife with conflict; the toxic mix of racial division, polarized politics, and a competitive presidential election produced a highly contentious campaign. Nevertheless, the two candidates differed in their penchant for discord. In a *New York Times* analysis published at the end of August 2020, Peter Baker and Maggie Haberman (2020b) write, "President Trump has been throwing accelerant on the fire of the nation's social unrest rather than trying to put it out, seeking confrontation rather than calm... From his time as a celebrity real estate developer, Mr. Trump has never been a conciliator, and he has long gravitated toward conflict and sought to escalate it."

Also in August 2020, when accepting the Democratic nomination for president in Milwaukee, Biden emphasized unity over division. He said,

> It is time for us, for we, the people, to come together. And make no mistake, united we can and will overcome this season of darkness in America... I'll work hard for those who didn't support me, as hard for them as I did for those who did vote for me. That's the job of a president, to represent all of us, not just our base or our party... America isn't just a collection of clashing interests, of red states or blue states. We're so much bigger than that, we're so much better than that.[27]

Given the conflictual nature of the 2020 presidential election as well as differences in the two candidates' preference for divisiveness, we hypothesize that people's level of conflict avoidance will serve as a lens for people to receive, interpret, and draw conclusions about the candidates and events of the campaign. To measure conflict avoidance, we rely on the "approach/avoidance component" of Goldstein's (1999) Conflict Communication Scale. This conflict avoidance scale includes five items where people are asked to indicate how much they agree with the following items on a four-point scale ranging from disagree strongly to agree strongly: (1) I hate arguments; (2) I find conflicts exciting; (3) I feel upset after an argument; (4) I enjoy challenging the opinions of others, and (5) arguments do not bother me.[28]

### Conspiracy Thinking

We turn to the fifth and final psychological predisposition: conspiracy thinking. Conspiracy thinking (also called conspiracy ideation or conspiracy mentality) is a stable predisposition that leads individuals to attribute "events to a secret plot by a covert alliance of powerful individuals

---

[27] abcnews.go.com/Politics/full-text-joe-bidens-2020-democratic-national-convention/story?id=72513129

[28] For items 1 and 3, people who strongly agree are rated as high on conflict avoidance. For items 2, 4, and 5, people who strongly disagree are rated as high on conflict avoidance. With our survey data, Cronbach's alpha for the conflict avoidance scale is .70. The mean (and standard deviation) of the conflict avoidance scale for our sample is 14.12 (3.11). The scale ranges from a low of 5 to a high of 20.

or to clandestine organizations rather than to more mundane human (in) activity or natural forces" (Imhoff and Bruder, 2014: 25). Conspiracy theories are universal and occur across time and cultures and in a wide variety of social settings (e.g., government, workplace, school).

One of the most enduring political conspiracies in the United States involves the assassination of President John F. Kennedy. The Warren Commission, authorized by President Lyndon Johnson and led by Chief Justice Earl Warren, investigated the assassination and concluded Lee Harvey Oswald acted alone in the assassination of Kennedy. These findings were supported, by and large, by additional investigations by the US Attorney General's Office in 1968, by the Rockefeller Commission in 1975 and by the US House of Representatives from 1978 to 1979. Nevertheless, people's suspicions about Kennedy's assassination persist more than fifty years after the event. For example, a survey commissioned by *FiveThirtyEight* in 2017 found 61 percent of respondents believed that Lee Harvey Oswald did not act alone.[29]

Additional conspiracies are widely circulated in the United States including: the moon landing in 1969 was faked, the George W. Bush Administration knew about the planned 9/11 terrorist attacks and let it happen, and President Obama was not born in the United States. More recent examples of conspiracy theories include the QAnon conspiracy claiming the world is run by a cabal of Satan-worshiping pedophiles. QAnon followers believe that this cabal includes top Democrats like Joe Biden, Hillary Clinton, Barack Obama and George Soros. According to the QAnon theory, "Donald J. Trump was recruited by top military generals to run for president in 2016 to break up this criminal conspiracy and bring its members to justice."[30]

During the COVID-19 pandemic, a number of conspiracies were disseminated regarding the virus, such as (1) COVID-19 is no worse than the flu; (2) wealthy elites intentionally spread the virus to win power and profit; and (3) wearing a mask makes people more susceptible to COVID-19 (Lewis, 2020). Additional conspiracy theories developed surrounding the safety and efficacy of the COVID-19 vaccines, including (1) the COVID-19 vaccine makes you magnetic; (2) the COVID-19 vaccine makes you infertile; (3) the government put a microchip in COVID-19 vaccines to track you; and (4) the COVID-19 vaccines rewrite your DNA (Cassata, 2020).

---

[29] fivethirtyeight.com/features/the-one-thing-in-politics-most-americans-believe-in-jfk-conspiracies/
[30] www.nytimes.com/article/what-is-qanon.html

There is a growing literature across a number of disciplines aimed at understanding the determinants of conspiratorial thinking among individuals (for a review see Douglas et al., 2019). Research suggests that conspiracy thinking is higher among people with lower levels of trust and higher levels of alienation (e.g., Goertzel, 1994; Imhoff and Bruder, 2014). Further, people's belief in conspiracy theories is highly sensitive to social context. For example, Republicans are more likely to believe in governmental conspiracies when there is a Democrat in the White House and Democrats are more likely to believe in governmental conspiracies when a Republican is president (e.g., van Prooijen and Douglas, 2018).

The media may play an important role in increasing levels of conspiracy thinking. Hollander (2018) reports exposure to Fox News is positively related to belief in conspiracy theories; Stempel, Hargrove, and Stempel (2007) find that the use of blogs and YouTube news channels stimulates conspiracy thinking; Walter and Drochon (2020) show that conspiracy thinking is higher when people turn to blogs and nonmainstream social media, compared to newspapers, for their news.

Regarding political attitudes and political behavior, researchers have linked conspiracy thinking to attitudes toward climate change (Uscinski and Olivella, 2017) and immigration (Gaston and Uscinski, 2018). Further, some studies demonstrate a positive relationship between conspiracy thinking and levels of political engagement (e.g., Imhoff, 2015; Imhoff and Bruder, 2014; Kim, 2019). However, Uscinski and Parent (2014) report that conspiracy thinking decreases people's likelihood of participating in conventional political activities while people higher in conspiracy thinking are more likely to support violence against the government.

During the 2020 campaign, Trump was aggressively promoting a conspiracy theory regarding voter fraud, especially mail voting. On July 2, 2020, Trump tweeted, "Mail-In Ballots will lead to massive electoral fraud and a rigged 2020 Election." By September 11, 2020, a fact-check by the *Washington Post* reported that Trump had "peddled imaginary threats about voting by mail" more than 100 times (Rizzo, 2020). By Election Day, Trump had made more than 150 false claims concerning "fraudulent ballots or the alleged dangers of mail-in voting" (Kessler and Rizzo, 2020). In the modern era, there has never been an incumbent president who openly and repeatedly disseminated conspiracy theories regarding the security of a US election. Therefore, we believe the 2020 presidential election is an ideal setting for examining how people's level of conspiracy thinking influences their interpretation of campaign information and evaluations of the ongoing political campaign.

To measure conspiracy thinking, we rely on the following three items from the Conspiracy Mentality Questionnaire: "I think that government agencies closely monitor all citizens"; "I think that events which superficially seem to lack a connection are often the result of secret activities"; and "I think that there are secret organizations that greatly influence political decisions" (Bruder et al., 2013: 5).[31] Respondents are asked to indicate their level of agreement with each of these statements on an eleven-point scale ranging from 1 = 0 percent – *certainly not* to 11 = 100 percent – *certain*.

To review, we argue that the availability of information from a variety of sources allow citizens to actively search for and assimilate information consistent with their psychological and political predispositions. We expect these predispositions to consistently influence how people interpret campaign information and evaluate campaign events, issues, and candidates. We also contend that people's psychological predispositions do not simply mirror their political proclivities. Instead, we expect that partisan attitudes will be orthogonal to psychological attitudes.

Relying on our original dataset, we examine the correlation between party identification and each of the five psychological predispositions.[32] The findings in Table 1.1 indicate that psychological predispositions are not simply a proxy for partisanship. We find the strongest correlations between partisanship and racial resentment and hostile sexism (.42 and .35, respectively). However, these correlations do not suggest that party identification is simply collinear with level of prejudice.[33] Further, the relationship between partisanship and authoritarianism, conspiracy thinking, and conflict avoidance is weak to nonexistent (i.e., .16, .10, .01, respectively).

We also look at the correlations among the five psychological predispositions. We see that the correlations between these constructs vary from a low of .03 (i.e., racial resentment and conflict avoidance) to a high of .47 (i.e., hostile sexism and racial resentment), with an average correlation of less than .18. The data in Table 1.1 suggest that the five psychological characteristics are tapping something different from partisanship,

---

[31] The Cronbach's alpha for the three-item conspiracy index is .81 with our survey data. The mean (and standard deviation) for the conspiracy scale in our sample is 17.99 (7.13). The scale ranges from a low of 0 to a high of 30.
[32] In the next section, we present more details regarding the timing, measurement, and waves of the panel survey.
[33] We will provide strong evidence for this claim in a large number of multivariate analyses where partisanship and psychological predispositions each contribute to explaining the variance in the dependent variables.

TABLE 1.1 *Correlations between party identification and psychological predispositions*

|  | Authoritarianism | Conspiracy thinking | Racial resentment | Hostile sexism | Conflict avoidance |
|---|---|---|---|---|---|
| Party identification | .16** | .10** | .42** | .35** | .01 |
| Authoritarianism |  | .14** | .23** | .27** | .10** |
| Conspiracy thinking |  |  | .11** | .22** | −.04* |
| Racial resentment |  |  |  | .47** | .03 |
| Hostile sexism |  |  |  |  | −.13** |

*Note:* The cell entries are Pearson correlation coefficients for the September wave of the panel survey (*n* = 3099).
\* $p < .05$
\*\* $p < .01$

and these psychological predispositions are not highly correlated with one another, with the exception of racism and sexism.

Throughout the book, we test the citizen-centered theory of campaigns with data from a three-wave panel study of more than 4,000 people interviewed in September, October, and immediately after Election Day in November 2020. We turn next to a description of the design and measurement of the panel survey.

DATA AND METHODS

The Panel Design and Sample

We designed a panel study where information is gathered from the same individuals at different points during the campaign to study the dynamics of the 2020 presidential campaign. According to Finkel (1995: 1), an important advantage of panel studies is that "change is explicitly incorporated into the design so that individual changes in a set of variables are directly measured." Brady, Johnston, and Sides (2006) explain that panel designs can isolate change when the waves of the panel straddle a "treatment" such as a presidential debate.[34] For untangling

[34] Brady, Johnston, and Sides (2006) do caution that the greater the time gap between panel waves, the harder it is to isolate campaign events. In our panel survey, respondents are interviewed in waves of less than one month apart, allowing us to more accurately separate the impact of specific events from rival factors. Experiments have been

causal relationships, such as how campaign events alter views about the competing candidates, panel designs have distinct advantages over cross-sectional designs. Precisely because we are measuring political attitudes for the same individuals across time, we can model how campaign events change people's attitudes.[35]

We conducted a three-wave panel survey during the 2020 presidential campaign with recruitment done by Dynata (formerly SSI) using an opt-in internet panel. Dynata maintains a large online panel of US adults. It uses invitations (e.g., email, web banners, phone alerts) to enroll people in research panels.[36] It screens and recruits participants with quotas (e.g., sex, age, ethnicity) in order to obtain a sample with demographics representative of the United States (Shaverdian et al., 2019). The opt-in sample is a nonprobability sample, and studies have shown that nonprobability samples can produce accurate results (e.g., Twyman, 2008; Vavreck and Rivers, 2008).

In Table 1.2, we provide a comparison of the demographic profile of the panel respondents with recent census data. The data in Table 1.2 show that the panel respondents are generally representative of the nation. However, they tend to be somewhat more educated, older, and more male compared to census numbers. In terms of partisanship, the panel respondents are somewhat more likely to identify with the Democratic party and less likely to call themselves independents, compared to a Gallup survey in the field during the 2020 presidential campaign.[37]

Respondents completed each wave of survey on the Qualtrics platform. We collected the first wave of the panel survey between September 1 and September 22, 2020, with 3,013, respondents completing the questionnaire (see Table 1.3). The second wave was conducted between October 4 and October 7, 2020, with 1,510 respondents completing the October

employed to examine the impact of campaign events (e.g., Arceneaux, 2010), but they are limited in their external validity (e.g., representativeness of the sample; artificiality of the settings, inability to look at stability of effects)

[35] Panel designs do have disadvantages, including panel attrition, panel conditioning, and panel selection bias (Lohse, Bellman, and Johnson, 2000). A recent study by Amaya, Hatley, and Lau (2021), looking at the PEW American Trends Panel, indicates that conditioning does not contribute significant error to panel estimates.

[36] Dynata uses a point system to incentivize participation in studies from their panel participants. Dynata panel members can buy items with their points, such as gift cards, or they can donate money to a preferred charity. For participation in each wave of our panel survey, Dynata panel members were given points equivalent to about $2.00.

[37] In the model estimations throughout the book, the sample is weighted based on the 2010 census data for region, sex, age, income, education, race, and ethnicity to produce results that reflect a nationally representative population of the United States.

TABLE 1.2 *Comparison of 2020 panel survey with census data and Gallup survey data*

|  | 2020 panel (*n* = 4,340) (in %) | Census[1](in %) |
|---|---|---|
| Education |  |  |
| Less than high school | 2 | 13 |
| High school | 23 | 27 |
| Some college | 20 | 21 |
| Associate degree | 10 | 8 |
| Bachelor's degree | 26 | 19 |
| Post-bachelor's degree | 20 | 11 |
| Income |  |  |
| Less than $25,000 | 18 | 17 |
| $25,000–$34,999 | 12 | 8 |
| $35,000–$49,999 | 14 | 12 |
| $50,000–$74,999 | 21 | 17 |
| $75,000–$99,999 | 16 | 12 |
| $100,000–$149,999 | 13 | 15 |
| $150,000–$199,999 | 5 | 8 |
| $200,000 or more | 3 | 10 |
| Sex |  |  |
| Male | 54 | 48 |
| Female | 46 | 51 |
| Age |  |  |
| 18–34 | 20 | 31 |
| 35–44 | 15 | 18 |
| 45–54 | 17 | 19 |
| 55–64 | 21 | 16 |
| 65 and older | 27 | 17 |
| Race/ethnicity |  |  |
| White | 65 | 60 |
| Black | 16 | 13 |
| Hispanic/Latino | 8 | 18 |
| Asian | 8 | 6 |
| Native American | 1 | 1 |
| Other | 2 | 3 |
| Party identification |  | Gallup data[2] |
| Democrat | 38 | 31 |
| Independent | 31 | 36 |
| Republican | 32 | 31 |

[1] Census data come from QuickFacts, www.census.gov/quickfacts/fact/table/US/PST045219
[2] Gallup data come from news.gallup.com/poll/15370/party-affiliation.aspx

TABLE 1.3 *Information about the panel survey design*

| Wave | September | October | October ("fresh sample") | November |
|---|---|---|---|---|
| Dates in field | 9/1–9/22 | 10/4–10/7 | 10/5–10/18 | 11/4–11/6 |
| Number of respondents | 3,013 | 1,510 | 1,298 | 2,153 |
| Average length (minutes) | 23.10 | 17.95 | 21.63 | 15.13 |

Total number of respondents = 4,311
Respondents in full panel (September–October–November) = 1,040

wave of the panel. We also collected a fresh sample of 1,298 respondents in October between October 5 and October 18, 2020. Finally, we recontacted all of the respondents for a final wave of the survey between November 4 and November 6, 2020, with 2,153 completed surveys. During the fall campaign, we collected survey data from 4,311 respondents, with 1,040 respondents completing each of the three waves of the panel survey. The September wave of the survey took about 23 minutes to complete (i.e., an average of 23.10 minutes). The October wave of the survey took somewhat less time, averaging almost 18 minutes (i.e., an average of 17.95 minutes), while the new wave of October respondents averaged just under 22 minutes (i.e., an average of 21.63 minutes). The November wave was the shortest survey, taking an average of 15.13 minutes to complete.

## The Survey Questionnaire

We ask a variety of different questions about politics and government, such as party identification, ideology, political knowledge, political trust, civic duty, and political engagement.[38] We also pose a series of questions about people's attention to news as well as their preference among different news outlets. Respondents are also queried about the most important problem facing the nation, the state of the economy, and concern about the COVID-19 pandemic and worries about the integrity of the election. Questions about support for racial justice protests and support for local police are also included in each wave of the survey.

[38] We rely on measures widely used in political science (e.g., the traditional American National Election Study seven-point party identification scale) as well as established survey measures to assess attitudes toward issues and current events (e.g., questions about racial justice protests).

The survey instrument also contains a number of questions about people's views of Trump and Biden, including approval of Trump's performance in office, feeling thermometer ratings for each candidate, assessments of the candidates' traits (i.e., leadership, integrity, empathy, and temperament), tone of each candidate's campaign, and views of each candidate's ability to deal with a variety of issues (e.g., COVID-19, race relations, the integrity of the election).

As discussed earlier, we include established measures to assess levels of racism (racial resentment) and sexism (hostile sexism), conflict avoidance, authoritarianism, and conspiracy thinking.[39] Finally, questions about standard demographic variables, including age, gender, education, income, religion, race, and ethnicity, are asked during the first wave of the survey.[40]

PLAN OF THE BOOK

### The Campaign Setting

We focus explicitly on two important events during the 2020 general election campaign. The initial event is the first presidential debate between Trump and Biden. Presidential debates have become routine events during campaigns, with debates occurring each presidential election year since 1976. Although they are highly scripted by the campaigns, detailed preparation is not always a strong predictor of how potential voters view the outcome. The first debate of 2020 was a doozy, and we examine how psychological and political predispositions influence people's views of the candidates' performances in the debate. Furthermore, since the debate occurred days before the launching of the second wave of our panel, we examine how views of the debate change people's overall evaluations of the candidates from September to October.

The second significant event is Trump's COVID-19 diagnosis and hospitalization. Trump's COVID-19 infection, unlike the debate, was unscripted and occurred well before the advent of vaccines, generating a great deal of discussion and concern about the health of the incumbent president. His diagnosis also fell between the September and October

---

[39] The battery of questions measuring each of the psychological predispositions are asked in the respondent's first wave of the panel survey.

[40] See Appendix A for a list of all the questions asked in each of the waves of the panel survey. The vast majority of the questions are asked in each of the survey waves, as indicated in Appendix A.

waves of our panel survey. This serendipitous timing provides us with analytical leverage to examine how Trump's contraction of the virus alters people's views about the COVID-19 pandemic as well as changing assessments of his ability to deal with the pandemic.

In addition to the COVID-19 pandemic, we examine two more issues during the fall campaign. The first issue, the protest movement against police brutality, was triggered by the murder of George Floyd by the Minneapolis police in May 2020. This event reignited the sustained, emotional, and complex issue of race in America in the midst of a presidential campaign and generated a great deal of discussion by the candidates about racial justice and policing. We measure attitudes toward the social justice movement as well as views of police during each wave of the panel, allowing us to examine dynamics in people's opinions and explore how views about racial justice and policing influence evaluations of the candidates over the course of the campaign.

Finally, we examine the issue of election integrity. This issue surfaced during the 2016 presidential campaign, but it became a focus of the 2020 campaign. For instance, during the course of the campaign, Trump and some members of the GOP questioned the legitimacy of voting by mail. While Trump's rhetoric about a "rigged election" was persistent and accelerated as Election Day approached, Biden and Democratic Party surrogates responded by emphasizing the safety and security of convenience voting. We explore the determinants of people's views about election integrity as well as citizens' assessments of each candidate's ability to ensure the legitimacy of the election results. Further, we explore how confidence in election integrity influences how people decide to cast their ballot: on Election Day, by mail, or via in-person early voting.

## An Analytical Road Map

In each of the next four chapters, we focus on one issue or event. In particular, Chapter 2 examines the September presidential debate; Chapter 3 centers on President Trump's COVID-19 diagnosis; Chapter 4 looks at attitudes toward social justice protests and policing; and Chapter 5 addresses the issue of election integrity. In each chapter, we employ the same basic analytical strategy.

First, we develop models to understand people's attitudes about each event and issue. So, for example, in Chapter 2, we present models explaining people's views about the performances of Trump and Biden in the first debate. Based on the citizen-centered theory of campaigns, we expect people's psychological predispositions and political proclivities (e.g., partisanship) to powerfully influence views about the event or issue. In these models, we also control for rival factors that may influence assessments. For instance, when we predict people's worries about COVID-19 in Chapter 3, we include demographic factors that may influence people's concern about the coronavirus. Second, we rely on the panel design to estimate how political and psychological predispositions, along with relevant rival factors, influence *changes* in people's views of each issue or event from September to October.[41] We conclude each chapter by looking at how assessments of the issue or event influence evaluations of the competing candidates in a baseline model and in a change model. For example, in Chapter 4, we examine how attitudes toward the social justice movement and views toward policing affect attitudes toward Trump and Biden in September. Then we develop change models to estimate how beliefs about police and racial justice protests influence changes in evaluations of Trump and Biden from September to October.[42]

In Chapter 6, we develop a comprehensive model to examine how each of the campaign issues and events, along with rival factors, predict evaluations of Trump and Biden in November. In these models, for example, we see that views of the candidates' debate performance in September continue to impact views of Trump and Biden in November. In addition, we estimate changes in people's evaluations of Trump and Biden from September to November and demonstrate that campaign issues and events powerfully alter views of the candidates. We conclude Chapter 6 by examining how the major elements of the campaign produce changes in vote intention from September to November.

We conclude the empirical chapters by demonstrating that the citizen-centered theory of campaigns improves our understanding of who voted in the 2020 election as well as how people decided to cast their vote (i.e., voting on Election Day or relying on convenience voting). In Chapter 7, we begin by predicting turnout where we include psychological predispositions as explanatory variables. Based on the vast literature on political engagement, we also include a series of additional factors (e.g., strength of partisanship, civic duty, political attention). We also predict people's likelihood of voting by mail (compared to on Election Day) and voting

---

[41] We do not look at changes in the views of the debate from September to October since the debate occurred at the end of September, after we had completed the initial wave of the survey.
[42] When estimating these baseline models and change models, we control for rival factors, including partisanship, economic assessments, and trait assessments of each candidate.

early (compared to on Election Day). We find that psychological predispositions play a powerful role, influencing people's decision to vote as well as affecting their reliance on convenience voting.

CHAPTER SUMMARIES

### Chapter 2. "A Hot Mess Inside A Dumpster Fire Inside a Train Wreck": Understanding the Impact of the First Presidential Debate

Presidential debates are now a fixture in the landscape of fall campaigns for the presidency. They attract worldwide media attention, as well as the interest of tens of millions of potential voters, and are held in close proximity to Election Day. In 2020, the first general election debate was a donnybrook. We find citizens develop clear opinions about who won the debate and who performed well; more people viewed Biden as the winner of the first debate and his performance ratings were significantly higher than Trump's ratings, except among Republicans. We also demonstrate that people who have low tolerance for conflict develop significantly more negative views of Trump's performance and are significantly more likely to consider Biden the winner of the debate. Furthermore, people's level of racism and conspiratorial thinking shape views of Trump's and Biden's performances during the first presidential debate. Finally, evaluations of the candidates' performance in the debate as well as people's views of who won the debate influence overall evaluations of Trump and Biden and produce significant changes in the ratings of Trump and Biden from September to October.

### Chapter 3. The Priming of COVID-19 during the Campaign: The Consequences of Trump's Coronavirus Diagnosis

The 2020 presidential campaign occurred in the midst of the first worldwide pandemic in 100 years. The pandemic engulfed the United States for the entire length of the campaign and the incumbent president was hospitalized with the virus at the height of the fall campaign. We show that people's concern about the coronavirus pandemic increased significantly after Trump contracted COVID-19. Furthermore, and consistent with the citizen-centered theory of campaigns, we find that psychological predispositions, along with political and demographic characteristics, substantively and significantly predict changes in worry about the coronavirus from September to October. For instance, people high in authoritarianism and conflict avoidance become significantly more worried about the coronavirus pandemic from September to October. Finally, we show that people are more likely to consider assessments of the candidates' competence for dealing with the coronavirus when developing overall evaluations of the candidates in October – after Trump's COVID-19 diagnosis – compared to September.

### Chapter 4. Protests against Police Brutality: How Attitudes about Racial Injustice and Policing Affected Campaign 2020

The murder of George Floyd at the hands of Minneapolis police over Memorial Day weekend ignited sustained protests across the country and placed the issue of race front and center. By September, more than two-thirds of our survey respondents report positive views of the Black Lives Matter movement. While the salience of race began to fade as the general election campaign unfolded, we find that political characteristics of citizens, such as party attachment and partisan media exposure, influence support for the social justice movement and support for law enforcement. Further, psychological predispositions consistently and significantly influence views of social protests and policing. For example, people's level of racial resentment produces powerful changes in their views of the protests and police from September to October. Finally, attitudes about racial justice and policing influence overall impressions of Biden and Trump, producing significant changes in people's views of the candidates during the first months of the fall campaign.

### Chapter 5. "A Rigged Election": How Views about Election Integrity Altered the Campaign

The incumbent president consistently and systematically sowed doubts about the integrity of the American electoral process throughout the 2020 presidential campaign. Trump's campaign tactic had effects on voters. We show that public confidence in the integrity of the election is much lower for Republicans and for people paying attention to conservative news compared to Democrats and consumers of left-leaning news. Further, a propensity to believe in conspiracy theories fuels doubts about the security of the election. In addition, we show that a number of psychological predispositions consistently influence people's assessments of Biden's and Trump's ability to safeguard the election, including people's level of racial resentment and level of hostile sexism. Finally, people's confidence in the security of the election is associated with positive changes in overall evaluations of Biden and negative changes in overall evaluations of Trump from September to October.

## Chapter 6. How the Campaign Shapes Voters' Decisions about the Candidates

We develop a comprehensive model where we include assessments of each campaign event (e.g., September debate) and issue (e.g., election integrity, worries about COVID-19) when predicting overall evaluations of Biden and Trump in November as well as changes in feeling thermometer scores from September to November. These models show that views about the first presidential debate and attitudes toward major campaign issues (i.e., election integrity, COVID-19, social justice protests) explain views of the candidates in November and predict shifts in evaluations over the length of the campaign. Finally, we estimate changes in vote preference from September to November and we find that elements of the campaign (e.g., views about the presidential debate, support for social justice protests) produce important changes in vote preferences.

## Chapter 7. The Impact of Campaign Messages on the Decision to Vote

We apply the citizen-centered theory of campaigns to help improve our understanding of participation in the 2020 election. We find a strong positive relationship between conflict avoidance and turnout, with people who dislike conflict participating in the election at a much higher rate than people who are more tolerant of conflict. We also demonstrate the significance of the campaign for understanding turnout; people who watched the September presidential debate, people who have higher levels of confidence in the election results, and people with more polarized views of the social justice movement are significantly more likely to vote in the general election. The citizen-centered theory of campaigns also informs our understanding of convenience voting. People who are more sympathetic to Trump (i.e., Republicans, people with less progressive views on race and gender) are more likely to heed his message of forgoing mail voting and going to the polls on Election Day. Further, people who dislike conflict are significantly more likely to rely on mail voting compared to voting on Election Day. Finally, views about the important issues of the campaign affect how people choose to cast a ballot; people who are more concerned about the COVID-19 pandemic and people with more confidence in the integrity of the election are more likely to vote by mail than in person on Election Day.

## Chapter 8. How Campaign 2020 Matters

We begin by highlighting the impressive evidence for the citizen-centered theory of campaigns. In particular, we find that psychological predispositions do not simply reinforce partisan orientation. Instead, these predispositions tap distinct characteristics, influencing how people view the events and issues of the campaign. We also make suggestions about how to study campaigns in the future. While the electoral context of 2020 highlighted particular psychological predispositions, future elections are likely to put a premium on alternative psychological predispositions (e.g., benevolent racism, need for affect). We encourage researchers to be more exhaustive, systematic, and consistent in exploring the impact of people's psychological predispositions during campaigns. We also review and speculate about how candidates' campaign strategies may have helped shape the outcome, especially when we consider the razor thin vote margins in a few key states. Specifically, it appears Trump's actions worked to his detriment both in who voted and in who they supported. Finally, given the events and rhetoric associated with the 2020 campaign, we conclude by assessing the health of our representative system of government where elections play a vital role.

2

# "A Hot Mess inside a Dumpster Fire inside a Train Wreck"

## Understanding the Impact of the First Presidential Debate

The first general election debate of 2020 took place on the evening of September 29, 2020, in Cleveland, Ohio, with more than seventy-three million viewers. According to Molly Ball and Charlotte Alter (2020) of *Time Magazine*, "It was like a tennis match gone horribly wrong: an aging pro who's a little rusty; a seasoned chair umpire; and an opponent on the other side of the court who just happens to be a rampaging rhinoceros. Some people will be appalled when the rhino starts trampling things. But others will root for the rhino." Stuart Emmrich (2020) of *Vogue* summarized the event with a different metaphor, comparing the debate to a *Bravo Housewives* reality show spinning out of control. He explained,

From the very beginning – with a scowling Donald Trump alternating between spewing lies and repeatedly interrupting Joe Biden; the former vice president retaliating in frustrated response ("Will you shut up, man?") and occasionally hurling insults of his own ("You're the worst president America has ever had"); and the outmatched moderator, Chris Wallace, completely unable to control the two men on the stage in front of him. (Emmrich, 2020)

A third metaphor, offered by Domenico Montanaro (2020) of *NPR*, was that the first presidential debate was supposed to be a boxing match. However, instead of a boxing match, we watched as President Trump was constantly jumping on the ropes, refusing to come down, while the referee (Chris Wallace) was continually trying to coax him off, and "Joe Biden was standing in the middle of the ring with his gloves on and a confused look on his face."

Immediately following the debate, ABC News host George Stephanopoulos said, "As somebody who's watched presidential debates for 40 years, as somebody who's moderated presidential debates, as somebody who's prepared candidates for presidential debates, as somebody who's covered presidential debates, that was the worst presidential debate I have ever seen in my life." Savannah Guthrie began the NBC News postdebate analysis by saying, "We need to just pause for a moment, and say, 'That was crazy.' What was that?" NBC News anchor Chuck Todd responded by explaining, "It was a train wreck. But it was a train wreck of the making of one person. I mean, we know who did it. President Trump did this." Lester Holt, also of NBC News, called the debate a "low point in political discourse." John Dickerson of CBS News said, "When the stakes were that high, the debate couldn't have been lower. It was not an equal opportunity experience. The president of the United States … was by far responsible for a greater share of the jaggedness at a time when America does not need jagged." Even Fox News host Sean Hannity conceded the debate did not go as well as people would have liked. And the next morning on *Fox & Friends First*, the political analyst Ron Meyer said, "Honestly, there wasn't much great about this debate. In my opinion, it could be one of the worst debates in televised American history" (Lopez, 2020).

The response to the first presidential debate was so overwhelmingly negative that the Commission on Presidential Debates (CPD) said that it would change the format of the remaining presidential debates. In a statement, the CPD said, "Last night's debate made clear that additional structure should be added to the format of the remaining debates to ensure a more orderly discussion of the issues. The CPD will be carefully considering the changes that it will adopt and will announce those measures shortly."[1]

In this chapter, we will examine people's reactions to the first general election debate. We will investigate how people viewed Trump's and Biden's performances and who people thought "won" the debate. Based on the citizen-centered theory of campaigns, we expect that people's political and psychological predispositions will drive their search for information, producing systematic differences in views of the competing candidates. In addition, given the salience of the debate, and the lopsided nature of the candidates' performances, we expect that people paying attention to the news will be more likely to develop negative views of Trump compared to Biden. Finally, by leveraging the power of the panel design, we will also investigate how the debate changed people's evaluations of the competing candidates.

Before turning to our results, we briefly review what we know about the impact of debates on voters during elections. Since the first televised

---

[1] www.debates.org/2020/09/30/cpd-statement-4/

presidential debate in 1960, scholars have been studying how presidential debates influence citizens' attitudes during electoral campaigns. Debates are distinct from other political events, exposing voters to presidential candidates for a sustained amount of time, usually ninety minutes to two hours. Furthermore, the news media, after the debate, focus extensively on the rival candidates' performances, their policy stands, their personalities, and their gaffes.

Every election season, the news media recall the famous debate moments of the past. These memories inevitably begin with the first televised debate between John F. Kennedy and Richard Nixon in 1960 where Kennedy's tan and healthy image contrasted dramatically to Nixon looking tired, with a five-o'clock shadow and a pallid complexion. In anticipation of the debate, Kennedy had spent time in the sun and also brought his own makeup artist to the television studio. Nixon, in comparison, was recovering from a stay in the hospital and refused an offer of makeup from Don Hewitt, the producer of the debate. Consequently, during the debate, Nixon could be seen sweating, while Kennedy looked cool and unflappable. While debate folklore claims that people watching on television thought Kennedy had won while people listening on radio thought Nixon was the winner, there is no empirical evidence collected at the time to support this contention (Campbell, 2010).[2]

Another legendary debate was the October 1976 debate between incumbent president Gerald Ford and challenger Jimmy Carter. During the debate, Ford answered a question about the Helsinki Accords by saying, "There is no Soviet domination of Eastern Europe and there never will be under a Ford administration." The moderator, Max Frankel of the *New York Times*, was stunned and responded, "I'm sorry, what? ... [D]id I understand you to say, sir, that the Russians are not using Eastern Europe as their own sphere of influence in occupying most of the countries there and making sure with their troops that it's a communist zone?" In response to Frankel, Ford remained firm, insisting that Poland, Romania, and Yugoslavia were free from Soviet interference (Gwertzman, 1976). Ford had meant to say that the spirit of the people of Eastern Europe had not been crushed during Soviet occupation (Graham, 2016). However, his gaffe followed him for the remainder of the campaign, and research by a GOP pollster suggests that

---

[2] Druckman (2003) conducted an experiment where he exposed student subjects randomly to an audio or television version of the 1960 presidential debate about 40 years after the debate and found that students developed more positive evaluations of Kennedy, relative to Nixon, in the television condition.

Ford's resurgence in public opinion polls during the summer of 1976 and never resumed after the debate gaffe (Steeper, 1978).

A final example of an important debate moment occurred during the last debate between incumbent president George W. Bush and Democratic challenger John Kerry in 2004. The moderator, Bob Schieffer, asked both candidates, "Do you believe homosexuality is a choice?" Senator Kerry answered the question by saying, "We're all God's children, Bob. And I think if you were to talk to [Vice President] Dick Cheney's daughter, who is a lesbian, she would tell you that she's being who she was, she's being who she was born as." Postdebate coverage of the debate focused intensely and negatively on Kerry mentioning the younger Cheney's sexuality. Relying on a multimethodological design, Fridkin et al. (2008) found that the news media's spin in the twenty-four hours following the 2004 debate persuaded potential voters to change their views about the rival candidates, especially their evaluations of John Kerry.

In the more than sixty years since the first televised presidential debate, researchers have conducted numerous studies and found that debates impacted voters in a variety of ways. For example, debates produce changes in (1) political knowledge (e.g., Benoit and Hansen, 2004; Jennings et al., 2020), (2) candidate evaluations (Lanoue and Schrott, 1989; Warner and McKinney, 2013; Yawn and Beatty, 2000), and (3) campaign interest and political engagement (McKinney, Rill, and Thorson, 2016). Presidential debates can even change people's vote preference, especially among people with less information and people with weaker attitudes (e.g., McKinney and Warner, 2013).

In addition, a number of factors can moderate the impact of debates on citizens' assessments of the candidates, including preexisting attitudes about the candidates (e.g., Schrott and Lanoue, 2013), voter characteristics, such as paying attention to the news (e.g., Benoit, Blaney, and Pier, 1998; Jarman, 2005), the political context, such as the nomination campaign versus the general election (see Hillygus and Jackman, 2003; McKinney and Carlin, 2004), and the nature of the news coverage (e.g., Fridkin et al., 2007).

## WHO WON THE FIRST 2020 PRESIDENTIAL DEBATE?

Several "instant polls" were conducted around the first general election debate in 2020. For these surveys, respondents are contacted before the debate and interviewed, and they agree to watch the debate. After the debate, these respondents are recontacted and they answer several questions about the debate.³ The results of the 2020 polls were unanimous: Biden won the debate. According to a CNN poll taken immediately after the debate, 60 percent of respondents thought Biden had won compared to 28 percent calling Trump the winner.⁴ While the margins were closer with a CBS News poll (48 percent calling Biden the winner and 41 percent claiming Trump had won),⁵ as well as a CNBC/Change Research poll (53 percent saying Biden had won and 29 percent calling Trump the winner),⁶ both polls found that more people viewed Biden as the winner compared to Trump. A poll conducted by Data for Progress found a twelve-point advantage for Biden, with 51 percent of the respondents saying Biden had won the debate while 39 percent of the respondents declared Trump the winner.⁷

In our survey, respondents interviewed in October were asked if they watched the first presidential debate.⁸ If the respondents indicated they watched the debate, they were asked a series of questions about the debate.⁹ We began by asking respondents "Regardless of who you are planning to vote for in the election, who did you think won the first presidential debate?" and respondents could answer "Joe Biden," "Donald Trump," or "It was a tie." Among the almost 1,800 respondents, 52 percent say Biden won the debate, 32 percent indicate Trump was the winner, and 16 percent of the respondents call the debate a tie between the candidates. These results are quite similar to a poll conducted by Data for Progress immediately following the debate.

Typical for the polarized environment in 2020 (e.g., Abramowitz and Saunders, 2008), Democrats and Republicans hold quite divergent assessments of who won the debate.¹⁰ The data in Figure 2.1 show that partisans believe their candidate had won the debate. However, even among partisans, we see evidence that Joe Biden is viewed as doing better than Donald Trump. While more than eight out of ten (82 percent) Democrats claim

---

[3] www.nytimes.com/2020/09/30/us/elections/in-instant-polls-taken-after-the-debate-biden-comes-out-on-top.html
[4] www.cnn.com/2020/09/29/politics/donald-trump-joe-biden-debate-poll/index.html
[5] www.cbsnews.com/news/who-won-debate-first-presidential-biden-trump/
[6] www.cnbc.com/2020/10/01/biden-leads-polls-voters-say-he-beat-trump-in-first-debate.html
[7] www.vox.com/2020/9/30/21495284/data-for-progress-debate-poll
[8] Sixty-eight percent of the October respondents indicated that they watched the first presidential debate.
[9] Given Prior's (2012) research showing respondents often overreport watching presidential debates, we need to be cautious when trying to estimate the impact of the first debate on citizens' attitudes.
[10] The relationship between party identification and debate assessments is statistically significant at $p < .001$ ($\square^2 = 232.9$, df = 4).

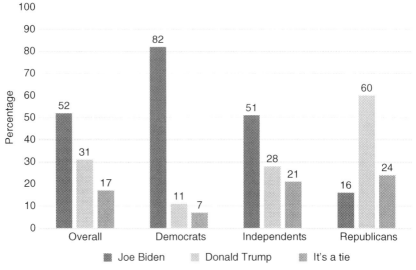

FIGURE 2.1 Who won the debate by partisanship

Biden won the debate, only six out of ten Republicans say Trump won the debate. Furthermore, while almost one in four (24 percent) Republicans call the debate a tie, less than one in ten (7 percent) Democrats make the same assessment. Finally, among independents, Biden is viewed as the winner more often than Trump. A majority of independents believe Biden won the debate (51 percent), while a little more than a quarter (28 percent) of these respondents state Trump won the debate.

## ASSESSMENTS OF THE CANDIDATES' PERFORMANCE IN THE 2020 PRESIDENTIAL DEBATE

We asked respondents to rate the candidates' debate performance on a scale from 1 to 10. The exact question wording was: "Thinking about the first debate, on a scale from 1 (very badly) to 10 (very well), how well did Donald Trump/Joe Biden perform in the debate?" Consistent with people's views about who won the debate, people's ratings of Joe Biden's performance are significantly higher than their evaluations of Donald Trump's performance during the debate. The data in Figure 2.2 indicate that respondents who report seeing the first debate rate Joe Biden significantly higher than Donald Trump. Biden's advantage is most dramatic among Democratic respondents and persists among independents. Among Republicans, Trump is given significantly higher ratings than Biden. Nevertheless, Democrats' ratings of Biden's performance (7.37)

## Views of the Candidates' Debate Performances

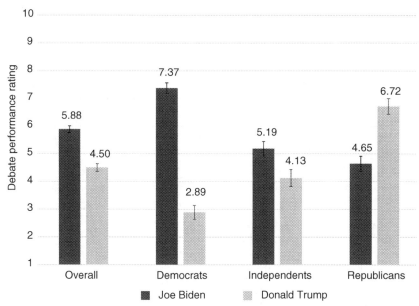

FIGURE 2.2 Debate performance rating by partisanship
Note: The mean debate performance ratings with 95% confidence intervals are displayed.

are significantly higher than Republicans' ratings of Trump's performance (6.72). These comparisons indicate that Biden is viewed as doing a better job than Trump during the first debate.

### Determinants of Debate Performance Ratings

We turn next to understanding how the political and psychological predispositions of citizens influence their view of Biden's and Trump's performances in the debate. We have already shown that partisanship is influential. In addition, because of the increases in polarization in today's political landscape, people often choose to pay attention to news reinforcing their existing predispositions. The emergence of cable television news programs, as well as internet news and social media sites, allows citizens to obtain news from like-minded sources (Peterson, Goel, and Iyengar, 2019).[11] Research examining the partisan nature of news shows

---
[11] While experimental and survey-based studies demonstrate partisan selective exposure (e.g., Levendusky, 2013; Stroud, 2011), the behavioral evidence (e.g., examining website visits, Twitter use) is mixed (e.g., Halberstam and Knight, 2016). Nevertheless, even if the partisan media's direct impact is relatively small, Druckman, Levendusky, and McClain (2018) show that the partisan media likely have an indirect effect via interpersonal communication.

that Fox News covers conservative issues and candidates more favorably, while MSNBC and CNN devote more positive coverage to liberal causes and candidates (e.g., Aday, 2010; Stroud, 2011).[12]

We expect that citizens who pay attention to sources only from the left will receive more critical news coverage of Trump's performance in the September debate compared to others who pay more attention to right-leaning media outlets. To illustrate, the postdebate analysis from left-leaning CNN began with Wolf Blitzer saying, "Clearly, this was the most chaotic presidential debate I've ever seen." Blitzer continues by praising Joe Biden, saying, "[Biden] clearly showed up today. He went head-to-head with the President of the United States who was often put on the defensive interrupting the vice president repeatedly."[13] Blitzer turned to CNN host Jake Tapper for his reaction to the first presidential debate. Tapper begins by saying, "That was a hot mess inside a dumpster fire inside a train wreck. That was the worst debate I have ever seen. In fact, it wasn't even a debate. It was a disgrace. And it's primarily because of President Trump." CNN correspondent Dana Bash, agreeing with Tapper, said, "That was a shitshow … Apologies for being maybe a little bit crude, but that was really the phrase that I'm getting from people on both sides of the aisle on text, and it's the only phrase that I can think of to really describe it." David Axelrod, former advisor to President Obama, continued by saying, "I don't think we've ever have seen a President of the United States completely lacking in shame. I mean, just shameless and obesely immoral. I mean, there's not a moral fiber in this man."

Sean Hannity of Fox News had a much different reaction to the debate. Hannity began his postdebate coverage by saying, "The very first presidential debate is now officially in the books and the extremely weak, the frail, the confused, kind of angry Joe Biden just got steamrolled by President Trump. Joe, flat out, refused to answer simple, basic fundamental questions, unable to respond to the President's beat downs. And he appeared flustered, irritated, and well, cranky. Joe, maybe he's past his bedtime, probably stayed up too late, needs his nap."[14] Hannity continues,

One thing I've concluded at the end of tonight is it's basically you're going to get a gladiator warrior fighter in Donald Trump, a guy that is going to go to battle

---

[12] See AllSides media bias of news outlets at www.allsides.com/media-bias/media-bias-ratings#ratings

[13] These quotations are from the postdebate CNN analysis transcript. See Blitzer (2020).

[14] These quotations are taken from a transcript of the Sean Hannity postdebate analysis on Fox News. See Hannity (2020).

like he has for the last four years, fighting for trade deals, fighting for his promises, getting the money for the wall, keep – you know, everything that he says he's going to do, including battling COVID.

One of Hannity's guests, Ari Fleisher, countered Hannity's assessment of the debate by explaining,

> I've got to say, we're not electing gladiators, and this shouldn't be a food fight. I think this was a train wreck tonight. Both candidates, too much interruption, too much back and forth. And that's just not good for the country. And so, it – there might be people who like to have this kind of thing for the entertainment value. I'm just not one of them.

Given the differences in the treatment of the candidates by news outlets with different partisan slants, we expect that people's partisan news diet will influence views of the candidates' performances in the debate. We examine partisan news consumption by asking "When it comes to staying up with the news, which of these news sources, if any, do you watch or consume regularly?" Respondents are offered a variety of responses, including MSNBC, CNN, Fox News, "other conservative news outlets, blogs, or websites," and "other progressive or liberal news outlets, blogs, or websites," as well as other sources.[15] We develop an index based on sources widely considered either liberal or conservative (e.g., Prior, 2012) where people who consume only liberal news sources are given the most positive score and people who consume only conservative news sources are given the most negative score.[16]

In addition to partisan news consumption, we expect people who are paying more attention to the news, generally, will be more likely to view Trump's performance in the debate more negatively than Biden's performance. We know that coverage of presidential debates is intense, dominating network and cable news cycles, online news sources, and social media sites like Twitter (e.g., Freelon and Karpf, 2015; Voth, 2017). Given the negative reaction from numerous pundits and news outlets (Lopez, 2020) as well as instant polls showing viewers thought Biden had won the debate (Bump, 2020), we hypothesize that people who are paying more attention to the news, regardless of the news source, will

---

[15] Additional response options are broadcast network news, Facebook, and Twitter.
[16] Specifically, people who say they pay attention to MSNBC, CNN, and other progressive or liberal news outlets and say they do not pay attention to Fox News or other conservative news outlets receive a score of 3 while people who say they pay attention to Fox News and other conservative news outlets and do not pay attention to MSNBC, CNN, or other liberal news outlets receive a score of –2.

develop more negative views of Trump and more positive views of Biden. We measure attention to news with the question "How often do you pay attention to news about politics and government affairs in a typical week?" with response options ranging from less than once a month (1) to every day (5).

We also examine the impact of the five psychological predispositions since we expect each of these predispositions to influence how people view the presidential debate and subsequent coverage of the event. To begin, given the confrontational nature of the first presidential debate of 2020, we expect that people who dislike conflict will develop more negative views of the candidates' debate performance. By virtually all accounts, the first debate between Trump and Biden was combative, as these headlines illustrate:[17]

**ABC News** First Presidential Debate between Trump and Biden Spirals into Chaotic Clash
**CBS News** First Debate Descents into Chaos as Trump and Biden Exchange Attacks
**CNBC** Vicious First Debate between Trump and Biden Offer Little on Policy, Lots of Conflict

Trump was particularly aggressive during the debate, frequently interrupting the moderator and Biden. In addition, he hurled insults at Biden, such as disparaging Biden's academic performance at the University of Delaware, saying, "He was the lowest or almost the lowest in your class. Don't ever use the word smart with me because you know what, there's nothing smart about you, Joe" (Sullivan, 2020). However, Biden also derided Trump during the debate, calling Trump a clown (twice) and declaring he was the worse president in US history (Martin and Burns, 2020). Given the conflictual nature of the debate, we expect people who disdain conflict to rate the candidates, and especially Trump, lower on the performance scale.[18]

We turn next to examining the impact of racial and sexist stereotypes on people's impressions of the candidates' performance in the debate. As discussed in Chapter 1, Trump has employed racist rhetoric before and during the length of his political career. We expect people who hold racist views will be more likely to view Trump's debate performance

[17] See abcnews.go.com/Politics/live-updates/first-presidential-debate/?id=73297227; www.cbsnews.com/live-updates/first-presidential-debate-trump-biden-wrap-up-moments/; www.cnbc.com/2020/09/29/first-presidential-debate-highlights-trump-vs-biden-.html
[18] See Chapter 1 for a discussion of how we are measuring the five psychological predispositions.

more favorably and will seek out information about the presidential debate reinforcing their views. Just as Donald Trump has made racist remarks, he also has a history of making sexist remarks as well as engaging in unwanted sexual contact before and during his political career. We hypothesize that people who hold sexist views about women may view Trump's debate performance in a more positive light and may search for information validating their preexisting attitudes.

In addition to conflict avoidance and racist and sexist attitudes, we expect that people who engage in authoritarian thinking will be more likely to develop favorable assessments of Trump compared to Biden. Trump's rhetoric often highlighted differences between Americans ("we") and "others," such as Mexicans, Muslims, immigrants, and minorities (Knuckey and Hassan, 2020). Such rhetoric is likely to appeal to people high in authoritarianism since the belief that certain groups are better than others and should wield more power is a central characteristic of authoritarianism (Smith, 2019).

Finally, we expect people who believe in conspiracies may develop more favorable impressions of Trump's performance in the first presidential debate. People high in conspiracy thinking may see Trump as an ally since he often disseminates conspiracy theories. In other words, we expect that Trump's penchant for conspiracy theories will resonate with people who engage in conspiratorial thinking, leading these individuals to rate Trump's debate performance more highly than people who are less likely to believe in conspiracies.[19]

## Explaining Debate Performance Ratings

We examine how the following forces influence people's impressions of Trump's and Biden's debate performances: campaign and political factors (e.g., partisanship, partisan media diet, news attention) and psychological predispositions (i.e., authoritarian tendencies, conspiracy thinking, racism and sexism, and conflict avoidance).[20] We present the results in Table 2.1, where we estimate one model explaining debate performance for each candidate.

---

[19] Lamberty, Hellmann, and Oeberst (2018) find people's level of conspiracy thinking is associated with voting for Trump in 2016.
[20] All of the independent variables in Table 2.1 are measured during the September wave of the panel, thereby increasing our confidence that the independent variables are influencing performance ratings measured in October. In estimating the models throughout this book, we do not include ideology because of the high correlation between party

TABLE 2.1 *Ordinary least squares regression predicting assessments of the candidates' debate performance*

|  | Donald Trump[1] |  | Joe Biden |  |
|---|---|---|---|---|
| *Political characteristics* |  |  |  |  |
| Attention to news | −.34 (.07)** | −.10 | .16 (.07)** | .06 |
| Partisan media | −.69 (.09)** | −.20 | .50 (.08)** | .17 |
| Party identification | .44 (.04)** | .31 | −.35 (.03)** | −.30 |
| *Psychological predispositions* |  |  |  |  |
| Authoritarianism | −.03 (.06) | −.01 | .10 (.06) | .05 |
| Conflict avoidance | −.18 (.02)** | −.17 | −.01 (.02) | −.01 |
| Conspiracy thinking | .07 (.01)** | .15 | .03 (.01)** | .07 |
| Hostile sexism | .04 (.03) | .03 | −.06 (.03)* | −.06 |
| Racial resentment | .16 (.02)** | .22 | −.09 (.02)** | −.15 |
| Constant | 3.32 (.56) |  | 7.54 (.54)** |  |
| $R^2$ | .46 |  | .29 |  |
| Number of respondents | 1,230 |  | 1,224 |  |

*Note:* The exact question wording for the dependent variables is: "Thinking about the first debate, on a scale from 1 (very badly) to 10 (very well), how well did (Donald Trump/Joe Biden) perform in the debate?" Attention to news ranges from low (1) to high (5). Partisan media ranges from −2 (only conservative news) to 3 (only liberal news). Party identification ranges from 1 (strong Democrat) to 7 (strong Republican). Authoritarianism ranges from 0 (low authoritarian thinking) to 4 (high authoritarian thinking). Conflict avoidance ranges from 5 (low conflict avoidance) to 20 (high conflict avoidance). Conspiracy thinking ranges from 0 (low conspiracy thinking) to 30 (high conspiracy thinking). Hostile sexism ranges from 4 (low sexism) to 16 (high sexism). Racial resentment ranges from 4 (low racial resentment) to 20 (high racial resentment). Each of the independent variables is measured during the September wave of the panel survey. For additional information about measurement, see the text.

[1] Unstandardized regression coefficients are followed by standard errors (in parentheses), followed by levels of statistical significance, and standardized coefficients.

** $p < .01$
* $p < .05$

We begin by looking at the political measures, starting with partisanship. As expected, partisanship strongly predicts how people rate the competing candidates' performance in the September presidential debate. The standardized coefficients indicate that party identification is the most

identification and ideology (e.g., the correlation is .64 for respondents in the October panel) and because including ideology does not substantively change the results presented in the models. In addition, we include demographic variables like age, gender, and race when they are theoretically important for the dependent variables of interest. In models where demographic variables are viewed as less theoretically important, we include the demographic variables only if their inclusion changes the impact of the psychological and political predispositions on the dependent variable.

important variable predicting both Trump's and Biden's ratings in the debate. For Trump, every one-point change in party identification is associated with almost a half-point change in the ten-point performance scale.[21] For Biden, the unstandardized coefficient is a bit smaller for party identification, with every one-point change in partisanship predicting about a one-third change in ratings of Biden's performance.

Similar to partisanship, we find that the news outlets people pay attention to powerfully predicts how they view Trump's and Biden's performances in the debate. For Trump, as one moves from watching only liberal news sources to watching only conservative news sources, ratings of his performance increase by 3.5 points on the ten-point performance scale. For Biden, the impact of the partisan media is not quite as powerful; moving from an exclusively conservative news diet to watching only liberal news sources increases his performance ratings by almost 2.5 points. Paying attention to the news, in general, decreases people's assessments of Trump's debate performance and increases positive views of Biden's performance. This finding supports our expectation that the news media's consensus regarding the outcome of the first debate affects people's views of the debate.

Moving to psychological predispositions, we see that people's level of conflict avoidance significantly influences their views of President Trump's performance but not of Joe Biden's performance ratings. These findings are consistent with reporting of the presidential debate since Trump's behavior was more frequently described as confrontational. Using the unstandardized regression coefficients presented in Table 2.1 to estimate Trump's performance ratings, we find that people who score the lowest on conflict avoidance rate Trump at more than 6 (6.23) on the ten-point performance scale, while people who score the highest on conflict avoidance rate Trump more than 2.5 points lower at 3.54 on the debate performance scale.[22] These results indicate that, controlling for a number of additional factors, people who dislike conflict are more likely to evaluate

---

[21] Party identification is measured with the following question: "Generally speaking, do you usually think of yourself as a Republican, Democrat, an Independent, or what?" Respondents are asked to place themselves on a scale ranging from strong Democrat (1) to strong Republican (7).

[22] When estimating the impact of conflict avoidance on predicting ratings of Trump's debate performance, we keep all remaining variables in the model at their means. Throughout this book, we keep all remaining variables in the model at their means when using the ordinary least squares regression coefficients to estimate predicted values.

Trump's debate performance much more negatively than people who are more tolerant of conflict.[23]

In addition to people's preference for conflict, we expect people holding more sexist and racist views to develop more positive views of Trump's debate performance. In contrast, people who score lower on measures of sexism and racism are expected to rate Biden's debate performance more favorably. We find that people's scores on the racial resentment scale strongly predict how people view the debate. The standardized regression coefficients indicate that racial resentment is among the most powerful variables in each of the models in Table 2.1.

We rely on the Ordinary Least Squares (OLS) regression coefficients in Table 2.1 to graphically display the impact of racial resentment on debate performance ratings (see Figure 2.3). In particular, when racial resentment is at a minimum, people rate Donald Trump's performance at about 3 on the ten-point scale. In contrast, people who score the highest on the racial resentment scale rate his performance at almost 6 on the debate performance measure. We see the opposite relationship when we look at respondents' perceptions of Biden. People who are high on racial

---

[23] The impact of psychological predispositions on people's views of the candidate's debate performance may be moderated or conditioned by people's partisan news diet. We estimate the conditional relationship between psychological predispositions and partisan news diet in the analyses throughout this book. We rely on Andrew Hayes' (2022) conditional process model and use his PROCESS macro to test for moderation effects. Since our measure of partisan news diet does not capture how often people pay attention to partisan news sources in a typical week, we need to be cautious when generalizing from our moderation analysis. When predicting Trump's debate performance, we find a negative and significant moderation effect for partisan news attention on racial resentment (coefficient = –.06, standard error = .01), hostile sexism (coefficient = –.06, standard error = .02), and conspiracy thinking (coefficient = –.023, standard error = .009). We find that the impact of these predispositions on ratings of Trump's debate is significantly more powerful and positive when people are consuming more conservative news. For example, among people who consume only conservative news, the effect of racial resentment on Trump's performance rating is .25 (with a standard error of .03). However, for people who consume only liberal news, the effect of racial resentment on Trump's performance ratings is insignificant (effect = .02 with a standard error of 04). For Biden's debate performance ratings, we find a significant and positive moderation effect for partisan news attention on racial resentment (coefficient = .06, standard error = .01), hostile sexism (coefficient = .05, standard error = .02), and conspiracy thinking (coefficient = –.026, standard error = .008). We find that the impact of these predispositions on ratings of Biden's debate is significantly more powerful and negative when people are consuming more conservative news. For example, the impact of racial resentment on views of Biden's debate performance is –.23 (with a standard error of .05) for people who consume only conservative news. However, among people who consume only liberal news, racial resentment has no effect on ratings of his debate performance (effect = .06 with a standard error of .04).

## Views of the Candidates' Debate Performances

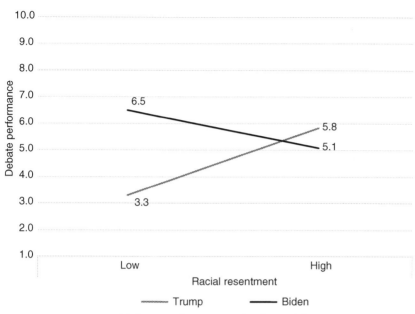

FIGURE 2.3 Debate performance rating by racial resentment

resentment score Biden in the middle of the ten-point debate performance scale, while people low on racial resentment rate him at about 6.5.

When we examine the effect of sexist attitudes on ratings of the candidates' debate performance, we find that hostile sexism scores do not significantly influence ratings of Trump's performance scores, although the coefficient is positive. However, people's level of sexism does alter views of Biden's debate performance. People who score low on the hostile sexism scale (e.g., people more likely to disagree with statements such as "most women interpret innocent remarks or acts as being sexist") rate Biden's performance in the debate significantly higher than people who score higher on the sexism measure. Overall, we see sexist and racist attitudes alter how people view the candidates' debate performance.

Finally, when we look at the psychological predispositions of authoritarianism and conspiratorial thinking, we find only partial support for our expectations. For example, we find that people's placement on the authoritarianism scale is not related to debate performance ratings for Trump or Biden. This contradicts our expectation that authoritarianism would be positively related to views on Trump's performance in the debate. Turning to conspiracy thinking, we find partial support for our expectations. People with high scores on the conspiracy thinking measure view Trump's debate performance more favorably. However, and not as expected, we also find a positive relationship between conspiratorial thinking and views about Biden's performance. The positive relationship is stronger for Trump than for Biden. The unstandardized coefficient for conspiracy thinking is more than two times larger in the model predicting Trump's debate performance than the model predicting Biden's debate performance.

Overall, the results show people's partisan predispositions and their political news choices influence how they view the candidates' performance in the debate. In addition, and central to the citizen-centered theory of campaigns, people's psychological predispositions systematically influence their views of the candidates' performance in the September debate, even after controlling for important political variables. Attitudes about race and gender as well as people's tendency to engage in conspiracy thinking shape how the debate is viewed. Finally, people's tolerance for conflict strongly predicts evaluations of Trump's performance.

### Explaining Judgments about "Who Won" the Debate

Psychological predispositions, along with partisanship and news consumption patterns, shape how people evaluate the performances of the rival candidate in the September debate. We turn next to see if these same forces significantly influence people's assessment of who won the debate. The results are presented in Table 2.2.[24] As in the earlier analysis, we find that people who pay more attention to the news are significantly more likely to view Biden as winning the debate. In addition, party identification and partisan news attention are predictably related to assessments of who won the debate. For example, as exposure to conservative news increases, relative to exposure to liberal news, people are more likely to consider Trump the victor of the debate (or, to use Sean Hannity's analogy, the "winning gladiator").

---

[24] Given the ordinal nature of the dependent variable (i.e., 1 = the respondent viewed Biden as the winner of the debate; 0 = the respondent considered the debate a tie; −1 = the respondent viewed Trump as the winner of the debate), we initially relied on ordinal regression to explain the variance in people's assessments of who won the debate. We replicated the analysis with OLS regression and the results do not differ depending on the analytical procedure. Therefore, we report the OLS results because of greater ease of interpretation.

TABLE 2.2 *OLS regression predicting "who won" the debate*

|  | Who won the debate?[1] |  |
|---|---|---|
| *Political characteristics* |  |  |
| Attention to news | .08 (.02)** | .09 |
| Partisan media | .15 (.02)** | .16 |
| Party identification | −.17 (.01)** | −.45 |
| *Psychological predispositions* |  |  |
| Authoritarianism | −.014 (.016) | −.02 |
| Conflict avoidance | .029 (.006)** | .10 |
| Conspiracy thinking | −.013 (.004)** | −.10 |
| Hostile sexism | −.01 (.01) | −.01 |
| Racial resentment | −.04 (.01)** | −.20 |
| Constant | .85 (.15)** |  |
| $R^2$ | .52 |  |
| Number of respondents | 1,121 |  |

*Note:* The exact question wording for the dependent variables is: "Regardless of who you are planning to vote for in the election, who did you think won the first presidential debate? Joe Biden (1) Donald Trump (−1) It was a tie (0)." Attention to news ranges from low (1) to high (5). Partisan media ranges from −2 (only conservative news) to 3 (only liberal news). Party identification ranges from 1 (strong Democrat) to 7 (strong Republican). Authoritarianism ranges from 0 (low authoritarian thinking) to 4 (high authoritarian thinking). Conflict avoidance ranges from 5 (low conflict avoidance) to 20 (high conflict avoidance). Conspiracy thinking ranges from 0 (low conspiracy thinking) to 30 (high conspiracy thinking). Hostile sexism ranges from 4 (low sexism) to 16 (high sexism). Racial resentment ranges from 4 (low racial resentment) to 20 (high racial resentment). Each of the independent variables is measured during the September wave of the panel survey. For additional information about measurement, see the text.

[1] Unstandardized regression coefficients are followed by standard errors (in parentheses), followed by levels of statistical significance, and standardized coefficients.

** $p < .01$
* $p < .05$

We also see that people's psychological predispositions significantly alter people's views regarding the outcome of the debate. Racial resentment continues to powerfully influence how people perceive the debate. Aside from party identification, level of racial resentment is the most powerful variable predicting views of who won and who lost the debate (i.e., the standardized coefficient of −.20 is the second largest in the model). In addition, we once again see that people's level of conflict avoidance alters how the debate is viewed. As people's dislike of conflict increases, they are significantly more likely to consider Biden the winner of the debate compared to Trump. Finally, and consistent with our analyses in Table 2.1, people's level of conspiracy thinking is negatively related to assessments about the debate. As conspiracy thinking increases, interpretations about who won the debate changes from favoring Biden to favoring Trump.[25]

Overall, the results presented in Tables 2.1 and 2.2 clearly demonstrate that people's evaluations of the candidates' performance in the debate, along with assessments of the outcome of the debate, are affected by traditional political variables as well as psychological predispositions.[26] These results support the citizen-centered theory of campaigns. As we theorized, by including psychological predispositions, we improve our understanding of how people evaluate significant campaign events, such as the first general election debate of 2020.

## THE ELECTORAL CONSEQUENCE OF THE FIRST 2020 PRESIDENTIAL DEBATE

We turn now to explore the impact of the debate on overall assessments of the competing candidates in October and changes in overall assessments between September and October. Looking ahead in the book, we will be conducting similar analyses in each of the next four chapters. More specifically, we will explore how views about COVID-19 (Chapter 3), the social justice protests (Chapter 4), and the issue of election integrity (Chapter 5) influence overall evaluations of Trump and Biden in October and changes in overall assessments across the campaign. In each chapter, we develop a "reduced" model where we isolate the impact of the specific issue or event examined in the chapter on overall impressions

---

[25] As we did earlier, we estimate the conditional relationship between partisan news diet and psychological predispositions on people's assessment of who won the debate. We find a significant moderation effect for racial resentment (coefficient = .02, standard error = .01), hostile sexism (coefficient = -.02, standard error = .01), conspiracy thinking (coefficient = .008, standard error = .002), and authoritarianism (coefficient = .03, standard error = .01). For example, the impact of conspiracy thinking on assessments of who won the debate is negative (i.e., favoring Trump) and significant for people who are exposed to more conservative news; the impact of conspiracy thinking on views of the debate winner becomes inconsequential for people who score 2 or higher on the partisan news index (two or more liberal sources, compared to conservative sources).

[26] While not everyone in our panel survey watched the October presidential debate, we have confidence in our results for a few reasons. First, more than two-thirds of the sample of respondents say they watched the first presidential debate. Second, when examining variables predicting whether people said they watched the debate, we find partisanship and their partisan news diet are *not* significantly related to debate watching. This suggests that we are not overrepresenting one side of the ideological spectrum. Nevertheless, since we cannot be sure that everyone who said they watched the debate actually watched the debate, we need to be cautious when generalizing from these results.

## The Electoral Consequences of the Debate

of the candidates, controlling for standard political variables. Finally, in Chapter 6, we develop a comprehensive model predicting overall evaluations of the presidential candidates where we include as independent variables each of the issues and events explored in the preceding chapters in order to explain evaluations of Trump and Biden in November.

In this chapter, we begin by examining the impact of the first presidential debate on people's "feeling thermometer" ratings of the two candidates in October.[27] Feeling thermometers have been used extensively by political scientists to assess citizens' impressions of the candidates (e.g., Markus and Converse, 1979). These measures are intuitive and easy for respondents to use and are powerfully related to voting decisions.[28] In the second analysis, we examine the impact of the debate on changes in feeling thermometer scores between September and October and we include ratings of the candidate's debate performance as well as assessments of who won the debate.

When examining the impact of the debate on impressions of the candidates after the debate, we include standard variables that may influence evaluations of the candidates in October.[29] We include a general assessment of the state of the national economy since retrospective economic assessments can influence views of presidential candidates (e.g., Fiorina, 1981; Kinder and Kiewiet, 1981).[30] In addition, we measure people's impressions of the candidates' personal traits because personality ratings often affect overall evaluations of presidential candidates during campaigns (e.g., Funk, 1996).[31] Third, we include the seven-point party

---

[27] Almost three-quarters of the panel respondents (i.e., 73 percent) completed the October wave of the survey within one week of the first debate.

[28] We ask respondents to rate political figures on the feeling thermometer in each of the waves of the survey. Respondents are told the following about the feeling thermometer: "Ratings between 51 degrees and 100 degrees mean that you feel favorable and warm toward the person. Ratings between 0 degrees and 49 degrees mean that you don't feel favorable toward the person and that you don't care too much for that person. You would rate the person at the 50-degree mark if you don't feel particularly warm or cold toward the person. If you come to a person whose name you don't recognize, you don't need to rate that person."

[29] The control variables (party identification, general economic assessment, and trait evaluations) are measured in the September wave of the panel.

[30] The exact question wording is "Now thinking about the economy in the country as a whole, would you say that over the past year the nation's economy has gotten better, stayed about the same, or gotten worse?" with options ranging from much worse (1) to much better (5).

[31] In particular, respondents are asked how well six traits describe each of the candidates. The six traits are: "strong leader," "cares about people," "good sense of humor," "honest," "hardworking," and "even-tempered." Respondents rate how well each trait describes Trump/Biden on a four-point scale ranging from "not well at all" (1) to "very well" (4). We sum ratings for each candidate across the six traits with the resulting index ranging from 6 to 24.

identification measure given the strong relationship between party attachment and feelings toward the presidential candidates (e.g., Campbell et al., 1960; Markus and Converse, 1979).

## DID THE DEBATE INFLUENCE IMPRESSIONS OF THE CANDIDATES IN OCTOBER?

We initially examine a static model to see if views about the debate, asked in the October wave of the survey, predict ratings of the candidates.[32] As the data in the top half of Table 2.3 show, people's views about the debate powerfully alter impressions of the candidates. For example, the unstandardized regression coefficient for debate performance suggests that every one-unit increase on the debate performance scale is associated with more than a four-point increase in October feeling thermometer ratings for Biden and Trump. Furthermore, the standardized regression coefficients in both the Trump and Biden models indicate that views about the candidate's debate performance are among the most important factors in these models.[33]

We can illustrate the impact of the debate by calculating the predicted values of the dependent variable (i.e., feeling thermometer scores for Trump and Biden) while varying people's debate performance ratings and people's views of who won the debate. We display the results in Figure 2.4. In the top figure, we vary debate performance from its low point (1) to its high point (10). Differences in debate ratings produce an expected change of about 40 points on the feeling thermometer scores for Biden and Trump. For example, people who rate Trump's performance as dismal (i.e., 1 on the ten-point debate performance scale) are estimated to rate Trump at 28.9 on the feeling thermometer in October. In contrast, people who view Trump's performance as stellar (i.e., 10 on the ten-point debate performance scale) are estimated to rate Trump at 67.2 on the October feeling thermometer. These results indicate the substantial impact people's assessments of the September debate have on changes in people's overall views of the candidate in October.

Like debate performance ratings, decisions about who won the debate strongly influence overall evaluations. Further, the unstandardized

---

[32] Our results do not substantively change if we measure the rival factors during the October wave of the survey. That is, both measures of debate performance significantly influence evaluations of Trump and Biden in October. We rely on the September measures of these rival factors in order to establish time-order.

[33] The standardized regression coefficients allow us to assess the relative strength of the different variables within each of the models.

TABLE 2.3 *Impact of the first debate on overall evaluations of the presidential candidates*

|  | Thermometer ratings in October[1] ||
|  | Trump thermometer | Biden thermometer |
| --- | --- | --- |
| *Debate factors* | | |
| Candidate's debate performance | 4.26 (.29)** | 4.56 (.28)** |
| Who won the debate | −7.65 (.95)** | 6.69 (.90)** |
| *Rival factors* | | |
| General economic assessment | .05 (.43) | .23 (.40) |
| Party identification | 1.91 (.28)** | −2.56 (.30)** |
| Trait assessment | 2.53 (.14)** | 2.26 (.13)** |
| Constant | −15.33 (1.83)** | .16 (2.65) |
| $R^2$ | .87 | .82 |
| Number of respondents | 1,003 | 994 |

|  | Changes in thermometer ratings from September to October[2] ||
|  | Trump thermometer | Biden thermometer |
| --- | --- | --- |
| *Debate factors* | | |
| Candidate's debate performance | 3.22 (.25)** | 3.31 (.24)** |
| Who won the debate | −7.40 (.81)** | 5.32 (.80)** |
| *Rival factors* | | |
| General economic assessment | 1.10 (.36)** | .52 (.35) |
| Party identification | 2.14 (.23)** | −2.51 (.25)** |
| Trait assessment | 2.82 (.11)** | 2.98 (.11)** |

(*continued*)

TABLE 2.3 (*continued*)

| | Changes in thermometer ratings from September to October | |
|---|---|---|
| | Trump thermometer | Biden thermometer |
| Intercept | −17.72 (1.52)** | −5.38 (2.28)** |
| Random effects | | |
| Variance of intercept | 127.68 (7.41)** | 143.98 (8.77)** |
| Variance of repeated measures (time) | 86.50 (3.63)** | 108.88 (4.64)** |
| Akaike information criterion | 18,409.11 | 18,347.34 |
| Log likelihood | 18,393.11 | 18,331.34 |
| Number of respondents | 1,159 | 1,130 |

*Note:* The dependent variable is the October feeling thermometer for each candidate, which ranges from 0 (very cold feelings for the candidate) to 100 (very warm feelings for the candidate). The candidate's debate performance ranges from 1 (the candidate performed very badly in the debate) to 10 (the candidate performed very well in the debate). Who won the debate values are −1 (Trump won the debate), 0 (the debate was a tie), and 1 (Biden won the debate). General economic assessment ranges from 1 (the economy has gotten much worse) to 5 (the economy has gotten much better). Party identification ranges from 1 (strong Democrat) to 7 (strong Republican). Trait assessment ranges from 6 (most negative) to 24 (most positive). Each of the rival factors is measured during the September wave of the panel survey.

[1] Unstandardized regression coefficients are presented with standard errors (in parentheses), followed by levels of statistical significance, and standardized coefficients.

[2] Estimated parameters of multilevel modeling (MLM) are presented with standard errors (in parentheses), followed by levels of statistical significance. In the MLM model, debate factors and the rival factors are fixed effects.

** $p < .01$

* $p < .05$

## The Debate Impact on Candidate Ratings in October

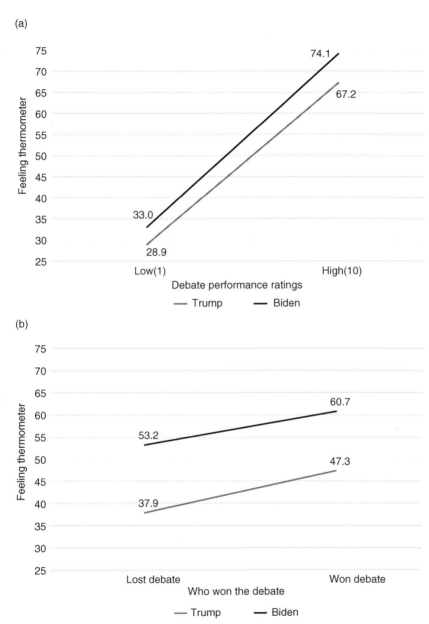

FIGURE 2.4 Impact of the first debate on October evaluations of the candidates

coefficients suggest that judgments about who won or lost the debate are somewhat more consequential for Trump than Biden (i.e., the unstandardized coefficient is −7.65 in the Trump model and 6.69 in the Biden model). Finally, the standardized coefficients show these assessments are as important as partisanship for understanding people's October evaluations of Biden and Trump.

As we did earlier, we estimate the impact of views about the debate winner by calculating the predicted values of the dependent variables (i.e., feeling thermometer scores for Trump and Biden) while varying the winner of the debate. We present these predictions at the bottom half of Figure 2.4. When we vary opinions about who won or lost the debate, we estimate Biden gains 13 points on the feeling thermometer when viewed as the winner of the debate, moving from 47.3 (i.e., when he is viewed as the loser) to 60.7 (i.e., when he is viewed as the winner). Trump gains more than 15 points on the feeling thermometer, moving from an estimated 37.9 on the feeling thermometer when he is viewed as the loser of the debate, compared to a score of 53.2 when he is classified as the winner.

### DID THE DEBATE PRODUCE CHANGES IN CANDIDATE EVALUATION FROM SEPTEMBER TO OCTOBER?

Now, we examine whether the first presidential debate produces *changes* in people's evaluations of Biden and Trump from September (before the debate) to October (after the debate). We rely on multilevel modeling (also called random effects models or linear mixed models) since we have repeated measures (i.e., feeling thermometer scores in September and feeling thermometer scores in October).[34] We report the results in the bottom half of Table 2.3.

These results once again demonstrate the importance of the September debate. Even controlling for rival forces like party identification, economic assessments, and trait evaluations, we demonstrate that evaluations of the candidates' performance in the debate as well as decisions about who won the debate produces significant changes in evaluations of the candidates. Further, and consistent with the static model, the impact of views of who won the debate is more substantial for Trump than for Biden (i.e., the estimated parameter measuring assessments of who won

[34] As Hair and Favero (2019) explain, OLS regression treats units of analysis as independent observations. However, with panel data, the units of observations (e.g., asking a respondent to rate Trump on the feeling thermometer in September and October) are not independent. Therefore, with OLS regression, the error terms may be correlated, leading to biased estimates of standard errors and increasing the risk of type 1 errors (i.e., rejecting the null hypothesis when the null hypothesis is correct). With multilevel modeling, the standard errors of the coefficients are unbiased, reducing the risk of type 1 errors. In subsequent chapters, when we are estimating change over time, we rely on multilevel modeling.

the debate is −7.40 in the Trump model and 5.32 in the Biden model). In the end, the debate most certainly advantaged Biden and hurt Trump with potential voters because evaluations of Trump's performance are more negative than those of Biden's performance and more people considered Biden the winner of the debate.

## CONCLUSION AND IMPLICATIONS

Shane Goldmacher (2020), a reporter for the *New York Times*, summarized the first debate by writing,

> Shouting, interruptions and often incoherent cross talk filled the air as Mr. Trump purposefully and repeatedly heckled and blurted over his rival and the moderator alike in a 90-minute melee that showcased the president's sense of urgency to upend a race in which polls show him trailing. Mr. Biden labored to get his points in over Mr. Trump's stream of interjections, turning directly to the camera for refuge from a scrum that hardly represented a contest of ideas. But Mr. Biden did not stumble, contradicting months of questions from the Trump campaign about his mental fitness, and Mr. Trump seemed to do little to bring over voters who were not already part of his base.

According to our analysis, Trump's confrontational style did not produce favorable ratings of his performance. We find that more people view Biden as the winner of the first debate and Biden's performance ratings are significantly higher than Trump's ratings, except among Republicans. We also demonstrate that people who have low tolerance for conflict develop significantly more negative views of Trump's performance and are significantly more likely to consider Biden the winner of the debate. Furthermore, people's level of racism and conspiratorial thinking shape views of Trump's and Biden's performances during the first presidential debate. We demonstrate that people's psychological predispositions, even in the face of powerful political controls, strongly affect impressions of the September debate.

Furthermore, we find citizens' views of the debate almost assuredly had electoral consequences. We show that evaluations of the candidates' performance in the debate as well as people's views of who won the debate influence overall evaluations of Trump and Biden and produce significant changes in ratings of Trump and Biden from September to October. While Biden did not emerge from the debate unscathed (e.g., telling a sitting president to "shut up" could be seen as crossing a line of decency), Trump's demeanor, the nature of his attacks, and his answers to questions posed by the moderator (e.g., refusing to condemn white supremacists) led people to view Trump's debate performance more negatively than his rival's performance. These assessments produce consequential changes in overall views of the candidates.

Our findings validate the importance of presidential debates. Especially if a debate is considered a lopsided affair, the winning candidate can reap significant electoral benefits, while the losing candidate will face lower evaluations and potentially less support at the polls. The first debate in the 2020 general election illustrates the power of campaign events. We expect that this "ugly" contest between the Republican incumbent and the Democratic challenger will be included in the history of consequential debate performances recounted by pundits, commentators, and journalists every election season.

The negative consequences of the poor debate performance may have lasted longer than a typical general election debate because Trump refused to agree to the second debate scheduled for October 15, 2020. The CPD announced that the second debate would be virtual after Trump tested positive for the coronavirus on October 2, 2020. Trump quickly rejected the plan for a virtual debate and said he would not show up. The planned third debate, scheduled for October 22, 2020, would become the second and final presidential debate. Thus, Trump's erratic and aggressive performance in the first debate would potentially persist in the public consciousness for up to three weeks until tens of millions of potential voters focused attention on the last debate.

Trump's contraction of COVID-19 changed the dynamics of the presidential campaign in the closing stretch of the election. In addition to precipitating the cancellation of a live second debate, the diagnosis focused attention anew on the pandemic during the final weeks of the campaign. Trump had repeatedly downplayed the severity of the COVID-19 pandemic. During the September debate, he said he wore a mask "when needed," he disparaged Biden for following social distance guidelines, and he contended that "we've had no negative effect" from large campaign rallies (Segers, 2020). Therefore, when Trump, along with his wife and son, and members of his inner circle tested positive for COVID-19 around the time of the first debate, the political ramifications of the pandemic became even more salient to the electorate. In Chapter 3, we examine how Trump's diagnosis and hospitalization changed people's views of the coronavirus outbreak as well as altered how people judged Trump's performance as president.

# 3

# The Priming of COVID-19 during the Campaign

## *The Consequences of Trump's Coronavirus Diagnosis*

Americans believed the COVID-19 pandemic was the most important problem facing the nation during the 2020 presidential campaign.[1] And President Trump himself contracted COVID-19 and was hospitalized during the home stretch of the campaign. His diagnosis and treatment occurred between the September and October waves of our panel survey, providing us with unique analytical leverage to examine how this crisis shaped voters' beliefs and behaviors during the fall election.

On Election Day 2020, the United States reported its second-highest count of new COVID-19 cases, with over 91,530 cases.[2] On the same day, hospitalizations topped 50,000 and more than 1,000 deaths were recorded. In addition, several states – including Ohio, Pennsylvania, Minnesota, Idaho, New Mexico, and Maine – logged record daily cases (Martin, 2020). The story of the COVID-19 deadly crisis, though, began almost a year earlier, on December 31, 2019, in Wuhan, China, when health officials notified the World Health Organization (WHO) of a cluster of pneumonia-like illnesses. On January 21, 2020, the Centers for Disease Control (CDC) confirmed the first case of COVID-19 in the United States: a thirty-five-year-old man living in Washington state tested positive for the coronavirus six days after returning from Wuhan. About a month later, on February 20, the CDC announced the

---

[1] news.gallup.com/poll/317765/satisfaction-among-americans-remains-nine-year-low.aspx

[2] The number of COVID-19 cases per day would be over three times this high in January 2021.

first COVID-19 death in the United States – a man in his fifties, also in Washington state.[3]

At the end of February 2020, in an interview on Fox News, Trump equated COVID-19 to the flu, saying, "This is a flu. This is like a flu...It's a little like a regular flu that we have flu shots for. And we'll essentially have a flu shot for this in a fairly quick manner." A few weeks later, on March 11, the WHO designated COVID-19 as a pandemic. On the same day, Tom Hanks announced that he and his wife, Rita Wilson, had contracted COVID-19; the NBA suspended their season; and a dozen states closed schools. On March 13, Trump declared a national emergency, allowing the government to release billions of dollars in federal aid to help state and local governments with their COVID-19 response. A week later, California became the first state to issue a stay-at-home order. During the next two months, forty-two states and territories would follow suit.

On March 16, Trump told Americans to avoid gathering in groups of more than ten and to stop eating in restaurants and taking nonessential trips for the next fifteen days. This is the closest the federal government would come to calling for a nationwide shutdown during 2020. A few days later, under pressure from political conservatives in his party, Trump said he was considering withdrawing the guidelines for social distancing, saying: "We cannot let the cure be worse than the problem itself." On March 19, he told a *Washington Post* editor, Bob Woodward, that he intentionally misled Americans by minimizing the danger of COVID-19: "I wanted to always play it down. I still like playing it down, because I don't want to create a panic." Woodward recounts this interview in his book released in September 2020.[4] By the end of March, the United States was the epicenter of the pandemic, with more than 81,000 cases and 1,000 deaths.

By April 11, the coronavirus death toll in the United States was the highest in the world. Four weeks after Trump declared the coronavirus outbreak a national emergency, twenty-two million Americans filed for unemployment aid – the steepest job loss since the Great Depression. A day later, on April 17, Trump tweeted "LIBERATE MINNESOTA," "LIBERATE MICHIGAN," and "LIBERATE VIRGINIA," supporting

---

[3] Information on the COVID-19 timeline comes from "A Brief History of COVID, 1 Year In" by Kaitlin Sullivan in *Everyday Health*, www.everydayhealth.com/coronavirus/a-brief-history-of-covid-one-year-in/, as well as "Sorrow and Stamina, Defiance and Despair: It's Been a Year," by Reis Thebault, Tim Meko, and Junne Alcantara in the *Washington Post*, www.washingtonpost.com/nation/interactive/2021/coronavirus-timeline/

[4] www.nbcnews.com/politics/donald-trump/trump-told-bob-woodward-he-knew-february-covid-19-was-n1239658

protesters who were ignoring social distancing guidance and demanding their states reopen. On April 23, Georgia became the first state to reopen businesses, and a week later, the federal government's social distancing guidelines expired and many states began reopening plans.

In mid-May, Trump announced "Operation Warp Speed," a partnership between federal agencies and private companies to produce and distribute a vaccine by the end of 2020. In the early summer, cases spiked across the southern United States, driven by young adults spreading the virus at social gatherings. During May, forty-three states began at least some form of reopening, hoping to boost their economies (seven states never had stay-at-home orders). By the end of May, coronavirus deaths in the United States surpassed 100,000.

The story only worsens across the summer of 2020. In June, in the West and South, more than a dozen states set records for new infections. Unemployment also hit a new record; for thirteen straight weeks, more than one million people filed for aid for the first time. On July 9, 2020, the WHO announced that COVID-19 may be airborne. Two days later, Trump wore a mask in public for the first time, more than three months after the CDC recommended face coverings for all Americans. A study during the month of July found that more than five million Americans lost their health insurance between February and May. Two vaccines, produced by Pfizer and Moderna, began large clinical trials while the official US death toll reached 150,000 by the end of July.

The Sturgis Motorcycle Rally in South Dakota on August 7, 2020, became a "superspreader" event, with nearly a half million people attending the weeklong rally, helping fuel a surge in cases across the Midwest. Cases traced back to the event were located in eighty-seven counties in Minnesota alone, according to a CDC report. At the end of August, infections surged on college campuses across the country. On September 11, Trump said the country had "rounded the final turn," but the country's top infectious disease doctor, Anthony Fauci, contradicted him the next day, saying, "I'm sorry, but I have to disagree with that." By September 20, the US death toll climbed past 200,000. On September 26, about 150 people gathered in the Rose Garden at the White House for a ceremony where Trump nominated Judge Amy Coney Barrett for the Supreme Court, followed by an indoor reception. A number of guests, including former New Jersey governor Chris Christie, former counselor to the president Kellyanne Conway, and Senators Mike Lee of Utah and Thom Tillis of North Carolina, tested positive for COVID-19 shortly after the event.

### DIFFERENCES BETWEEN BIDEN AND TRUMP CAMPAIGNING DURING THE PANDEMIC

During the general election campaign, Trump held large rallies, mostly outdoors, where supporters were often tightly packed together, with few wearing masks. He also frequently flouted local ordinances about crowd size and social distancing when holding campaign rallies (Boburg, 2020). A study by Bernheim et al. (2020) investigated the effects of eighteen large Trump rallies held between June 20 and September 22, 2020, and concluded that these rallies may have resulted in more than 30,000 cases of COVID-19 and potentially led to more than 700 deaths, although not necessarily among people attending the rallies. In addition to these large rallies, Trump's campaign resumed in-person fundraising events in June. Perhaps his most infamous fundraising event took place at his New Jersey golf club only a few hours before he tested positive for the coronavirus. He did not wear a mask during the event and mingled with the crowd of about 150 donors, going table to table shaking hands with attendees (Choma, 2020).

The Republican National Committee (RNC), coordinating with Trump's presidential campaign, had an active field organization. During the campaign, more than 280 offices opened across the country. Elliott Echols, the RNC's national field director, said the Republican party held more than 31,000 in-person campaign events between June and September 2020 (Dawsey, Scherer, and Linskey, 2020). By mid-October, the campaign had knocked on over 22.5 million doors, averaging 2 million doors per week in the closing weeks of the campaign (Hinckley, 2020).

By the fall, the importance of mask-wearing to fight the spread of the COVID-19 pandemic had been clearly established by medical authorities. Studies suggested that masks could save lives by limiting the chances of both transmitting and contracting the coronavirus as well as potentially reducing the severity of infection if people did become ill (Peeples, 2020). Nevertheless, Trump's mask-wearing during the campaign was inconsistent; he first wore a mask in public on July 12 when he met with wounded soldiers and healthcare workers at Walter Reed military hospital (Mason, 2020). However, in the first presidential debate in late September, in front of more than seventy-three million viewers, Trump made fun of Biden for regularly wearing a mask, saying "I don't wear masks like him. Every time you see him, he's got a mask. He could be speaking 200 feet away from it and he shows up with the biggest mask I've seen" (Cathey, 2020).

Trump was accurate about Biden's approach to masks. Biden was rarely seen in public without a mask. In addition, the Biden campaign had shunned large crowds because of the pandemic and held "drive-in" rallies where supporters could maintain social distance (Dawsey, Scherer, and Linskey, 2020). Biden's efforts highlighted his desire to listen to the medical experts and keep his supporters and staff safe. In keeping with his efforts to "follow the science," his field organization was largely virtual. Two weeks before Election Day, the Biden digital operation had reached over thirty-seven million people with calls and text messages, mostly in battleground states (Alter, 2020). To disseminate campaign materials in battleground states, the Biden campaign set up "voter activation centers," where people wore masks and social distanced while picking up literature and yard signs. In the final month of the campaign, they began in-person canvassing operations but with safety concerns "front and center." According to Jen O'Malley Dillon, Biden's campaign manager, "We're now expanding on our strategy in a targeted way that puts the safety of communities first and foremost and helps us mobilize voters who are harder to reach by phone now that we're in the final stretch and now that Americans are fully dialed in and ready to make their voices heard" (Peeples, 2020).

The diverging approaches of the Biden and Trump campaigns reinforce the conflicting arguments of the Democratic and Republican parties. According to Melissa Michelson, an expert on get-out-the-vote methods, "By not engaging in door knocking, or minimal door knocking, Democrats are sending a message – reminding people that we are in a pandemic" (Hinckley, 2020). This reminder helps to prime voters to think about Trump's handling of the COVID-19 outbreak, a strategy that may have helped Biden on Election Day. Republicans, in contrast, were trying to emphasize a return to normal life and they did not want to focus attention on the ongoing pandemic during the final weeks of the campaign.

The differences between the Republican and Democratic presidential candidates were mirrored among their partisans. According to data collected by PEW over the course of the campaign, partisan differences in the percentage of people who viewed the coronavirus outbreak as a major threat to the health of the US population emerged early and stayed relatively stable through Election Day.[5] Early in the pandemic, in March,

---

[5] www.pewresearch.org/short-reads/2020/11/06/2020-election-reveals-two-broad-voting-coalitions-fundamentally-at-odds/

59 percent of Democrats (and Democratic leaners) and 33 percent of Republicans (and Republican leaners) viewed the pandemic as a major threat to the health of US residents. By June, the gap had widened, with 82 percent of Democrats (and Democratic leaners) and only 43 percent of Republicans (and Republican leaners) viewing the coronavirus pandemic as a major threat to the health of the US population. This wide division persisted through Election Day 2020.

### THE CASE OF DONALD TRUMP CONTRACTING COVID-19

Just before 1:00 a.m. (EST) on Friday, October 2, 2020, President Donald Trump tweeted, "Tonight, @FLOTUS and I tested positive for COVID-19. We will begin our quarantine and recovery process immediately. We will get through this TOGETHER!" (Liptak et al., 2020). By late afternoon on Friday, October 2, Trump was admitted to Walter Reed hospital for treatment related to the coronavirus. At the time of the diagnosis, more than 200,000 Americans and more than 1 million people worldwide had died from complications from the coronavirus disease.

Trump's diagnosis and hospitalization dominated news coverage for days, with some news reports questioning the president's effectiveness in dealing with the pandemic both nationally and within the White House. For example, the *New York Times* published an article on October 2 with the headline "Trump Tests Positive for the Coronavirus" and the subheadline "The president's result came after he spent months playing down the severity of the outbreak that has killed more than 207,000 in the United States and hours after insisting that 'the end of the pandemic is in sight'" (Baker and Haberman, 2020a).

The political ramifications of Trump's diagnosis were being discussed across the media landscape. For example, an article published by the Associated Press on October 1 explained that "Trump's diagnosis was sure to have a destabilizing effect in Washington, raising questions about how far the virus had spread through the highest levels of the U.S. government." Similarly, the October 2 article in the *New York Times* suggested:

[President Trump's] positive test could prove devastating to his political fortunes given his months of playing down the enormity of the pandemic even as the virus was still ravaging the country and killing about 1,000 Americans every day. He has repeatedly predicted the virus was "going to disappear," asserted that it was under control and insisted that the country was "rounding the corner" to the end of the crisis. He has scorned the advice of scientists, saying they were mistaken about the severity of the situation. For months, Mr. Trump has refused to wear a mask in public on all but a few occasions and has repeatedly questioned their effectiveness. (Baker and Haberman, 2020a)

Fox News produced dozens of stories discussing the unfortunate timing of Trump's COVID-19 diagnosis and downplayed the illness, suggesting that the president's advisors sent Trump to the hospital in "an abundance of caution." Trump himself described his recovery, after spending three nights at Walter Reed National Military Medical Center, as quick and easy (Barrabi, 2020). In fact, hours before his release from the hospital, he tweeted, "Don't be afraid of Covid. Don't let it dominate your life." Meanwhile, the disease had already killed more than 210,000 Americans (Kolata and Rabin, 2020).

In this chapter, we examine how people's views of the COVID-19 pandemic changes over the course of the campaign. First, we compare people's concern about the coronavirus before and after Trump's diagnosis with COVID-19. Second, we examine how political factors, psychological predispositions, and demographic characteristics influence people's worries about the coronavirus. Finally, we examine whether Trump's diagnosis alters the criteria people use to evaluate his ability to deal with COVID-19 as well as people's general impressions of Trump.

To be sure, a number of scholars have studied the impact of events occurring during a campaign on citizens' attitudes and voting decisions (e.g., Shaw, 1999; Hillygus and Jackman, 2003; McKinney and Warner, 2013; Weinschenk and Panagopoulos, 2016). For instance, Karol and Miguel (2007) examined the electoral cost of the Iraq War on support for President Bush in the 2004 presidential election and found support for President Bush was lower in states with higher numbers of Iraq War casualties. Similarly, Campbell (2005) found that the unpopularity of the Iraq War in 2004 led Bush to underperform based on other political considerations (see also Pomper, 2005).

We also know that economic conditions can influence the political prospects of candidates competing for president (see Gomez and Wilson, 2001; Healy and Lenz, 2014; Vavreck, 2009). Singer (2011) examined the impact of the economic recession during the 2008 presidential election and found that citizens who were hardest hit by the Great Recession and those who were anxious about future economic setbacks were most likely to consider the economy when casting their vote. In other words, these individuals were highly likely to consider John McCain and Barack Obama's abilities to deal with the economy when voting in the 2008 election.

These studies are motivated by the theoretical framework of "retrospective voting." The theory explains that incumbent presidents are held accountable by citizens at the ballot box for events taking place during their tenure in office. V. O. Key (1966) captured the logic of "retrospective voting" by explaining that citizens "are not fools" and act as "a rational god of vengeance and reward."[6] Fiorina (1981) elaborated and expanded on the framework of retrospective voting, finding consistent evidence that voters hold candidates and parties responsible for their records in office.[7] We believe that retrospective voters are likely to consider Trump's handling of COVID-19 when casting their votes since the crisis emerged under his watch and dominated headlines for most of 2020. Trump's positive COVID-19 diagnosis links the crisis directly to him in a personal way rarely seen in campaigns, highlighting Trump's inability to keep himself and his family safe from the pandemic sweeping the country. We expect that people's views about the COVID-19 pandemic will influence evaluations of Trump.

We examine how people's views about the importance of COVID-19 as an important issue change over the length of the campaign. We expect the salience of COVID-19 as an issue to spike after Trump tests positive for the coronavirus. Furthermore, we will examine whether people are more likely to consider COVID-19 when assessing Trump's performance *after* he contracted the coronavirus. In other words, we explore the following question: Did Trump's positive diagnosis "prime" citizens to weigh COVID-19 considerations more heavily when evaluating his candidacy?

Iyengar and Kinder (1987) first introduced the notion of priming in their classic study of agenda-setting. In particular, they show that the news media, by focusing on certain issues, alter the criteria citizens think about when evaluating political figures. Since the publication of Iyengar and Kinder's pioneering work, a number of scholars have documented priming effects during political campaigns (e.g., Claibourn, 2008; Jacobs and Shapiro, 1994; Matthews, 2019; Schaffner, 2005).

Our panel survey is well-suited for examining whether President Trump's COVID-19 diagnosis and hospitalization changes people's

---

[6] Some research suggests that US presidents are penalized electorally for negative economic trends but are not often rewarded for positive economic trends (e.g., Kiewiet, 1983; Nannestad and Paldam, 1997, but see Lewis Beck, 1988).

[7] Healy and Malhotra (2013) review the literature on retrospective voting and suggest a more nuanced picture where retrospective voters sometimes (but not always) hold incumbents responsible for positive and negative outcomes during their time in office.

views of the pandemic as well as alters the criteria people use to evaluate Trump's performance. In particular, the first wave of the panel survey ended on September 22, 2020, and the second wave of the panel began on October 4, 2020, two days after Trump's diagnosis. This timing is ideal for us to examine how people's concern about COVID-19 changes across this time period as well as how concern about COVID-19 influences people's assessments of Trump's ability to deal with the pandemic and whether these assessments influence overall impressions of Trump's job performance.

## CHANGES IN CITIZENS' VIEWS OF COVID-19 AS AN IMPORTANT PROBLEM

We begin by looking at respondents' views about the most important problem facing the nation. When we look at the results of the September and October surveys, we see some stability and some movement in people's issue priorities (see Figure 3.1). People's mentions of the economy stayed stable from September to October, with 21 percent of the respondents identifying the economy as the most important issue during both periods. Issues related to race are mentioned by 11 percent of respondents in September but fall by almost half (i.e., to 6 percent) in October. General concerns about healthcare are the fourth most frequently mentioned issue in September but rises slightly in October. During both September and October, the coronavirus easily tops people's policy agenda. However, as we expected, following Trump's positive COVID-19 diagnosis, people's concern about the pandemic increases from 29 percent in September to 35 percent in October.

We can assess changes in views regarding COVID-19 more authoritatively by taking advantage of the September–October panel. In particular, we can analyze whether the same people alter their views regarding the severity of the coronavirus pandemic after Trump contracted COVID-19. When we restrict our analysis to the panel respondents, we find a significant increase in respondents mentioning the coronavirus as the most important issue facing the nation in October compared to September. While less than one-third (31 percent) of the panel respondents mention the coronavirus in September, this proportion increases to 38 percent in the October wave of the survey.[8]

---

[8] This difference is statistically significant ($p < .001$) based on the paired-sample $t$-test.

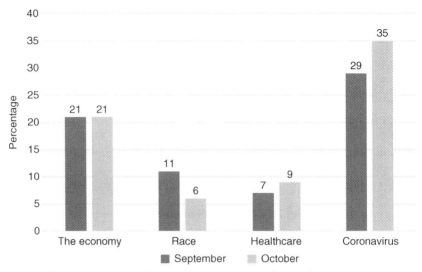

FIGURE 3.1 The most important issue facing the country

As discussed earlier, Trump continually downplayed the danger of COVID-19. For instance, on February 7, 2020, he said, "[W]hen we get into April, in the warmer weather – that has a very negative effect on that, and that type of a virus."[9] Then, on February 27, he explained that the outbreak would be temporary and "It's going to disappear. One day, it's like a miracle – it will disappear." On June 17, when new cases in the United States were averaging 20,000 a day, Trump proclaimed that the pandemic is "fading away. It's going to fade away." A few weeks later, on July 2, when the country's daily cases had doubled to about 50,000, the president said the pandemic is "getting under control." Around this same time, he also said that "99%" of COVID-19 cases are "totally harmless" and children are "virtually immune" to COVID-19.

Given Trump's repeated claims stressing the pandemic was under control, his refusal to endorse a mask mandate, and his downplaying the danger of COVID-19, we expect Republicans to be less worried about the coronavirus pandemic compared to Democrats and independents.[10] Nevertheless, we expect people's views of COVID-19 as a pressing

---

[9] See Paz (2020) for a list of President Trump's claims about the coronavirus pandemic.
[10] A number of studies have shown that Republicans were less concerned about the coronavirus pandemic than Democrats. Republicans were also less likely than others to engage in mitigation strategies such as mask-wearing and social distancing (e.g., Camobreco and He, 2022; Clinton et al., 2021; Gadarian, Goodman, and Pepinsky, 2022; Jones and McDermott, 2022)

## Changes in Citizens' Views of COVID-19

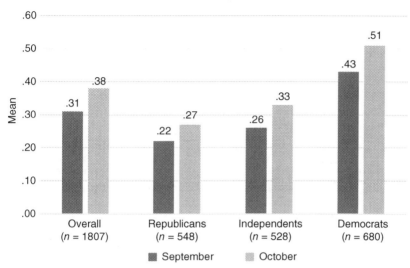

FIGURE 3.2 COVID-19 as the most important issue facing the country by partisanship

national problem, regardless of partisan affiliation, to increase after the president contracted COVID-19. The data in Figure 3.2 support our contention. First, we see that in both September and October, Republicans are least likely to mention the coronavirus as the most important issue facing the nation while Democrats are far more likely to mention this issue, with independents in the middle. Second, and as expected, we see a significant increase in people mentioning COVID-19 as a pressing national problem in October compared to September. Among Republicans, independents, and Democrats, our panel respondents become significantly more likely to mention the coronavirus as a national concern in the days and weeks following Trump's diagnosis.

We can further explore whether Trump contracting coronavirus affects respondents' views about the seriousness of the coronavirus pandemic. In particular, we compare people who answered the October survey within one week of Trump's diagnosis to people who answer the survey later in October. If Trump's diagnosis affected people's views about the pandemic, we expect people interviewed early in October to mention COVID-19 as the most important problem facing the nation more frequently than people interviewed later in the month.[11] This is exactly

---

[11] The timing of Trump's COVID-19 diagnosis may have covaried with other factors or events, making it difficult to isolate Trump's diagnosis as the event leading people to see the pandemic as the most important problem facing the nation. For example, perhaps

what we find: 38 percent of the respondents answering the October survey within days of Trump's diagnosis say that the coronavirus is the most important problem, compared to 31 percent of respondents responding within the next few weeks.[12]

UNDERSTANDING CITIZENS' CONCERN
ABOUT THE COVID-19 PANDEMIC

Based on the citizen-centered theory of campaigns, we expect that people's predispositions (e.g., political characteristics, psychological predispositions) will influence their views about events and issues. We have already shown that partisan attachment influences whether people mention COVID-19 as the most important issue facing the nation. We look beyond partisanship to develop a more comprehensive model to explain people's worries about the coronavirus. Initially, we create a COVID-19 worry index composed of two questions: (1) "How concerned are you, if at all, about the coronavirus or COVID-19 outbreak," with response options ranging from "not at all concerned" to "extremely concerned, and (2) "Thinking about the United States as a whole, what do you think is the most important problem facing the country today?" We differentiate between people who mention COVID-19 as the most important problem and people who do not mention COVID-19.[13]

---

Trump's COVID diagnosis covaried with an increase in COVID rates in the country. According to the CDC tracker, national coronavirus figures were relatively flat during the first week in October; cases and deaths would not increase significantly until late October (see covid.cdc.gov/covid-data-tracker/#trends_weeklycases_7daydeathspe r100k_00). Therefore, we do not think changes in national COVID cases and deaths can explain increases in concern about the coronavirus pandemic. Trump's diagnosis did covary with the White House event celebrating Amy Coney Barrett's nomination to the Supreme Court. While we cannot separate whether people's increase in COVID concern between September and October is a response to Trump's diagnosis or to the "superspreader" event at the White House, the public did not learn about the number of COVID-19 cases tied to the event until Trump's diagnosis was announced. Further, news attention to Trump's diagnosis likely dwarfed the amount of coverage devoted to cases attributed to the White House event.

[12] The difference between the two groups ($n = 1,692$ for people answering the survey in the first week after Trump's diagnosis; $n = 1,410$ for people answering the survey in the following weeks of October) is statistically significant at $p < .001$ ($X^2 = 18.94$, df = 1). These respondents include panel respondents as well as new October respondents.

[13] The concern about COVID-19 question ranges from 1 to 5. For the most important problem question, people who identified COVID-19 are coded as 1 and all other responses are coded as 0. We standardize each measure and then combine the two measures into an COVID-19 worry index.

## Political Characteristics

To explain respondents' responses to the worry index, we include three indicators to capture the political characteristics of respondents: party identification, partisan news diet, and attention to the news. Just as we expect Republicans to be less concerned about the coronavirus pandemic than Democrats, we expect people who are paying attention to right-leaning news outlets to be less worried about COVID-19 compared to people exposed to left-leaning news.[14] To illustrate differences in coverage of the COVID-19 pandemic across different news sources, we randomly select a weekday during the month of September and compare the lead story across these news sources.

We look at the lead stories for September 17, 2020, on three news programs: *Tucker Carlson Tonight* on Fox News, MSNBC's *All In with Chris Hayes*, and NBC's *Nightly News with Lester Holt*. Each of these news programs included a lead story about COVID-19. However, the content of coverage deviated sharply on Tucker Carlson's show on Fox News compared to the coverage on MSNBC and NBC News. In particular, Tucker Carlson began his newscast by reporting a "coronavirus coverup," suggesting that top city officials in Nashville, Tennessee, hid key health statistics showing that restaurants and bars do not encourage the spread of COVID-19. Carlson continues by saying:

So why are they so afraid to tell us the real numbers? You know the answer. The more data you have about the virus, the more facts, the more science, the less frightened you may be...If you knew the details, you might realize that getting a drink at a bar in Nashville or for that matter, sending their children to school in person poses very little risk to anyone...As of tonight, the restrictions, terrible policy decisions made by stupid and dishonest politicians like Mayor John Cooper of Nashville and many more like him are causing far more harm to this country and this population than the virus itself has caused...But many Americans, because of the information encouraged by the left, which is misinformation, it is propaganda...they don't know what this pandemic actually looks like. They are told lies and they believe them.[15]

In contrast, Chris Hayes began his broadcast summarizing the state of the pandemic before introducing Dr. Anthony Fauci (Director, National Institute of Allergy and Infectious Disease), saying,

---

[14] Unless otherwise noted, the measurement of variables in our models is the same as in previous chapters.
[15] See Carlson (2020a).

There's no denying the U.S. has had a disastrous response to the virus. The numbers don't lie. We are now on the cusp of hitting 200,000 deaths due to the coronavirus in this country. That horrific death toll represents a far higher per capita mortality rate than most of the rest of the world. And while we have come down from our peak of cases in the summer, thank God, we look to be now plateauing at nearly 40,000 new cases per day, a huge number. We're also losing almost 1,000 Americans every day still.[16]

Turning to the *NBC Nightly News*, Lester Holt began his broadcast focusing on Trump's COVID-19 response by saying,

Good evening. Who and what to trust? Increasingly, these are urgent questions tonight as the country nears two hundred thousand COVID-19 deaths amid a troubling disconnect at the top. Tonight, a day after President Trump publicly contradicted his top health officials about the virus and a vaccine, a former member of the White House Coronavirus Task Force tonight has broken ranks, blasting the President for what she calls a flat-out disregard for human life.[17]

So, lead stories on FOX, MSNBC, and NBC all focused on the coronavirus pandemic, but only Tucker Carlson on FOX News suggested that the dangers of the pandemic were being overblown.

Finally, we expect overall news attention to influence people's views about the coronavirus outbreak since news about the escalating cases and the daily death count was pervasive across a wide range of news outlets. Furthermore, the fact that the president, his family, and close associates contracted COVID-19 during the first week in October dominated the news. Therefore, we expect that people who pay more attention to the news are more likely to be exposed to concerning information about the coronavirus outbreak, leading these individuals to be more worried about COVID-19.

### Psychological Predispositions

We expect psychological predispositions to influence people's concern about the coronavirus. We begin with people's level of conspiracy thinking. It may be the case that people high in conspiracy thinking will be more likely to believe arguments that the coronavirus is a hoax and is not dangerous. For example, Rush Limbaugh, a popular conservative radio host said, "It looks like the coronavirus is being weaponized as yet another element to bring down Donald Trump. Now, I want to tell you the truth about the coronavirus. ... Yeah, I'm dead right on this.

[16] See Hayes (2020).
[17] See Holt (2020).

The coronavirus is the common cold, folks" (Chiu, 2020). If people high in conspiracy thinking are more likely to think the coronavirus is not a dangerous virus, they are unlikely to express worries about the COVID-19 pandemic. Douglas (2021) identifies a negative relationship between beliefs in COVID-19 conspiracies and willingness to comply with mitigation strategies (e.g., mask-wearing, social distancing), suggesting conspiracy thinking may decrease views of COVID-19 as a threat.

On the other hand, alternative conspiracies were disseminated about the coronavirus pandemic during 2020, painting a more dangerous view of the outbreak (Lewis, 2020). For example, a conspiracy theory emerged early in the outbreak saying that the virus was created in the Wuhan lab as part of China's covert biological weapons program (Knight, 2021). A belief that the coronavirus was a biological weapon launched by the Chinese government may produce more worries about the COVID-19 pandemic, not less. Consistent with our expectation, Imhoff and Lamberty (2020) find that the relationship between COVID-19 conspiracy beliefs and mitigation behaviors depends on the nature of the conspiracy theory. In particular, people who believe conspiracy theories about the virus being manufactured in a laboratory are more likely to engage in preventive actions, compared to people who believe in "hoax" conspiracy theories.[18] Given these findings regarding the importance of people's beliefs in a specific type of COVID-19 conspiracy, we are agnostic about whether conspiracy thinking, in general, will increase or decrease worries about coronavirus pandemic.

Level of authoritarianism may also be related to worries about COVID-19. Again, we develop two alternative hypotheses. First, people with higher levels of authoritarianism, who are more likely to be deferential to authority (e.g., Solt, 2012), may be more receptive to Trump's repeated assertations that the pandemic is under control. Further, these individuals may be especially responsive to Trump's rhetoric since Trump has displayed authoritarian tendencies (e.g., using the military to quell peaceful protests). Therefore, individuals high in authoritarianism may echo Trump's downplaying of COVID as a serious health threat.[19] Research by Prichard and Christman (2020) support this expectation, reporting a negative relationship between right-wing authoritarianism (RWA) and concern about COVID-19.

---

[18] Also see Bierwiaczonek, Gundersen, and Kunst's (2022) meta-analysis examining the role of conspiracy beliefs for COVID-19 health responses.
[19] Prichard and Christman (2020) find that RWA is associated with less concern about COVID-19.

Alternatively, people high in authoritarian thinking may be *more* worried about the coronavirus pandemic. We know people high in authoritarianism express a greater fear of death, are more likely to view the world as a dangerous place (Jost et al., 2017), and are especially sensitive to threat (e.g., Deason and Dunn, 2022). Therefore, level of authoritarianism may be positively associated with concern about the health threats of COVID-19. Hartman et al. (2021), examining respondents in the United Kingdom and Ireland, report a positive relationship between RWA and worries about the coronavirus pandemic. As with conspiracy thinking, we develop two rival expectations: (1) Increases in authoritarianism will be associated with less worries about COVID-19 and (2) increases in authoritarianism will be associated with more worries about COVID-19.

Turning to levels of prejudice, the impact of the COVID-19 pandemic negatively affected some people more acutely than others. Racial and ethnic minority groups were at higher risk for getting sick and dying from COVID-19 (Niño and Hearne, 2022). News about these health inequities were highlighted across news outlets. For example, in the summer of 2020, a story titled "Blacks hospitalized with coronavirus at a rate four times higher than whites" appeared on the Fox News website. Similarly, racial and ethnic minorities were more likely to be working in industries defined as essential during the pandemic, such as food and agriculture.[20] The pandemic also revealed gender disparities; women held 76 percent of healthcare jobs (McNicholas and Poydock, 2020) and one out of every four women reported becoming unemployed during the pandemic, twice the rate of men.[21] Given the gender, racial, and ethnic disparities associated with the coronavirus pandemic, we expect that people who score lower on racism and sexism indices may be more worried about COVID-19. In other words, people with favorable views of women and minorities will likely be more concerned about the welfare of these groups during the COVID-19 crisis, producing higher levels of worry about the coronavirus.

Finally, level of conflict avoidance may also influence people's level of worry about the coronavirus. According to research on the Big Five personality traits, people who are high in conflict avoidance are high in neuroticism (e.g., Gerber et al., 2010, 2011; Sydnor, 2019). Further, a number of studies have established a link between neuroticism and elevated distress during pandemics (Taylor, 2022), including the COVID-19

---

[20] www.epi.org/blog/who-are-essential-workers-a-comprehensive-look-at-their-wages-demographics-and-unionization-rates/
[21] www.washingtonpost.com/us-policy/2020/07/29/childcare-remote-learning-women-employment/

pandemic (e.g., Kumar and Tankha, 2022; Lee and Crunk, 2022). For example, Troisi et al. (2021) find that people who are high in neuroticism (or low in emotional stability) are more fearful of COVID-19 because these individuals are more sensitive to stress and threats of infection. Similarly, Aschwanden et al. (2021) find that people high in neuroticism are more concerned about the coronavirus pandemic in March 2020. Given the strong positive association between intolerance of conflict and neuroticism, we hypothesize that people high in conflict avoidance will be more worried about COVID-19.

## Demographic Characteristics

Since demographic groups were differentially affected by COVID-19, we include measures for the age, gender, and race and ethnicity of the respondent. We expect older people, minorities, and women to be more concerned about the pandemic, since they are more likely to be deleteriously affected by the virus (e.g., Cohen, 2020; Niño and Hearne, 2022).

## RESULTS: EXPLAINING WORRY ABOUT COVID-19

We turn to our analysis explaining people's worries about COVID-19. We present two models in Table 3.1. In the first model, we look at how political characteristics, psychological predispositions, and demographic characteristics influence worries about COVID-19 in October. In the second model, we examine how these factors influence changes in people's concern about COVID-19 from September to October.[22] In the static model, we see that party identification strongly influences whether people are worried about the coronavirus. Even though COVID-19 is not a political issue, the standardized coefficients in the model indicate that party identification is the most powerful variable in the equation. As people move from strongly identifying with the Republican party to strongly identifying with the Democratic party, people's level of worry about COVID-19 increases significantly.

[22] In each of the models, we measure the independent variables during the September wave of the panel. In the first model (i.e., the static model), we rely on ordinary least squares (OLS) regression to estimate worries about COVID-19 in October. In the second model (i.e., the change model), we rely on MLM. As discussed in Chapter 2, the assumptions for OLS regression may be violated with panel data (i.e., the standard errors may be biased), so we rely on MLM where the standard errors of the coefficients are unbiased. Because the results of the OLS analysis and MLM analysis are different when estimating the change model in Table 3.1, we present the MLM results.

TABLE 3.1 *Explaining citizens' worries about COVID-19*

| | Worries about COVID-19 – October[1] | | Worries about COVID-19 – changes from September to October[2] |
|---|---|---|---|
| *Political characteristics* | | | |
| Attention to news | .18 (.03)** | .14 | .24 (.02)** |
| Partisan media | .30 (.05)** | .16 | .31 (.04)** |
| Party identification | −.12 (.02)** | −.17 | −.10 (.01)** |
| *Psychological predispositions* | | | |
| Authoritarianism | .14 (.03)** | .11 | .13 (.02)** |
| Conflict avoidance | .04 (.01)** | .09 | .05 (.01)** |
| Conspiracy thinking | −.01 (.01) | −.01 | .01 (.01) |
| Hostile sexism | −.07 (.01)** | −.12 | −.03 (.01)** |
| Racial resentment | −.04 (.01)** | −.11 | −.05 (.01)** |
| *Demographic characteristics* | | | |
| Age | .004 (.002)** | .04 | .002 (.002) |
| Gender | .06 (.07) | .02 | .02 (.05) |
| White | −.25 (.07)** | −.07 | −.21 (.06)** |
| Intercept | .03 (.26)** | | −.70 (.20) |
| Random effects | | | |
| Variance of intercept | | | 1.33 (.05)** |
| Variance of repeated measures (time) | | | .71 (.02)** |
| Model fit | | | |
| Akaike information criterion | | | 16,104.058 |
| Log likelihood | | | 16,076.058 |
| $R^2$ | | .22 | |
| Number of respondents | 1,841 | | 2,876 |

*Note:* Worries about COVID-19 is an index based on two questions: (1) concern about the coronavirus and (2) naming COVID-19 as the most important issue facing the nation. Attention to news ranges from low (1) to high (5). Party identification ranges from 1 (strong Democrat) to 7 (strong Republican). Partisan media ranges from −2 (only conservative news) to 3 (only liberal news). Authoritarianism ranges from 0 (low authoritarian thinking) to 4 (high authoritarian thinking). Conflict avoidance ranges from 5 (low conflict avoidance) to 20 (high conflict avoidance). Conspiracy thinking ranges from 0 (low conspiracy thinking) to 30 (high in conspiracy thinking). Hostile sexism ranges from 4 (low sexism) to 16 (high sexism). Racial resentment ranges from 4 (low racial resentment) to 20 (high racial resentment). Age is an interval measure. Gender is coded 1 for female and 0 for male. White is coded 1 for white respondents and 0 for minorities. Each of the independent variables is measured during the September wave of the panel survey. For additional information about measurement, see the text.

[1] Unstandardized regression coefficients are presented with standard errors (in parentheses), followed by levels of statistical significance, and standardized coefficients.
[2] Estimated parameters of multilevel modeling are presented with standard errors (in parentheses), followed by levels of statistical significance. In the MLM model, political characteristics, psychological predispositions, and demographic characteristics are fixed effects.

** $p < .01$
\* $p < .05$

## Results: Explaining Worry about COVID-19

Similarly, we see that people's partisan news consumption alters concern about the pandemic, with people consuming only conservative news sites indicating significantly less worry about the coronavirus than people paying attention to liberal news outlets. Finally, and as expected, general attention to news promotes more concern about COVID-19 since news during this period focused on the dangers of the coronavirus.

With regard to the psychological predispositions of authoritarianism and conspiracy thinking, we developed rival explanations suggesting that these two predispositions may lead to increases *or* decreases in worries about the coronavirus. We find that level of conspiracy thinking is not related to worries about COVID-19 in October. However, we find that people's level of authoritarianism is significantly and positively related to worries about the pandemic. In particular, people's placement on the worry index changes more than half a point when we compare people with a low score on the authoritarian scale (i.e., a score of 0) to people with a high score (i.e., a score of 4). These results support prior research on authoritarianism, indicating that people with a propensity for authoritarian thinking are more fearful of death and more likely to see the world as a dangerous place.[23]

Just as authoritarianism is positively related to worry about COVID-19, we find people high in conflict avoidance are significantly more concerned about the coronavirus than people who are less aversive to conflict. In particular, people high in conflict avoidance are predicted to score six-tenths of a point on the COVID-19 worry index compared to people receiving the lowest score on the conflict avoidance scale.

We also find that people with more stereotypical views of women and minorities are less worried about the detrimental effects of the virus. Levels of both sexism and racism are significantly and negatively related to concern about the coronavirus. Looking at the impact of people's level of hostile sexism, people with the lowest score on the sexism scale are expected to receive a score of .22 on the worry index while people who

---

[23] We find the positive relationship between authoritarianism and worry about COVID-19 is significant when we look at only Republicans (the unstandardized coefficient for authoritarianism is .12 with a standard error of .06), only Democrats (the unstandardized coefficient for authoritarianism is .19 with a standard error of .05), and only independents (the unstandardized coefficient for authoritarianism is .09 with a standard error of .05). Further, when we replicate the analysis in Table 3.1 to examine whether partisanship conditions the impact of authoritarianism on worries about COVID-19, we find that the interaction coefficient does not reach statistical significance (the unstandardized coefficient for the interaction term is .046 with a standard error of .034). Finally, consistent with our findings, Hartman et al. (2021) report a positive and significant relationship between authoritarianism and concern about the coronavirus.

receive the maximum score on the sexism scale are predicted to receive a score of −.62, a drop of almost a full point on the worry index.[24]

Moving to the demographic factors, we find that as people age they become significantly more worried about the pandemic. In addition, minorities are more concerned about the coronavirus than whites, controlling for all the rival factors in the model. And the coefficient for gender is positive, as hypothesized (e.g., women are expected to be more worried about the coronavirus than men), but the relationship is far from statistically significant.

The second model in Table 3.1 estimates change in worries about COVID-19 from September to October. The panel data across this critical period of the campaign allow us to take a close look at how Trump's diagnosis changes attitudes about the pandemic. We find that as people's news consumption increases and as their attention to left-leaning news sources increases, people become more concerned about COVID-19 from September to October. Similarly, Democrats are more likely than Republicans to become more concerned about the coronavirus pandemic after Trump's diagnosis.

Turning to people's psychological predispositions, we again find that people who score higher on the authoritarian measure and the conflict avoidance scale become significantly more worried about COVID-19 in October compared to September. We also see that people's levels of sexism and racism significantly predict changes in concern about the coronavirus.[25] More specifically, as people's stereotypical views of

---

[24] We explore whether the impact of psychological predispositions on worries about COVID-19 is moderated by people's partisan news diet. We find a significant interaction effect for two of the five predispositions: racial resentment (coefficient = .04, standard error = .01) and hostile sexism (coefficient = .05, standard error = .01). The moderation analysis indicates racist and sexist views more powerfully reduce worries about COVID-19 among people who pay more attention to conservative news. For example, the impact of hostile sexism on worries about the coronavirus is negative and significant (effect = −1.0 with a standard error of .02) for people who pay more attention to conservative than liberal news (i.e., a score of −1 on the partisan news index). For people who consume nonpartisan news or an equal amount of liberal and conservative news, hostile sexism continues to diminish worries about COVID-19, but the impact is smaller (effect = −.04 with a standard error of .01). Among people who pay more attention to liberal than conservative news (i.e., a score of 1 on the partisan news index), level of hostile sexism does not influence people's concern about the coronavirus (effect = .01 with a standard error of .02).

[25] We explore the interaction between partisan news consumption and psychological predispositions on changes in worries about COVID-19. We find a significant interaction effect for one of the five predispositions: racial resentment (coefficient = .03, standard error = .01). The moderation analysis indicates the impact of racial resentment on reducing worries about COVID-19 is more powerful among people who pay more attention to conservative news.

women and minorities increase, they become significantly less worried about COVID-19 as the campaign progresses. These results support our contention that it is vital to consider people's psychological predispositions, in addition to political factors, when seeking to understand their views about the salient issues dominating campaigns. These variables are important predictors of change even in the face of stiff control variables. Finally, minorities become significantly more concerned about COVID-19 after Trump's diagnosis, reflecting their greater vulnerability to the ravages of the virus.

## THE PRIMING OF COVID-19 IN THE WAKE OF TRUMP'S DIAGNOSIS

We turn next to examining whether Trump's COVID-19 diagnosis makes the coronavirus pandemic more salient to citizens when evaluating his performance as president. In other words, does Trump's diagnosis "prime" people's worries about COVID-19? We begin by looking at people's confidence in Trump's ability to handle the public health impact of the coronavirus outbreak, with responses ranging from not at all confident (1) to very confident (4). In general, people express doubt in Trump's ability to deal with the pandemic, with respondents averaging a score of 2 ("not too confident") on the four-point scale. Further, confidence in Trump's capability to deal with the COVID crisis declines significantly from September to October among our panel respondents.[26]

To examine whether people's worries about COVID-19 became more consequential for understanding assessments about Trump, we begin by predicting respondents' confidence in his ability to deal with the coronavirus pandemic. We measure worries about COVID-19 as we did in the previous analysis (i.e., Table 3.1). If Trump's COVID-19 diagnosis primed people to think about COVID-19 more seriously when evaluating his ability to deal with the pandemic, then the index assessing worries about the coronavirus should more powerfully influence assessments of Trump's performance on COVID-19 in October compared to September.

[26] Among panel respondents, the difference between September's confidence ratings (2.2 with a standard error of .03) and October's responses (2.1 with a standard error of .02) is statistically significant based on the paired-sample $t$-test ($t = 3.15$, $p < .01$). In contrast, panel respondents' confidence in Biden's ability to deal with COVID-19 is static ($t = -.75$, ns) from September (2.6 with a standard error of .03) to October (2.6 with a standard error of .03).

When predicting people's views of Trump's ability to deal with the coronavirus, we need to control for rival factors that may influence their evaluations. We control for people's partisan affiliation since Republicans are more likely to have confidence in Trump's ability to deal with the COVID-19 pandemic compared to Democrats.[27] We also include an index measuring people's assessments of Trump's personality characteristics since trait assessments often alter views of presidential candidates (e.g., Fridkin and Kenney, 2011; Funk, 1996). Finally, we include a general assessment of the state of the national economy since retrospective assessments of the economy can powerfully influence views of the incumbent president (e.g., Fiorina, 1981; Kinder and Kiewiet, 1981).

With these measures in hand, we turn to predicting people's confidence in Trump's ability to handle the public health impact of the coronavirus outbreak in September and October.[28] We present the results in Table 3.2.[29] In the September model, we see that people's worries about COVID-19 do not significantly influence people's assessment of Trump's ability to deal with the pandemic. However, the same model in October yields quite different findings. In the October model, worries about COVID-19 significantly and negatively influence assessments of Trump's handling of the pandemic. In fact, according to the standardized coefficients, concern about COVID-19 is more important than partisanship for predicting confidence in Trump's ability to deal with COVID-19. These findings support our hypothesis that the issue of COVID-19 was primed among the public in October after Trump was infected, leading people to weigh their views about the coronavirus more heavily when developing impressions of Trump's handling of the crisis.[30]

---

[27] See Chapter 2 for more details regarding the measurement of each of these rival factors.
[28] In the September model, all of the independent variables and the dependent variable are measured during the September wave. And in the October model, the independent variables and dependent variable are measured in October. In these analyses, we want to see if worries about COVID-19 – measured at the same time as confidence in Trump's ability to deal with COVID-19 – are more powerful in October than September.
[29] The dependent variable is ordinal, ranging from 1 to 4. We estimate the equations in Table 3.2 with ordinal regression and with OLS regression. The results from the two analyses are substantively similar. We present the OLS results in Table 3.2 because of the greater ease of interpretation.
[30] We replicate the analysis in Table 3.2, predicting Biden's ability to deal with the coronavirus pandemic. We find that that the impact of worries about COVID-19 on people's assessments of Biden's ability to deal with the pandemic are stable from September to October (i.e., the coefficient for COVID-19 worries is .05 with a standard error of .01 in the September model and .05 with a standard error of .02 in the October model). These results suggest that worries about COVID-19 are not primed for people's assessments of Biden's ability to deal with the pandemic.

TABLE 3.2 *Impact of worries about COVID-19 on Trump's ability to deal with the pandemic*[1]

|  | September |  | October |  |
|---|---|---|---|---|
| *COVID-19* |  |  |  |  |
| Worries about COVID-19 | −.006 (.01) | −.01 | −.070 (.008)** | −.09 |
| *Rival factors* |  |  |  |  |
| General economic assessment | .164 (.012)** | .18 | .154 (.011)** | .16 |
| Party identification | .019 (.008)** | .04 | .015 (.007)* | .03 |
| Trait assessment of Trump | .129 (.003)** | .69 | .130 (.003)** | .71 |
| Constant | .05 (.04) |  | .433 (.06)** |  |
| $R^2$ |  | .68 |  | .75 |
| Number of respondents |  | 2,455 |  | 2,605 |

*Note:* The dependent variable is people's confidence in Trump's ability to handle the public health impact of the coronavirus outbreak, with responses ranging from 1 (not at all confident) to 4 (very confident). Worries about COVID-19 is an index based on two questions: (1) concern about the coronavirus and (2) naming COVID-19 as the most important issue facing the nation. General economic assessment ranges from 1 (the economy has gotten much worse) to 5 (the economy has gotten much better). Party identification ranges from 1 (strong Democrat) to 7 (strong Republican). Trait assessments of Trump is a composite index of six traits ranging from 6 to 24. For more information about measurement, see the text.

[1] Unstandardized OLS regression coefficients are presented with standard errors (in parentheses), followed by levels of statistical significance, and standardized coefficients.

** $p < .01$
* $p < .05$

Turning to the rival factors, measures assessing people's evaluations of Trump's personality characteristic powerfully influence views of Trump's ability to deal with the pandemic in both September and October. For instance, in September and October, for every one-point change in the trait index, we expect a .13 increase in evaluations of Trump's ability to deal with the COVID-19 crisis. Economic assessments also color people's views about Trump's competence for handling the pandemic in September and October. Finally, partisan attachment influences people's assessments of Trump's ability to deal with the coronavirus, with Republicans developing more positive views of Trump in September and October compared to other respondents.

Next, we look for evidence of priming when we estimate people's approval of Trump as president. In particular, we examine whether people's assessments of Trump's handling of the coronavirus pandemic more powerfully influence evaluations of Trump's job performance in

TABLE 3.3 *Impact of COVID-19 views on presidential approval of Donald Trump*[1]

|  | September |  | October |  |
|---|---|---|---|---|
| COVID-19 |  |  |  |  |
| Trump's ability to deal with pandemic | .295 (.016)** | .30 | .412 (.016)** | .41 |
| Rival factors |  |  |  |  |
| General economic assessment | .070 (.010)** | .08 | .033 (.010)** | .03 |
| Party identification | .111 (.006)** | .08 | .065 (.005)** | .12 |
| Trait assessment of Trump | .084 (.003)** | .45 | .083 (.003)** | .45 |
| Constant | −.121 (.029)** |  | −.106 (.024)** |  |
| $R^2$ |  | .79 |  | .84 |
| Number of respondents |  | 2,426 |  | 2,592 |

*Note:* The dependent variable is people's approval of Donald Trump on a four-point scale ranging from strongly disapprove (1) to strongly approve (4). Trump's ability to deal with the coronavirus pandemic is measured on a scale ranging from 1 (not at all confident) to 4 (very confident). General economic assessment ranges from 1 (the economy has gotten much worse) to 5 (the economy has gotten much better). Party identification ranges from 1 (strong Democrat) to 7 (strong Republican). Trait assessments of Trump is a composite index of six traits ranging from 6 to 24. For more information about measurement, see the text.

[1] Unstandardized OLS regression coefficients are presented with standard errors (in parentheses), followed by levels of statistical significance, and standardized coefficients.
** $p < .01$
\* $p < .05$

October than September.[31] We include the same control variables in these models (i.e., trait evaluations, general economic assessments, and party identification).

We see assessments of Trump's COVID-19 performance significantly influence overall approval in both September and October (see Table 3.3). Nevertheless, and as expected, the unstandardized coefficient for Trump's COVID-19 response is larger in October (.412) than September (.295). This finding clearly demonstrates people are giving more weight to Trump's ability to deal with the pandemic when evaluating Trump's performance as president in October compared to September. Furthermore,

---

[31] The exact question wording is "Do you approve or disapprove of the way Donald Trump is handling his job as president?" with options ranging from strongly approve (4) to strongly disapprove (1). We estimate the equations in Table 3.3 with ordinal regression. The results are substantively similar to the OLS results; we present the OLS results in Table 3.3 because of the greater ease of interpretation.

the unstandardized coefficients for the control variables decrease in size during this period. Also, the performance of the model, as indicated by the $R^2$, is higher in October than in September, indicating the greater predictive value of assessments of Trump's COVID-19 response on his job approval.[32]

In one final test of the priming hypothesis, we examine whether attitudes about the candidates' ability to deal with the pandemic influence overall evaluations of the candidates more powerfully in October than September. In this final analysis, we estimate views of Trump and Biden. To measure overall evaluations, we rely on the feeling thermometer ratings ranging from 0 (feel very cold toward the candidate) to 100 (feel very warm toward the candidate). As we have done in earlier analysis, we control for assessments of candidates' personal traits, economic performance evaluations, and people's partisan attachment. We expect that views about the candidate's ability to deal with COVID-19 will become more consequential for overall views of Trump from September to October. In contrast, we do not expect COVID-19 assessments to more significantly influence overall impressions of Biden in October compared to September. In other words, we expect people's ratings of Trump's ability to deal with COVID-19 to be primed for general evaluations of Trump (and not Biden) after he contracts the virus.

The findings in Table 3.4 confirm our expectations. While Trump's ability to handle the coronavirus outbreak significantly influences people's scores on his feeling thermometer in both September and October, COVID-19 assessments are more powerful in October.[33] The unstandardized coefficient for COVID-19 assessments is 4.63 in September, indicating that every one-point decrease on the confidence measure is associated with less than a five-point decrease on the Trump feeling thermometer. In October, in contrast, every one-point decrease in COVID-19 assessments is associated with more than an eight-point drop (i.e., 8.37) on the feeling thermometer. We find the impact of COVID-19 assessments on overall evaluations of Trump to almost double in size from September to October, with his coronavirus diagnosis and hospitalization occurring between the September and October waves of the panel survey.

---

[32] As in Table 3.2, we find that views about Trump's personality traits and economic assessments powerfully influence approval of Trump. Similarly, party identification strongly alters people's approval ratings of Trump.
[33] Clarke, Stewart, and Ho (2021) and Shino and Smith (2021) find that concerns about COVID-19 hurt Donald Trump at the ballot box.

TABLE 3.4 *Impact of views about COVID-19 on overall evaluations of the presidential candidates*[1]

|  | Feeling thermometer ratings for Trump |  |  |  | Feeling thermometer ratings for Biden |  |  |  |
|---|---|---|---|---|---|---|---|---|
|  | September |  | October |  | September |  | October |  |
| COVID-19 |  |  |  |  |  |  |  |  |
| Ability to deal with pandemic | 4.63 (.54)** | .14 | 8.37 (.53)** | .25 | 6.42 (.57)** | .21 | 3.56 (.48)** | .11 |
| *Rival factors* |  |  |  |  |  |  |  |  |
| General economic assessment | 2.17 (.34)** | .07 | 0.82 (.32)* | .03 | .25 (.29) | .01 | -.06 (.29) | -.01 |
| Party identification | 3.82 (.21)** | .22 | 3.45 (.18)** | .19 | -3.51 (.21)** | -.22 | -3.95 (.19)** | -.24 |
| Trait assessment | 3.56 (.11)** | .58 | 3.35 (.10)** | .54 | 3.12 (.11)** | .54 | 3.76 (.09)** | .63 |
| Constant | -33.74 (.96)** |  | -36.20 (.80)** |  | .48 (1.93) |  | -.95 (1.85) |  |
| $R^2$ | .79 |  | .84 |  | .75 |  | .78 |  |
| Number of respondents | 2,419 |  | 2,588 |  | 2,315 |  | 2,474 |  |

*Note:* The dependent variable is feeling thermometer ratings (ranging from 0 to 100) for Donald Trump and Joe Biden. The candidate's ability to deal with the coronavirus pandemic is measured on a scale ranging from 1 (not at all confident) to 4 (very confident). General economic assessment ranges from 1 (the economy has gotten much worse) to 5 (the economy has gotten much better). Party identification ranges from 1 (strong Democrat) to 7 (strong Republican). Trait assessments of the candidate is a composite index of six traits ranging from 6 to 24. For more information about measurement, see the text.

[1] Unstandardized OLS regression coefficients are presented with standard errors (in parentheses), followed by levels of statistical significance, and standardized coefficients.

** $p < .01$
* $p < .05$

# The Priming of COVID-19 after Trump's Diagnosis

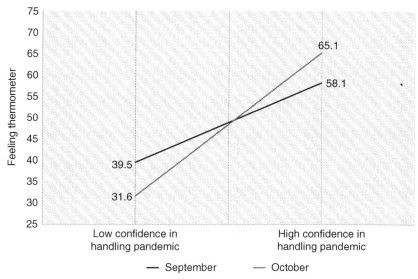

FIGURE 3.3 Impact of Trump's ability to handle COVID-19 on his feeling thermometer scores in September and October

We estimate the impact of the coronavirus ratings by calculating the predicted values of the dependent variable (i.e., feeling thermometer scores for Trump) when we vary people's views of Trump's ability to deal with COVID-19 from not at all confident (1) to very confident (4). We display the results in Figure 3.3. The slope of the line is steeper in October than September. More specifically, in October people who give Trump the lowest ratings on his COVID-19 response are expected to rate Trump at 31.6 degrees on the feeling thermometer whereas people who strongly approve of Trump's handling of the pandemic are expected to rate Trump more than 30 degrees higher on the feeling thermometer, at 65.1 degrees. In September, the difference in ratings between people who have no confidence in Trump's COVID-19 response and people who are very confident is less than 20 degrees on the feeling thermometer.

Since we know assessments of Trump's performance on COVID-19 declined significantly between September and October, the greater weight people attached to coronavirus when evaluating Trump is politically damaging. Not only do ratings of Trump's COVID-19 response decline from September to October but people weigh these coronavirus assessments more heavily in October compared to September.

Turning to Biden's thermometer ratings, we find people's views of Biden's ability to deal with the pandemic significantly influence his ratings in September and October. However, unlike Trump, the impact of COVID-19 assessments is less consequential for Biden in October compared to September. In particular, the unstandardized coefficient measuring people's views of Biden's ability to deal with COVID-19 is 6.42 in September, indicating that every one-point increase on the COVID-19 measure is associated with more than a six-point increase on the Biden feeling thermometer. In October, in contrast, every one-point increase in COVID-19 assessments is associated with less than a four-point increase (i.e., 3.56) on the Biden feeling thermometer.

### CONCLUSION AND IMPLICATIONS

The panel design we deployed in combination with the timing of Trump's COVID-19 diagnosis and hospitalization provides us with unique analytical leverage to see how this event shaped the 2020 presidential campaign. We have shown that people's concern about the coronavirus pandemic increased significantly after Trump contracted COVID-19. Between the September and October waves of the panel survey, people are more likely to mention the coronavirus as the most important issue facing the nation and they are more likely to be concerned about the COVID-19 outbreak. Furthermore, and consistent with the citizen-centered theory of campaigns, we find that psychological predispositions, along with political and demographic characteristics, substantively and significantly predict changes in worrying about the coronavirus between September and October. For instance, people high in authoritarianism and conflict avoidance and people holding less sexist and less racist attitudes become significantly more worried about the coronavirus pandemic from September to October.

Finally, we find impressive evidence for priming; people are more likely to weigh COVID-19 assessments when evaluating Trump's performance in October compared to September. These results suggest that Trump's COVID-19 diagnosis increased the salience of the pandemic among potential voters and encouraged citizens to consider Trump's ability to handle the health crisis when developing overall evaluations of the president. Since people's views about Trump's ability to deal with the coronavirus were negative (i.e., 45 percent of respondents in October said they were "not at all confident" that Donald Trump could handle the public health impact of the coronavirus outbreak), increasing the public focus on the pandemic most certainly hurt him electorally.

A raging pandemic would be tough for any president running for reelection. Trump's approach to the coronavirus outbreak, however, may have been particularly problematic. He repeatedly played down the danger of the pandemic: He ignored the advice of medical experts by refusing to wear a mask, he held a number of large campaign rallies, and he hosted public events at the White House. So, when Trump contracted the virus, his approach to the pandemic was highlighted and underlined for voters. That is, people may have viewed his sickness as a vivid illustration of his failure to control the virus nationally.

It is possible to speculate, though, that if Trump had conscientiously followed the protocols recommended by his Coronavirus Task Force and still contracted COVID-19, voters may have been more likely to blame the virus than Trump. And it is quite likely that Trump would not have become ill at all if he had followed recommended mitigation protocols. Furthermore, citizens may have rallied around the president in a show of solidarity, perhaps even increasing his popularity among the electorate. Presidents often receive boosts in their support in the wake of a significant crisis, as President H. W. Bush did in the wake of Operation Desert Storm or President George W. Bush did after 9/11 (Hetherington and Nelson, 2003). So if Trump was viewed favorably in terms of his handling of the pandemic, priming of the coronavirus may have possibly produced a more favorable view of his reelection candidacy.

In Chapter 4, we turn to another important issue raised during the 2020 presidential election: the issue of racial justice and police brutality. The murder of an unarmed Black man by white police officers in Minneapolis spurred a summer of social protests aimed at highlighting the issue of police brutality and encouraging reforms in policing across the country. We examine changes in people's support for these protests as well as their attitudes toward police over the course of the campaign. We also explore how the issues of race and policing influence people's views of the competing presidential candidates. And, consistent with the citizen-centered theory of campaigns, we continue to show that people's psychological predispositions powerfully and consistently influence views of race and policing.

# 4

## Protests against Police Brutality

*How Attitudes about Racial Injustice and Policing Affected Campaign 2020*

The most enduring, systematic, perplexing, tragic, and unresolved issue facing the nation is equality and justice for all Americans, irrespective of race. The nation faced trauma and reckoning on this issue again in the summer of 2020 and witnessed the largest racial justice protests in more than fifty years (Brownstein, 2020). Protests erupted after the murder of George Floyd while in the custody of the Minneapolis police on May 25, 2020. Floyd, a forty-six-year-old Black man was arrested about 8 p.m. after allegedly using a counterfeit $20 bill at a local Cup Foods. A cellphone video of the incident showed a police officer, Derek Chauvin, pinning Floyd to the ground with his knee on the back of Floyd's neck for more than nine minutes while a handcuffed Floyd repeats "I can't breathe" and eventually loses consciousness and later dies at a local hospital (Bogel-Burroughs, 2021).

Even though a surge of COVID-19 cases was underway, hundreds of protestors began demonstrating in Minneapolis on May 26, 2020. Demonstrators targeted the precinct station where Derek Chauvin and the three other officers involved in Floyd's death worked. Some businesses in the area where George Floyd was killed were set on fire. Protests continued in the city of Minneapolis during the next days and weeks. During these protests, police often used tear gas and fired rubber bullets into crowds to break up demonstrations (Reuters, 2020).

On May 29, 2020, President Trump delivered an ultimatum to Minneapolis protesters, suggesting that the military could use armed force to suppress riots. Trump called the protesters "thugs" and tweeted, "When the looting starts, the shooting starts." Soon, Floyd's murder acted as a catalyst and protests spread across the country, including large peaceful protests as well as some instances of violence (Taylor, 2021).

One very high-profile protest occurred near the White House in Washington, DC, on the evening of June 1, 2020. Several thousand people were peacefully protesting the police killing of George Floyd in Lafayette Park (Colvin and Superville, 2020).[1] President Trump had announced earlier in the day that he would be addressing the nation from the White House Rose Garden around 6:30 p.m., thirty minutes before a mandatory 7:00 p.m. curfew in DC. A gathering of law enforcement, including US Secret Service agents, Park Police, and National Guardsmen, stood near the protestors, with many officers in full riot gear. A few minutes before 6:30 p.m., the law enforcement personnel began marching toward the protesters, forcing the protesters to retreat, firing tear gas and deploying flash bangs to disperse the protestors from the park.

A few minutes later, Trump began to speak in the Rose Garden, explaining, "I am your president of law and order and an ally of all peaceful protesters." He continued, "As we speak, I am dispatching thousands and thousands of heavily armed soldiers. We are putting everybody on warning." Moments later, he walked from the White House grounds, crossing Lafayette Park, which had been cleared of protestors moments earlier. In his trek, Trump was accompanied by several senior aides, including Defense Secretary Mark Esper, Attorney General William Barr, and Joint Chiefs of Staff Mark Milley, who wore military fatigues.

Trump stopped in front of St. John's Church, a landmark building that had been damaged in a protest fire a day earlier. In front of the church, he raised a Bible and spoke. "We have a great country," he said. "Greatest country in the world." Then he encouraged his senior aides to join him for another round of photos before walking back to the White House. Days later, DC's mayor Muriel Bowser had "Black Lives Matter," the signature phrase associated with a growing movement advocating against racially motivated police violence, emblazed in giant yellow letters on the street across from the White House.

The number and size of the protests during the summer of 2020 echoed the civil unrest following the assassination of Dr. Martin Luther King in April 1968. A wave of marches and protests erupted across the country in small, medium, and large cities throughout the summer. According to a report in the *New York Times*, the Black Lives Matter (BLM) protests may have peaked on June 6, 2020, when half a million people turned out

---

[1] We rely on an Associate Press report to describe the events of June 1st. See apnews .com/article/donald-trump-ap-top-news-dc-wire-religion-politics-15be4e293cde be72c10304feoec668e4

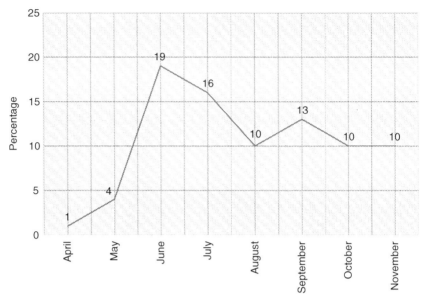

FIGURE 4.1 Race relations as the most important problem in 2020

in about 550 places across the United States. Public opinion polls estimate that between fifteen and twenty-six million people in the United States participated in demonstrations over the death of George Floyd and other victims between May 26 and June 28, 2020 (Buchanan, Bui, and Patel, 2020).

The public largely supported the peaceful protests against racial injustice over the summer. A poll conducted in the wake of George Floyd's death showed that 67 percent of respondents strongly or somewhat approved of the BLM movement, with 92 percent of Democrats (or respondents who lean Democratic) and 37 percent of Republicans (or Republican leaners) approving the movement. However, by September, support for the movement had declined significantly, with 55 percent of respondents strongly or somewhat approving the movement. In September, support of Democrats for the movement remained relatively stable at 88 percent (including leaners), while support among Republicans and Republican leaners dropped over 20 points, to 16 percent (Thomas and Horowitz, 2020).

We see a similar trend when we examine Gallup data regarding the most important problem facing the nation.[2] The trend in Figure 4.1 shows that when respondents are asked to name the most important national problem, less than 5 percent identify race relations as a

---

[2] For more information on the Gallup poll data, see news.gallup.com/poll/329711/racial-justice-concerns-persist-months-floyd-death.aspx

significant problem before the killing of George Floyd. But in the wake of Floyd's death and subsequent racial justice protests, concerns about race relations increase with about one in five people saying that the issue is the most important problem facing the nation in June 2020. However, by late summer, the public's concern about race relations drops precipitously, with only 10 percent of respondents naming race relations as the most important problem facing the nation in October.

In this chapter, we examine how attitudes about protests supporting racial justice, views about BLM, and attitudes toward the police vary over the length of the general election campaign. We examine how political characteristics and psychological predispositions influence people's views of police and racial justice issues during the 2020 campaign. This is the first time since 1968 that civil unrest of a sizeable scale stretched across the year of a presidential election campaign. Our panel study once again provides us with strong analytical leverage to explore citizens' attitudes about support for the BLM movement as well as support for protests against police violence in September, October, and November.[3] We also ask people about their views of police in each of the waves of our survey, allowing us to examine fluctuations in support for police during this turbulent period.[4]

We begin by looking at people's support for protests against police brutality. The data in Figure 4.2 show people's support for racial justice protests was highest at the start of the fall campaign but dropped significantly by October, holding stable through Election Day. We see the same pattern whether we look at support for the BLM movement, in particular, or support for protests against police brutality, more generally.

When we look at support for police during the same period, we find the opposite pattern. The data in Figure 4.3 illustrate that people's

---

[3] The exact wording for the question assessing attitudes toward the BLM movement is "Do you support or oppose the Black Lives Matter movement?" with responses ranging from strongly disapprove (1) to strongly approve (5). The exact wording for the question measuring attitudes toward racial justice protests is "Thinking about George Floyd's death and recent protests. In general, do you approve or disapprove of the recent protests against police violence in response to Floyd's death?" Response options ranged from strongly disapprove (1) to strongly approve (5). In October and November, the question wording changes slightly, given additional deaths of Black men by police, to "Thinking about recent protests that have occurred after incidents where African Americans have been harmed or killed by police, do you approve or disapprove of the recent protests against police violence?" Response options are unchanged.
[4] The exact question wording to measure approval of police is "Do you approve or disapprove how the police in your community are doing their job?" with response categories ranging from strongly disapprove (1) to strongly approve (4). To measure confidence in police, we ask "How much confidence, if any, do you have in police officers acting in the best interests of the public?" Response options vary from no confidence at all (1) to a great deal of confidence (4).

96    *Views about Racial Justice Protests and Policing*

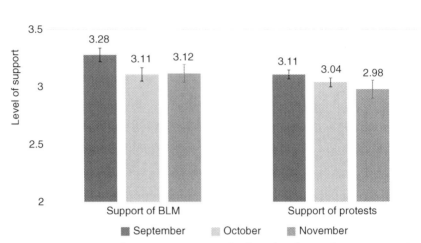

FIGURE 4.2 Support for protests against police brutality during the 2020 campaign
Note: We present the means with 95% confidence intervals.

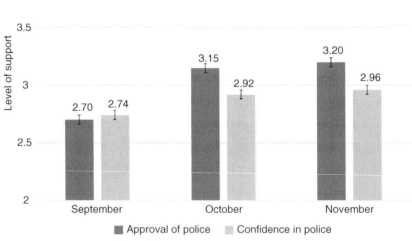

FIGURE 4.3 Support for police during the 2020 campaign
Note: We present the means with 95% confidence intervals.

support for how police in their community are doing their jobs as well as people's confidence in police officers acting in the best interest of the public increases significantly from September to October and then stays relatively stable throughout the rest of the campaign season. As the death of George Floyd and the nightly protests against police brutality retreated from prominence on television news programs, on the front pages of newspapers, and on social media sites, people's views of the police became more favorable.

## EXPLAINING CITIZENS' ATTITUDES TOWARD SOCIAL JUSTICE PROTESTS AND POLICING

We examine the impact of citizens' political characteristics, psychological predispositions, and demographic factors to gain a better understanding of how the presidential campaign affected people's views of racial justice protests as well as their views of police.

### Political Characteristics

We expect that people's partisanship will influence their views about social justice protests and views of policing. Public opinion data show Democrats are much more supportive of the BLM movement than Republicans (e.g., Boudreau, MacKenzie, and Simmons, 2022; Drakulich and Denver, 2022; Drakulich et al., 2020) while Republicans have more favorable attitudes toward the police (e.g., Jones, 2013; Socia et al., 2021).[5]

These partisan differences align with historical differences in the policy positions of the two major parties. The Democratic party has a longer history of fighting racial injustice (Lyman, 2020) while the Republican party has been considered the "law-and-order" party since Richard Nixon's 1968 run for the presidency (Lynch, 2020). During the length of the 2020 campaign, the two major party candidates articulated divergent messages regarding their support for racial justice protests. For example, Trump declared himself the president of law and order (Lemire, Colvin, and Suderman, 2020) and said demonstrators protesting racial injustice "are looking for trouble" and companies supporting BLM are "weak" and led by "weak people." In a tweet in July 2020, he called BLM "a symbol of hate," and in September he gave a speech at the National Archives where he said calls for racial equality are "attempting to demolish" the "treasured and precious inheritance" of our nation (Gomez, 2020).

---

[5] For instance, Drakulich et al. (2020) find people more concerned about biased policing and more supportive of reforming police practices are more likely to vote for Hillary Clinton in 2016.

Biden's messaging, in contrast, emphasized the historical importance of both serving as the vice president of the first Black president and choosing Senator Kamala Harris as the first Black woman to be nominated by a major political party. He acknowledged the problem of systemic racism during the campaign and released a plan to eliminate racial disparities as well as expand the Justice Department's ability to address police misconduct (Gomez, 2020).

Given these differences between the parties and the Democratic and Republican candidates, we expect party identification to be negatively related to support for social justice protests (e.g., strong Democrats who are coded a 1 will be most supportive of social justice protests, while strong Republicans who are coded as 7 will be least supportive) and positively related to support for police.

Similarly, we expect people's consumption of partisan news to influence their views about police brutality protests since left-leaning and right-leaning news sources presented the protests and policing in dramatically different ways (Kilgo and Mourão, 2019). For instance, on September 1, 2020, the following was the opening segment on Tucker Carlson's (2020b) show on FOX News:

If you've watched the show over the past few months, you know that we have fixated – sometimes with the exclusion of other important things – on the riots and disorder that have paralyzed many American cities. We haven't done this for partisan reasons. Honestly, it is a presidential year, but the threat that we're facing is deeper and more significant than any single election. Political violence is the greatest threat we face. It is more dangerous than any virus or any foreign adversary. It could literally end this country.

We've told you who is responsible for the violence. We didn't need to tell you, you knew it, and it is obvious no matter what the professional liars are now claiming on television. The main suspect for example in the most recent political assassination in Portland has a BLM logo tattooed on his neck. He is not hiding what team he's on. None of them are… Why would kids raised in the fairest country in the world support a violent revolutionary group like BLM, whose program consists mainly of destroying things?

On the same evening, on *Anderson Cooper 360°* on CNN (Berman, 2020), the opening segment began by focusing on the shooting of Jacob Blake in Kenosha, Wisconsin. John Berman, Anderson Cooper's guest host for the evening, began the newscast by saying:

The President of the United States traveled to Kenosha, Wisconsin today where a white police officer shot a Black man, Jacob Blake seven times in the back… Never once, neither there nor during the rest of the visit did the President utter Jacob Blake's name, not once. I'm not sure he has ever said Blake's name. I'm not sure he knows it. What does that tell you about his views on the pain being felt by so many African-Americans?

And when asked about the larger issue of race and policing...here's how the President responded, "Frankly, I think the police do an incredible job and I think you do have some bad apples...and you do have the other situation, too, where they're under this tremendous pressure and they don't handle it well. They call it choking and it happens." Choking. It's an interesting choice of words. Horrifying when he compares it to missing a golf putt as he also did. And point of fact, choking is what was inflicted on Eric Garner during an arrest for selling loose cigarettes and on George Floyd by a police officer's knee on his neck. It's the reason you hear protesters chanting, "I can't breathe," but safe to say that's not exactly front of mind for the President.

These stories appeared on the exact same day, showing that the major news programs on CNN and FOX News presented completely different slants on the issue of police brutality and social justice protestors. These striking differences motivate our expectations that people's partisan media diet will significantly influence views of social injustice protests as well as support for policing.[6]

We also explore whether people's attention to news, in general, influence their support for the social justice movement and support for police. In Chapter 2, given the lopsided nature of the debate, we argue (and find) that attention to news is related to more negative assessments of Trump's performance and more positive views of Biden's performance. In Chapter 3, given the overwhelmingly negative coverage about the COVID-19 pandemic, we expect (and find) that people who pay attention to the news are more worried about the coronavirus. For the issues of social justice protests and policing, we expect less news attention and less homogenous coverage. Therefore, we are agnostic about whether news attention will influence support for social justice protests and support for police.

### Psychological Predispositions

According to the citizen-centered theory of campaigns, people's psychological predispositions will influence support for social protest movements and support for police. Most importantly, we expect people's feelings of racial resentment will influence support for the BLM movement and racial injustice protests. As discussed earlier, racial resentment is a form of racism that rests on the view that Black people do not try hard enough

---

[6] Experimental data suggest that differences in news media frames of police violence against Black victims can significantly alter views of the police and views of the victim (see Boudreau, MacKenzie, and Simmons, 2019; Fridkin et al., 2017).

to overcome obstacles and they want to take opportunities that they have not earned (Kinder and Sanders, 1996). People who hold these types of anti-Black attitudes are less likely to support protests against racial injustice (Stepp and Castle, 2021). Furthermore, we expect that people who have higher levels of racial resentment will be more supportive of police, as numerous studies have documented (e.g., Carter and Cora, 2016; Morris and LeCount, 2020; Strickler and Lawson, 2022). For instance, Drakulich et al. (2020) find the relationship between support for police and voting for Trump in 2016 mainly among people scoring high on the racial resentment scale.[7] Finally, sexist attitudes, like racist attitudes, are driven by people's anti-egalitarian attitudes (Sidanius, Pratto, and Brief 1995); therefore, we expect people who score higher on the hostile sexism scale will be less supportive of a movement promoting racial justice.

In addition, people's level of authoritarian and conspiratorial thinking may be related to support for social justice protests and support for police. First, since authoritarian thinking is a preference for social conformity over autonomy, we expect that people who score higher on the authoritarian scale will be less likely to support protests against the status quo and more supportive of law enforcement. Second, and less straightforward, we expect that people who are more likely to engage in conspiracy thinking will be *more* supportive of protests against police brutality and *less* supportive of police.[8] We argue that because people who engage in conspiracy thinking are less trustful of institutions, including the federal government and law enforcement (Miller, Saunders, and Farhart, 2016), and they will be more supportive of antiestablishment protests. Similarly, since people who engage in conspiracy thinking believe that people in power are malevolent and conceal "evil-doing" with lies (Sutton and Douglas, 2014: 256), these individuals will be less supportive of institutions – like law enforcement.

We also expect that people's tolerance of conflict may influence support for social justice protests and support for police. We offer two rival hypotheses. First, the goal of the social justice protest movement in 2020 was to bring attention to the issue of police brutality and advocate for reforms to reduce police violence against minorities, especially Black

---

[7] Mullinix, Bolsen, and Norris (2021) also find that people high in racial resentment are less likely to blame police when they are exposed to news stories and videos depicting racially charged instances of police use of force.
[8] Research indicates that authoritarian and conspiracy thinking may not be strongly correlated. See Berinsky (2012), Oliver and Wood (2014), Uscinski and Parent (2014), but also see Richey (2017).

men. Therefore, we hypothesize that people who want to avoid conflict will be more supportive of a movement seeking to reduce violence. On the other hand, research by Harlow et al. (2020) shows that BLM protests are often framed as rioting, with news coverage focusing on violence, property damage, and confrontations with police. Therefore, we develop an alternative hypothesis: People high in conflict avoidance will develop less favorable views of the social justice protests given common news coverage of these protests.

Regarding conflict avoidance and support for police, we expect people high in conflict avoidance to be less supportive of the police for two reasons. First, the social justice movement during the summer of 2020 showcased high-profile incidents of police brutality, including the deaths of George Floyd, Ahmaud Arbery, Rayshard Brooks, Dion Johnson, and Breonna Taylor at the hands of police (Fausset, 2021). Second, episodes of police violence were vividly illustrated during several peaceful protests in the summer and fall. For example, in the peaceful protest at Lafayette Park across the street from the White House, federal law enforcement flooded the street with clouds of tear gas, fired stun grenades, set off smoke bombs, and shoved demonstrators with shields and batons (Lang, 2020). The entire incident was broadcast in real time across cable and network news stations.

## Demographic Characteristics

Turning to the demographic characteristics of citizens, we expect minorities to be more supportive of the protests than whites. Polling data by PEW in June of 2020 show that support for BLM protests among Black respondents averaged about 86 percent, support among Latinos averaged 77 percent, and support among whites was lower at 60 percent.[9] Another poll conducted by Kaiser Family Foundation (KFF) at the same time found a similar racial division: 84 percent of Black respondents supported the protests against police violence, compared to 61 percent of white respondents.[10] Support for earlier civil rights movements yielded similar differences along racial lines; during the civil rights movement and Black power movement of the 1960s, Black citizens were more supportive of these movements than whites (e.g., Bobo, 1988).

---

[9] www.pewresearch.org/social-trends/2020/06/12/amid-protests-majorities-across-racial-and-ethnic-groups-express-support-for-the-black-lives-matter-movement/

[10] www.kff.org/report-section/kff-health-tracking-poll-june-2020-racism-protests-and-racial-disparities/

With regard to support for law enforcement, a long line of research shows that approval of police is significantly higher among whites than minorities (e.g., Tuch and Weitzer, 1997). In a poll conducted by Gallup after the killing of George Floyd, 56 percent of white respondents and only 19 percent of Black respondents said that they had "a great deal" or "quite a lot" of confidence in the police.[11] While there has been a racial gap in support for police since Gallup began asking this question in 1993 (i.e., in 1993, 60 percent of white respondents had confidence in the police, compared to 34 percent of Black respondents), the thirty-seven-point racial gap in 2020 is the largest gap reported during the nearly thirty-year period.

Consistent with public opinion data measuring confidence in police, a number of experimental studies show racial differences in how people respond to episodes of police violence. Crabtree and Yadon (2022) find that white respondents' views of police remain relatively neutral when given news about a fatal police shooting. Similarly, McGowen and Wylie (2020) find Blacks are more likely than whites to express anger in response to a police shooting and are more likely to place blame on the police officer involved in the shooting. Jefferson, Neuner, and Pasek (2021) also find clear racial differences in response to scenario describing a police shooting of a Black man. For instance, white respondents are more likely than Black respondents to view the officer's actions as appropriate while Blacks are more likely than whites to think the officer should be charged.[12]

Since we expect Black respondents to be particularly supportive of the social justice movement of 2020 and especially negative in their views of police, we examine whether Black respondents, other minority respondents, and white respondents differ in their assessments of the protests and their evaluations of police.

Turning to age, we expect younger people to be more supportive of social justice issues than their older counterparts (Parker, Graff, and Igielnik, 2019) and older respondents to be more likely to view police in a favorable light (e.g., Brown and Benedict, 2002; Socia et al., 2021). Finally, women may be more supportive of the social justice movement than men. According to surveys conducted during the summer of 2020,

---

[11] news.gallup.com/poll/317114/black-white-adults-confidence-diverges-police.aspx
[12] Jefferson et al. (2020) examined whether racial motivated reasoning or racial differences in prior beliefs and expectations affect Black and white respondents' reactions to the experimental scenario. While they find evidence for both mechanisms, they report slightly stronger support for individuals in different racial groups "interpreting novel information in ways that were shaped by preexisting beliefs and expectations." (Jefferson et al., 2020: 1178).

women were somewhat more likely than men to support the BLM protests (e.g., Fahs and Swank. 2022). Further, women are more supportive of social justice issues, in general, than men (e.g., Lizotte, 2020). However, a long line of research on political engagement suggests that women are less likely to engage in protests than men (e.g., Dodson, 2015), indicating women may be less likely to approve of protests as a form of political activity. Regarding support for police, the evidence is mixed; some studies show a gender gap in approval of police, while other studies find gender has no effect on perceptions of police (Brown and Benedict, 2002).

## UNDERSTANDING CITIZENS' SUPPORT FOR RACIAL JUSTICE PROTESTS

### Support for Social Justice Protests

We measure support for the social justice protests by developing an index based on citizens' support for the BLM movement and approval of protests against police brutality. The index ranges from 2 (strongly oppose) to 10 (strongly support).[13] We seek to explain people's level of support for social justice protests in September as well as changes in support from September to October. To explain people's placement on the social justice index, we examine people's political characteristics, psychological predispositions, and demographic characteristics.[14]

We begin by looking at support for racial justice protests in September (first column in Table 4.1). As expected, we see that people's partisan affiliation strongly influences support for racial justice protests. According to the unstandardized coefficient for party identification, support for racial justice protests increases more than 2 points (i.e., $-.31 * 7 = 2.17$) as we move from strong Republican identifiers (coded as 7) to strong Democratic identifiers (coded as 1). We also see that people's partisan media diet significantly influences people's views about the protests. People who are exposed to liberal news treatment of BLM and police brutality cases are more supportive of racial justice protests than people watching a more critical view of the protests on news programs like FOX News. Finally, attention to the news, in general, is associated with significantly more positive views of racial justice protests in September.

---

[13] Cronbach's alpha for the social protests index is .86.
[14] All of the independent variables are measured during the September wave.

TABLE 4.1 *Explaining support for social justice protests*

| | Support for protests (September)[1] | Support for protests (Changes from September to October)[2] |
|---|---|---|
| *Political characteristics* | | |
| Attention to news | .26 (.03)** | .18 (.03)** |
| Partisan media | .27 (.06)** | .34 (.05)** |
| Party identification | -.31 (.02)** | -.22 (.02)** |
| *Psychological predispositions* | | |
| Authoritarianism | -.01 (.03) | -.02 (.03) |
| Conflict avoidance | .04 (.01)** | -.02 (.01)* |
| Conspiracy thinking | .025 (.006)** | .027 (.005)** |
| Hostile sexism | -.16 (.02)** | -.13 (.02)** |
| Racial resentment | -.26 (.01)** | -.30 (.01)** |
| *Demographic characteristics* | | |
| Age | -.032 (.002)** | -.03 (.01)** |
| Black | .52 (.14)** | .63 (.12)** |
| Gender | -.35 (.08)** | -.17 (.07)* |
| White | -.37 (.09)** | -.11 (.09) |
| Intercept | 11.99 (.30)** | 12.61 (.27)** |
| Random effects | | |
| Variance of intercept | | 2.47 (.08)** |
| Variance of repeated measures (time) | | .91 (.03)** |
| Model fit | | |
| Akaike information criterion | | 17,532.85 |

104

Log likelihood                                17,502.85
R²                            .54
Number of respondents       2,824              2,827

*Note:* The dependent variable is support for social justice protests, which ranges from 2 (low) to 10 (high). All independent variables are measured in September. Attention to news ranges from low (1) to high (5). Partisan media ranges from −2 (only conservative news) to 3 (only liberal news). Party identification ranges from 1 (strong Democrat) to 7 (strong Republican). Authoritarianism ranges from 0 (low authoritarian thinking) to 4 (high authoritarian thinking). Conflict avoidance ranges from 5 (low conflict avoidance) to 20 (high conflict avoidance). Conspiracy thinking ranges from 0 (low conspiracy thinking) to 30 (high in conspiracy thinking). Hostile sexism ranges from 4 (low sexism) to 16 (high sexism). Racial resentment ranges from 4 (low racial resentment) to 20 (high racial resentment). Age is measured in years. Black is 1 for Black and 0 for other. Gender is 1 for female and 0 for male. White is 1 for white and 0 for other. For more details about measurement, see the text.

[1] Unstandardized regression coefficients are presented with standard errors (in parentheses), followed by levels of statistical significance, and standardized coefficients.

[2] Estimated parameters of multilevel modeling are presented with standard errors (in parentheses), followed by levels of statistical significance. In the MLM model, political characteristics, psychological predispositions, and demographic characteristics are fixed effects.

\*\* $p < .01$
\* $p < .05$

Among people's personality predispositions, we find that level of racial resentment is strongly and negatively related to support for the social protests. According to the standardized coefficients, racial resentment is by far the most important variable explaining support for BLM and the social justice protests. We illustrate the importance of racial resentment by calculating the predicted values of the dependent variable (i.e., support for racial justice protests) when we vary racial resentment from low (4) to high (20). We find that when racial resentment is at a minimum, people's score on the social protests index is 8.62. However, when racial resentment is at its maximum, support for protests drops in half to 4.46. We also find evidence for our expectation that support for social protests is negatively related to level of sexism. In particular, people scoring high on the hostile sexism scale are less supportive of protests against social injustice compared to people who score low on the sexism measure.

In addition, and as hypothesized, we find that people who engage in conspiracy thinking are more supportive of racial justice protests. Further, we find that conflict avoidance is significantly related to support for the social justice movement, with people who want to avoid conflict being more supportive of a movement seeking to reduce violence. Finally, although we expected that people high in authoritarianism would be less supportive of protests against police brutality, we fail to find a significant relationship.[15]

Looking at the demographic characteristics of citizens, we find that Blacks, compared to other minorities, are significantly more supportive of racial justice protests, while whites are less supportive of racial justice protests than non-Black minorities. Women are less supportive of the BLM protests, once we control for political and psychological predispositions. Finally, and as expected, we find support for protests declines significantly with the age of the respondent.

---

[15] We explore whether the impact of psychological predispositions on support for racial justice protests is moderated by people's partisan news consumption. We find a significant interaction for one of the five psychological predispositions: racial resentment. While racial resentment has a negative impact on support for racial justice protests at all levels of partisan news attention, the impact of racial resentment on support for the protests becomes significantly more powerful as people's preference for conservative news increases. For example, the impact of racial resentment on support for racial justice protests is more than two times larger for people who pay attention exclusively to conservative news sources (effect = -.39, standard error = .02) compared to people who consume only liberal news (effect = -.18, standard error = .03). (In this example, we compare people who score -2 on the partisan news index to people who score 3 on the partisan news index.)

## Changes in Support for Social Justice Protests

We have shown how political factors and psychological predispositions influence baseline support for racial justice protests in September 2020. We turn now to explaining changes in citizens' support for these protests over the course of the campaign. To model changes in support for racial justice protests from September to October, we rely on multilevel modeling.[16] The dependent variable is *change* in level of support for the protests from September to October and we examine the same independent variables included in the earlier analysis.

We expect that people's political characteristics will explain changes in people's views of the protests. Once again, we find that people's partisan affiliation leads to expected changes in support for protests against police brutality (see second column in Table 4.1). Furthermore, we see people's partisan news diet leads to changes in views of the protests, with people exposed to liberal-leaning news sites becoming more supportive of social justice demonstrations during the campaign compared to people who pay attention to right-leaning sources of news. These findings suggest that as the campaign intensifies, people become more polarized in their political views, leading to predictable changes in people's assessments of the social protest movement. Finally, paying attention to the news, in general, is associated with increases in support for racial justice protests.

The results in Table 4.1 also show that psychological predispositions are important determinants of changes in support for social justice protests. People's level of racial resentment is significantly related to changing opinions about the protests. More specifically, people with higher levels of racial resentment become less supportive of the protests over the course of the campaign, while people with less racial resentment become more supportive. We also find that people's sexist attitudes are linked to less support for social justice protests from September to October.

Furthermore, the results in Table 4.1 show that conspiracy thinking is related to changes in support for the protest movement. In particular, as conspiracy thinking increases, favorability toward racial justice protests increases significantly over the course of the campaign. Finally, we find that conflict avoidance is significantly associated with changes in support for the protest movement. However, unlike the static model in Table 4.1, where conflict avoidance is positively associated with support for the

---

[16] See the discussion in Chapter 2 regarding the utility of relying on MLM when modeling changes in attitudes for respondents in a panel survey.

racial justice movement, the results of the change model suggest that conflict avoidance is negatively related to support for the protests against police brutality, with people who are least tolerant of conflict becoming less supportive of racial justice protests from September to October. Finally, and consistent with the static model, level of authoritarianism is not related to changes in support for racial justice protests.[17]

Turning to demographic characteristics, we find that people's age is related to changes in support, with young people increasing their support of protests against racial injustice from September to October compared to older respondents. Black respondents, compared to non-Black respondents, become significantly more likely to endorse the social justice movement over the two months of the fall campaign. Being white, in contrast, is not related to changes in support for the protest movement from September to October. Finally, and similar to our static model, we find that men are more likely than women to become more supportive of the protests over time.

This analysis demonstrates quite convincingly that citizens' attitudes toward the racial protest movement are changing in a systematic fashion across the campaign. This is interesting given the standard belief in 2020 that people's attitudes toward politics in general are stable and hardened around partisan attachments and candidate support. Contrary to the conventional wisdom, we find that attitudes toward racial justice shift across the fall campaign, with political factors, psychological predispositions, and demographic characteristics playing a central role in explaining these fluctuations.

We turn next to examining people's attitudes toward the police. We have shown that people's views of the police became more favorable over the course of the campaign. In our next analysis, we will show how political characteristics, psychological predispositions of citizens, and demographic factors influence support for police during the 2020 campaign.

## UNDERSTANDING APPROVAL OF POLICE

We expect that variables leading to greater support for social justice movements would also contribute to declines in support for police. To

---

[17] We explore whether the impact of psychological predispositions on changes in support for racial justice protests are more powerful for people paying attention to partisan news. As with the static model, we find a significant positive interaction between racial resentment and partisan news, suggesting that the impact of racial resentment on decreases in support for the protests becomes more powerful as people's preference for conservative news increases.

# Understanding Approval of Police

measure support for police, we develop an index where we combine answers to two questions: (1) level of job approval for police in the community and (2) level of confidence that police officers are acting in the best interests of the public. The resulting index ranges from 2 (low approval) to 8 (high approval).[18]

As we did when explaining social protests, we begin with a baseline model explaining support for police in September. The data in the first column of Table 4.2 show a positive relationship between party identification and attitudes toward the police, with Republicans reporting more positive views of police than Democrats. We also find that people's partisan media diet is related to attitudes toward law enforcement, with people exposed to conservative news adopting significantly more favorable views toward the police compared to those who consume news from liberal sources. Further, people's attention to news, in general, is associated with more favorable views of police.

Turning to psychological predispositions, we find that each of the psychological factors are significantly related to support for police. People who express higher levels of racial resentment are significantly more likely to view the police in a positive light. Racial resentment is by far the most influential variable in the model, according to the standardized coefficients. In addition, we find a modest positive relationship between level of hostile sexism and support for police. Further, and as hypothesized, people who score higher on the conspiracy index are less likely to view the police in a positive light. This is consistent with our expectation that people who engage in conspiracy thinking will be less trustful of institutions, such as law enforcement. Conflict avoidance is also associated with less support for police, perhaps because of the high-profile incidents of police brutality during the summer and fall of 2020. Finally, and as hypothesized, we find that people with more authoritarian attitudes are significantly more supportive of police in the September wave of the panel.[19]

Finally, white respondents, compared to minorities, are considerably more positive toward the police. In fact, the unstandardized coefficient indicates that white respondents are almost one-third of a point (i.e., .30 of a point) higher on the six-point police index, holding everything else constant. We also find that age significantly influences views of the police,

---

[18] Cronbach's alpha for the police approval index is .79.
[19] We explore whether the impact of psychological predispositions on support for police is moderated by people's partisan news consumption. We fail to find a significant interaction for any of the five psychological predispositions.

TABLE 4.2 *Explaining support for police*

| | Support for police (September)[1] | Support for police (Changes from September to October)[2] |
|---|---|---|
| *Campaign characteristics* | | |
| Attention to news | .19 (.03)** | .14 (.02)** |
| Partisan media | -.19 (.05)** | -.05 (.04) |
| Party identification | .14 (.01)** | .15 (.01)** |
| *Psychological predispositions* | | |
| Authoritarianism | .14 (.03)** | .10 (.02)** |
| Conflict avoidance | -.05 (.01)** | -.02 (.01)* |
| Conspiracy thinking | -.014 (.004)** | -.005 (.004) |
| Hostile sexism | .02 (.01)* | -.01 (.01) |
| Racial resentment | .14 (.01)** | .12 (.01)** |
| *Demographic characteristics* | | |
| Age | .008 (.002)** | .016 (.002)** |
| Black | .02 (.11) | -.37 (.10)** |
| Gender | -.14 (.06)** | -.04 (.05) |
| White | .30 (.07)** | .29 (.07)** |
| Intercept | 2.42 (.23)** | 2.44 (.21)** |
| Random effects | | |
| Variance of intercept | | 1.19 (.05)** |
| Variance of repeated measures (time) | | .94 (.03)** |

| | |
|---|---|
| Model fit | |
| Akaike information criterion | 15,565.369 |
| Log likelihood | 15,535.369 |
| $R^2$ | .33 |
| Number of respondents | 2,737   2,770 |

*Note:* The dependent variable is support for police and ranges from 2 (low) to 8 (high). All independent variables are measured in September. Attention to news ranges from low (1) to high (5). Partisan media ranges from −2 (only conservative news) to 3 (only liberal news). Party identification ranges from 1 (strong Democrat) to 7 (strong Republican). Authoritarianism ranges from 0 (low authoritarian thinking) to 4 (high authoritarian thinking). Conflict avoidance ranges from 5 (low conflict avoidance) to 20 (high conflict avoidance). Conspiracy thinking ranges from 0 (low conspiracy thinking) to 30 (high in conspiracy thinking). Hostile sexism ranges from 4 (low sexism) to 16 (high sexism). Racial resentment ranges from 4 (low racial resentment) to 20 (high racial resentment). Age is measured in years. Black is 1 for Black and 0 for other. Gender is 1 for female and 0 for male. White is 1 for white and 0 for other. For more details about measurement, see the text.

[1] Unstandardized regression coefficients are presented with standard errors (in parentheses), followed by levels of statistical significance, and standardized coefficients.

[2] Estimated parameters of multilevel modeling are presented with standard errors (in parentheses), followed by levels of statistical significance. In the MLM model, political characteristics, psychological predispositions, and demographic characteristics are fixed effects.

** $p < .01$
* $p < .05$

with older respondents being more likely to view the police in a positive light. Finally, women are less supportive of police than men; this result is consistent with a long line of research showing that women are less likely than men to favor the use of force in domestic areas, including the use of police to quell civil disturbances (e.g., Norrander, 2008).

### Changes in Support for Police

We turn next to explaining changes in perceptions of the police from September to October. As we did earlier when examining the dynamics of support for social justice protests, we rely on multilevel modeling to explain *changes* in support for police from September to October (see the second column in Table 4.2). The results in Table 4.2 show that eight of the ten independent variables included in the model significantly explain changes in support for police. We find that partisanship produces positive changes in views of the police, with Republicans becoming more favorable over time. However, compared to the change model explaining support for social protests, we find that people's partisan media diet is less important for explaining changes in views of police. The type of news media consumption may be less influential for explaining support for police because news attention for law enforcement issues (e.g., defunding the police) was less pervasive than coverage of social protests (e.g., BLM, social justice protests) during the campaign.

To measure news attention to issues related to policing versus issues related to social justice protests, we searched the evening news broadcasts across fourteen networks between September 1, 2020, and November 3, 2020.[20] In particular, relying on the Vanderbilt Television News Archive, we used the following terms to search for stories about social justice protests: "police brutality protests," "social justice protests," and "Black Lives Matter." Similarly, to search for stories related to the police, we used the following terms: "police," "police brutality," "Defund the Police." We found almost three times as many news stories about social justice protests than stories about policing. We identified 514 stories mentioning social justice protests and 176 stories discussing police-related issues. These results support our contention that news media messages about the police were less pervasive, clarifying why the partisan media message

---

[20] The following networks were included in the search: ABC, NBC, CBS CNN, PBS, FOX News, MSNBC, C-SPAN, CNBC, Univision, Bloomberg, Telemundo, BET, and FOX Business Network.

failed to explain changes in support for law enforcement from September to October.

We also see that views about race continue to have an impact on changes in views of the police, with people scoring high on racial resentment becoming more favorable to police from September to October. Level of authoritarian thinking is also important for explaining variations in people's approval of police during the fall campaign; people with high levels of authoritarian thinking become more supportive of law enforcement from September to October. We also find, as hypothesized, a negative relationship between conflict avoidance and support for police. People who are least tolerant of conflict are more likely to develop negative views of law enforcement over the campaign period. Finally, while level of conspiracy thinking predicted baseline support for police in October, we do not find that people's propensity for conspiracy thinking produces significant changes in their support of law enforcement.[21]

Finally, age continues to explain changes in people's views; as age increases, people become more supportive of law enforcement during the fall campaign. Second, Black respondents are more likely than other non-Black minorities to become significantly less supportive of police during the last months of the campaign. Third, white respondents, compared to non-Black minority respondents, become significantly more positive in their views of law enforcement from September to October. Overall, the results of the change model in Table 4.2 support the citizen-centered theory of campaigns. People's political and psychological predispositions, along with demographic characteristics, powerfully predict variations in people's views of police during the fall campaign.

## THE ELECTORAL CONSEQUENCES OF RACIAL JUSTICE PROTESTS

We conclude by looking at how attitudes toward racial protests as well as attitudes toward law enforcement influence people's evaluations of the presidential candidates. To measure overall evaluations of the candidates, we rely on the feeling thermometer scores. We include as independent variables (1) people's level of support for racial justice protests

---

[21] We explore whether the impact of psychological predispositions on changes in support for police are more powerful for people paying attention to partisan news. We find a significant negative interaction between racial resentment and partisan news, suggesting that the impact of racial resentment on increases in support for police becomes more powerful as people's preference for conservative news increases.

(i.e., the dependent variable in Table 4.1) and (2) people's support for police (i.e., the dependent variable in Table 4.2). The candidates' approaches to the issue of race could not be more different. Beason (2020), staff writer for the *Los Angeles Times*, explains the contrast:

> Trump has consistently downplayed the role of racism in American life while simultaneously attacking protesters, making racist and xenophobic comments and claiming he's done more for Black people than any other president 'with the possible exception of Abraham Lincoln.' Biden has positioned himself as a crusader for racial justice who'll use the presidency to correct long-standing social inequities and restore the climate of relative tolerance that marked his two terms as vice president under President Obama. He's chosen as his vice-presidential running mate California Sen. Kamala Harris, setting her up to become the first person of color and the first woman to hold that position if elected. At the Cleveland debate, he again vowed to stand up to racists – including Trump.

Given the far greater priority given to the issue of race by Biden than Trump, we expect people who are most supportive of the goals of the social protest movement to be more likely to develop negative attitudes toward Trump and positive attitudes toward Biden. In addition, since Trump and Republican surrogates delivered campaign messages painting Biden as weak on crime and supporting defunding the police, while Trump repeatedly portrayed himself as the "law and order" president, we expect support for police will be linked to more favorable views of Trump and more negative views of Biden.[22]

In addition to variables measuring support for social justice protests and support for police, we once again include a series of control variables: (1) assessments of candidates' personal traits, (2) economic performance evaluations, and (3) party identification. We present two sets of models in Table 4.3. In the first set of models (see the top half of Table 4.3), we predict overall evaluations of Trump and Biden in the September wave of the survey. In the second set of models (see the bottom half of Table 4.3), we predict changes in evaluations of each candidate from September to October.[23] We begin with a discussion of the September model.

In the model predicting evaluations of Trump and Biden in September, we find that people's support for social justice protests is negatively related to overall evaluations of Trump. In fact, when we

---

[22] For example, the following advertisements, sponsored by the America First Action Committee (a single-candidate super political action committee in support of Trump) paint Biden as supporting defunding the police: youtu.be/AUeuPbsmHmE youtu.be/MW3UZfNlAc8

[23] In each of the models in Table 4.3, the independent variables are measured in September.

TABLE 4.3 *Impact of views of protests and police on overall evaluations of the presidential candidates*

| | Thermometer ratings in September[1] | |
|---|---|---|
| | Trump thermometer | Biden thermometer |
| *Attitudes toward police and protests* | | |
| Support for protests | -1.53 (.17)** | .99 (.20)** |
| Support for police | .07 (.27) | -1.05 (.27)** |
| *Rival factors* | | |
| General economic assessment | 3.45 (.34)** | .94 (.33)** |
| Party identification | 2.78 (.23)** | -3.17 (.23)** |
| Trait assessment | 4.03 (.09)** | 3.81 (.09)** |
| Constant | -18.91 (2.16)** | 2.77 (2.39) |
| $R^2$ | .80 | .73 |
| Number of respondents | 2,323 | 2,238 |

| | Changes in thermometer ratings from September to October[2] | |
|---|---|---|
| | Trump thermometer | Biden thermometer |
| *Attitudes toward police and protests* | | |
| Support for protests | -1.48 (.15)** | 1.31 (.18)** |
| Support for police | .21 (.24) | -.76 (.24)** |
| *Rival factors* | | |
| General economic assessment | 2.56 (.31)** | .69 (.29)* |

*(continued)*

TABLE 4.3 (*continued*)

Changes in thermometer ratings from September to October

| | Trump thermometer | Biden thermometer |
|---|---|---|
| Party identification | 2.94 (.20)** | −3.35 (.21)** |
| Trait assessment | 4.01 (.08)** | 3.75 (.08)** |
| Intercept | −19.77 (1.90)** | 1.51 (2.17) |
| Random effects | | |
| Variance of intercept | 206.54 (8.28)** | 207.78 (9.06)** |
| Variance of repeated measures (time) | 101.30 (3.59)** | 123.37 (4.49)** |
| Akaike information criterion | 34,008.19 | 32,684.51 |
| Log likelihood | 33,992.19 | 32,668.51 |
| Number of respondents | 2,430 | 2,315 |

*Note:* The dependent variable is feeling thermometer ratings (ranging from 0 to 100) for Donald Trump and Joe Biden. Support for social protests ranges from 2 to 10. Support for police ranges from 2 to 8. General economic assessment ranges from 1 (the economy has gotten much worse) to 5 (the economy has gotten much better). Party identification ranges from 1 (strong Democrat) to 7 (strong Republican). Trait assessment ranges from 6 (most negative) to 24 (most positive). All independent variables are measured in September. For more details about measurement, see the text.

[1] Unstandardized regression coefficients are presented with standard errors (in parentheses), followed by levels of statistical significance, and standardized coefficients.
[2] Estimated parameters of multilevel modeling are presented with standard errors (in parentheses), followed by levels of statistical significance. In the MLM model, attitudes toward police, attitudes toward social protests, and the rival factors are fixed effects.

** $p < .01$
* $p < .05$

## Electoral Consequences of Racial Justice Protests

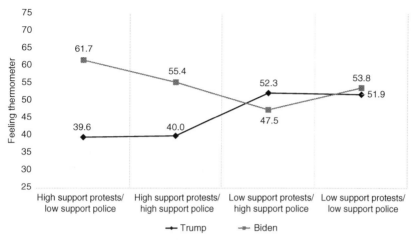

FIGURE 4.4 Impact of support for social justice protests and support for police on feeling thermometer ratings of Trump and Biden in October

compare people who are least supportive of the racial justice movement to those who are most supportive, we estimate a drop in evaluations of Trump of more than 12 points on the feeling thermometer. While Trump's overall evaluations are damaged by people who support the social justice movement, Biden's evaluations are helped by attitudes toward the movement. The unstandardized coefficient for support for social protests in the Biden model indicates that every one-point increase in support for the racial justice movement is associated with a one-point increase in Biden's feeling thermometer score. Finally, support for police does not significantly alter overall evaluations of Trump in September, but people's attitudes toward the police are significant and negative in the model predicting overall evaluations of Biden in September.

To examine the dual impact of attitudes toward the racial justice movement and attitudes toward policing on evaluations of Trump and Biden, we derive point estimates relying on the coefficients in Table 4.3.[24] The data in Figure 4.4 show that Trump's feeling thermometer ratings are lowest among people highly supportive of protests against police brutality, regardless of their attitudes toward the police. Trump's ratings are estimated to be about 40 on the feeling thermometer among these respondents, more than 15 points below Biden's estimated ratings.

---

[24] We vary support for the racial justice movement from low (2) to high (10) and vary support for police from low (2) to high (8).

In contrast, for people who do not support the racial justice movement, evaluations of Biden decline significantly, especially among people who also have very favorable views of police. For instance, we see a fourteen-point drop in Biden's feeling thermometer scores when we compare people with highly favorable attitudes about the protest movement and negative feelings about police, on the one hand, to people with positive feelings about the police and unfavorable attitudes about the protests, on the other hand. Finally, views of Trump are significantly more positive (above 50 on the feeling thermometer) among people who are least supportive of the social justice movement, irrespective of their attitudes toward the police.

Overall, the issues of race and policing play an important role for understanding impressions of Biden and Trump in September. We turn next to examining changes in evaluations of Trump and Biden from September to October (i.e., the models in the bottom half of Table 4.3). In this analysis, we look at whether attitudes toward protests against racial injustice and views about policing influence *changes* in people's impressions of the candidates during the fall campaign. We see similarities between the static model for September and the change model for October. First, when looking at changes in evaluations of Trump from September to October, we see a negative relationship between attitudes toward racial justice and changes in views of Trump. That is, as people become more supportive of the social justice movement, they become significantly more negative in their views of Trump over the first months of the fall campaign. Second, people's support for police does not alter overall evaluations of Trump during the course of the campaign. Trump's portrayal of himself as a friend of law enforcement does not produce more favorable changes in people's views of his candidacy. Nevertheless, he is penalized for his position on racial justice protests, with people supportive of these protests becoming significantly more critical in their view of Trump over the first two months of the general election campaign.

For Biden, we see that attitudes toward racial justice protests are associated with positive changes in evaluations of the Democratic nominee from September to October. And, similar to the static model, support for police is significantly and negatively related to changes in evaluations of Biden. However, unlike the static model, the size of the estimates for support for social protests and support for police suggests that the impact of attitudes toward the protest movement is more consequential for explaining changes in views of Biden.

## CONCLUSION AND IMPLICATIONS

The 2020 summer of protests pushed issues of race front and center in the presidential campaign, leading more than two-thirds of people to report positive views of the BLM movement in the wake of the death of George Floyd. While the salience of race faded as the general election campaign unfolded, we find that political characteristics of citizens strongly affect people's views of the racial justice protests and opinions about the police. For instance, party attachment and partisan media exposure influence views of the social justice movement as well as people's support for law enforcement. Also, consistent with the citizen-centered theory of campaigns, we find that psychological predispositions consistently and significantly influence both views of social protests and policing. For example, level of racial resentment produces powerful changes in people's views of the protests and police from September to October.

Furthermore, we find that attitudes about racial justice and views of policing influence impressions of Biden and Trump. Even after controlling for a number of factors, like partisanship, we show that views about race and policing produce substantive changes in people's ratings of the competing candidates. We believe that issues revolving around racial justice, by influencing evaluations of the candidates, likely altered voters' decision-making at the ballot box.

In the years since George Floyd's death, Derek Chauvin, the police officer who knelt on Floyd's neck for more than nine minutes, was found guilty of second-degree unintentional murder, third-degree murder, and second-degree manslaughter. Chauvin also pleaded guilty to violating Floyd's civil rights. He was sentenced to twenty-two-and-half years in prison in June 2021.[25] In addition, Thomas Lane, J. Alexander Kueng, and Tou Thao were convicted of depriving Floyd of his civil rights. Kueng and Thao were also convicted of not intervening to stop their fellow officer (Derek Chauvin) from using excessive force.[26] Lane pleaded guilty in May 2022 to a state charge of aiding and abetting second-degree murder and was sentenced to three years in prison. Kuening pleaded guilty and Thao was found guilty on state charges of aiding and abetting

---

[25] www.npr.org/sections/trial-over-killing-of-george-floyd/2021/06/25/1009524284/derek-chauvin-sentencing-george-floyd-murder
www.npr.org/2022/05/05/1096822662/judge-accepts-plea-deal-in-derek-chauvins-civil-rights-case
[26] www.nbcnews.com/news/us-news/jury-reaches-verdict-federal-trial-3-officers-george-floyds-killing-rcna17237

second-degree murder and second-degree manslaughter; Kuening was sentenced to just over three years in prison while Thao was given nearly a five-year sentence.[27]

The killing of George Floyd placed a focus on systematic racism and police brutality, as well as broader concerns around social injustice. More than thirty states and many large cities have created new rules for policing, including banning neck restraints and requiring police officers to intervene when another officer is using extreme force. And the US House of Representatives passed a bill named for George Floyd that would limit police use of force as well as make it easier to prosecute police officers for misconduct. However, the legislation was never passed by the US Senate (Leonhardt and Philbrick, 2021). On the second anniversary of the death of George Floyd, President Biden signed an executive order aimed at reforming police practices. The order creates a national registry of officers fired for misconduct, encourages state and local police to tighten restrictions on chokeholds and no-knock warrants, and requires law enforcement to stop the use of excessive force when they see it and administer medical aid to the injured. The family of George Floyd was at the White House for the signing of the executive order (Pettypiece, 2022).

While there have been some changes since Floyd's death, the pace of police violence has not slowed. According to Mapping Police Violence, from May 2020 to May 2021, there were at least 1,068 police killings across the country – averaging three killings every day (Haddad, 2021). Moreover, in the first seven months of 2022 police have killed more than 700 people, Further, there has only been eight days in the first seven months of the year with no deaths at the hands of police (Asher, 2022).

Attitudes toward BLM have become more polarized, with Republicans becoming less supportive of BLM than they were in 2020 while support among Democrats remains higher than it was before Floyd's death but lower than immediately after the incident. Support for law enforcement has rebounded over this time period, with most people indicating a high degree of trust in law enforcement, at least compared to immediately after Floyd's death. Most people both disagree with calls to "defund" or abolish police departments and agree to some changes in policing, such as banning chokeholds (Leonhardt and Philbrick, 2021).

---

[27] www.nytimes.com/2022/05/18/us/thomas-lane-george-floyd.html
www.usatoday.com/story/news/nation/2023/08/07/tou-thao-sentenced-george-floyd-death/70541218007/

## Conclusion and Implications

We highlight statistics regarding police violence as well as efforts to alter public policy and shifts in public opinion, as a reminder that the nation's long struggle with equality for all of its citizens remains unsettled and often near the top of the national agenda. Candidates for the presidency will need to focus on these issues well into the future. The 2020 campaign, because of the highly publicized death of George Floyd at the hands of police only five months before the November election, forced candidates to take clear stands on the issues of racial justice and police brutality. This is not the first campaign where these types of events occurred during an election year; unfortunately, it will almost certainly not be the last. In our representative democracy, where the vital concept of equality remains a contested issue and solutions remain contentious and complex, citizens are paying attention to candidates' messages and these messages are influencing decisions at the ballot box.

In Chapter 5, we turn to another salient issue in the 2020 campaign: the question of the integrity of the election results. We will show that, consistent with the citizen-centered theory of campaigns, political characteristics and psychological predispositions significantly influence people's confidence in the integrity of the election. Further, these citizen characteristics powerfully alter ratings of Trump's and Biden's ability to guarantee the integrity of the election. Finally, we show that people's views about the integrity of the election influence evaluations of Trump and Biden in September and motivate changes in opinions of the rival candidates over the course of the campaign.

# 5

## "A Rigged Election"

### *How Views about Election Integrity Altered the Campaign*

Years before Donald Trump entered politics, he began questioning the integrity of US presidential elections. In 2012, when Democrat Barack Obama beat Republican Mitt Romney, Trump wrote a series of election night tweets challenging the election results and calling for a revolution (Kelsey, 2016). For example, he tweeted, "This election is a total sham and a travesty. We are not a democracy!" He also claimed falsely that Obama had lost the popular vote to Romney while winning the Electoral College vote.

In 2016, when Trump lost the Iowa caucus to Ted Cruz in the opening contest for the Republican nomination for president, he once again complained about election fraud on Twitter, saying, "Ted Cruz didn't win Iowa, he stole it. That is why all of the polls were so wrong and why he got far more votes than anticipated. Bad!" And "Based on the fraud committed by Senator Ted Cruz during the Iowa Caucus, either a new election should take place or Cruz results nullified" (Smith, 2020).

During the 2016 general election campaign, at rallies, during television and radio interviews, and on Twitter, Trump accelerated his claims that the "system was rigged." In October 2016, he tweeted, "The election is absolutely being rigged by the dishonest and distorted media pushing Crooked Hillary – but also at many polling places – SAD." Around the same time, at a rally in Wisconsin, he asserted, "Remember, we are competing in a rigged election. They even want to try and rig the election at the polling booths, where so many cities are corrupt and voter fraud is all too common" (Collinson, 2016).

During the final presidential debate between Trump and Clinton, Trump twice declined to say whether he would accept the election's

## The Impact of Election Integrity on the Campaign 123

outcome, flouting the country's tradition of a losing candidate's concession after the votes are counted. Clinton called Trump's answer "horrifying" and said Trump "is denigrating and he is talking down our democracy. And I, for one, am appalled that somebody who is the nominee of one of our two major parties would take that kind of a position" (BBC, 2016). Even after Trump won the 2016 general election, with Clinton conceding, he continued to complain about massive voter fraud, saying, "In addition to winning the Electoral College in a landslide, I won the popular vote if you deduct the millions of people who voted illegally" (Twitter, on November 27, 2016). However, Trump lost the popular vote to Clinton by nearly three million votes and no systematic evidence of voter fraud was ever established (Seipel, 2016).

In 2020, Trump framed his discussion of a rigged election mostly by claiming (without evidence) that mail voting would lead to massive voting fraud. He first made this claim in April 2020, but repeated it 144 times according to an analysis by the *Washington Post* (Kessler and Fox, 2021). In May, Trump made a similar assertion on Twitter when he said, "The United States cannot have all Mail In Ballots. It will be the greatest Rigged Election in history. People grab them from mailboxes, print thousands of forgeries and 'force' people to sign. Also, forge names. Some absentee OK, when necessary. Trying to use Covid for this Scam!" In an August 19 speech, he said, "The only way they're going to win is by a rigged election. I really believe that." And then in a campaign rally a few weeks later, he repeated, "It's a rigged election. It's the only way we're going to lose." A few days later in a press interview, Trump doubled down on his accusations, saying, "You're going to see something with these ballots. You're going to see corruption like you've never seen. You're going to see a rigged election."

Relying on the *Washington Post* database documenting Trump's false or misleading claims (see www.washingtonpost.com/graphics/politics/trump-claims-database/), we track Trump's claims about a rigged election during the 2020 election campaign. The data in Figure 5.1 illustrate that Trump maintained a steady drumbeat of unsubstantiated claims of election fraud and these assertions increased as Election Day approached.

On NBC's Town Hall on October 15, Trump made the following false claims about election irregularities:

And you can tell these clowns that are always looking and investigating and everything else, the ballots are a big problem for our country because they can be reproduced a lot easier than breaking into computer sites. The fake ballots that everybody is talking about all over the world. It's so crazy what's going on.

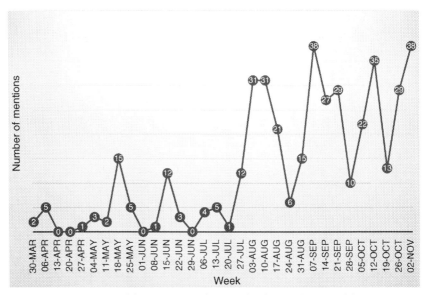

FIGURE 5.1 Weekly mentions of "rigged" election by Donald Trump

Look at these ballots that are being messed around. Tens of thousands of ballots are already fraudulent.

When I see thousands of ballots, right, unsolicited ballots being given out by the millions and thousands of them are dumped in dumpsters and when you see ballots with the name – Trump military ballots from our great military and they're dumped in garbage cans.

It's a crooked deal, it's a rigged deal. You see it every day, new, new, uh, new ballots are coming out that are thrown in garbage cans with the name Trump on it. You see it every day. But when you bring it up they say, 'Oh, he's against our constitution, he's against our freedom.' No, they're against our freedom. But it's very rigged.[1]

The repeated rhetoric about voter fraud and a rigged election had a predictable effect on the electorate. In particular, Republicans were much less confident than Democrats about the integrity of the election. Gallup polling conducted in the last few weeks of the 2020 election indicated that about three-quarters (74 percent) of Democrats said they were very or somewhat confident that "votes for president will be accurately cast and counted in this year's election." In contrast, less than half of Republicans (44 percent) claimed they were very or somewhat confident in the accuracy of the election (McCarthy, 2020).

---

[1] www.rev.com/blog/transcripts/donald-trump-nbc-town-hall-transcript-october-15

In this chapter, we rely on our survey to examine three key questions: (1) What are the determinants of people's confidence in the integrity of the election? (2) Who has confidence in Trump's and Biden's ability to ensure the veracity of US elections? (3) How do beliefs about election integrity influence overall evaluations of Trump and Biden? We measure people's confidence in the election once in the October wave of the survey. The question tapping people's confidence in each candidate's ability to maintain the integrity of election is asked in September and October, allowing us to examine how political factors as well as psychological predispositions influence people's level of confidence in the election at different points in the campaign.

UNDERSTANDING THE DETERMINANTS OF CONFIDENCE IN THE INTEGRITY OF THE ELECTION

A small and rapidly growing literature has begun to explore forces leading people to perceive election fraud. First, people's attitudes toward the rival candidates, coupled with the outcome of the election, influence opinions about the integrity of an election. Known as the "winner's effect," several researchers have demonstrated, using divergent methodologies (e.g., experiment, surveys) and looking at different elections, that citizens who voted for the winning candidate experience greater gains in confidence in elections following an election compared to people who voted for the losing candidate (e.g., Atkeson and Saunders, 2007; Beaulieu, 2014; Levy, 2021; Sinclair, Smith, and Tucker, 2018; Uscinski and Parent, 2014; Wang and van Prooijen, 2022).

In the context of the 2020 election, during the length of the fall campaign, Biden was consistently leading Trump in public opinion polls. According to Real Clear Politics polling averages, Biden's lead over Trump never dipped below 5 percentage points from August 1 through Election Day and reached an advantage of more than 10 points in mid-October.[2] Therefore, during the campaign period, we expect that Trump supporters will demonstrate less confidence in the legitimacy of the election compared to Biden supporters, since Biden was considered the front-runner.

Relying on polling data from Monmouth University, we see evidence of the "winner" and "loser" effect during the 2020 election.[3] As the data

---

[2] See www.realclearpolitics.com/epolls/2020/president/us/general_election_trump_vs_biden-6247.html
[3] See www.monmouth.edu/polling-institute/reports/?s=confidence%20in%20election

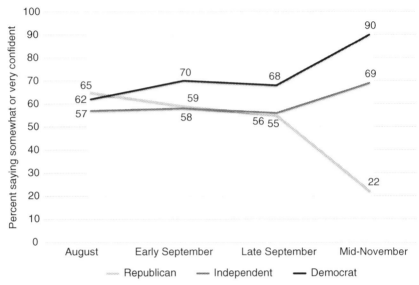

FIGURE 5.2 Partisan differences in confidence in the integrity of the 2020 election

in Figure 5.2 illustrate, Democrats and Republicans expressed similar levels of confidence in the integrity of the election in August. However, partisan differences began to emerge by early September, growing during the length of the campaign and exploding after the election. After the November election, 90 percent of the Democrats polled expressed confidence that the election was "conducted fairly and accurately." In contrast, only one in five Republicans indicated confidence in the integrity of the election in the weeks following Election Day.

Consistent with public opinion polling, Berlinski et al. (2023) utilize a survey experiment to show that exposure to claims of vote fraud after the 2018 election reduced confidence in the integrity of the election, especially among Republicans and Trump supporters.[4] Since Trump repeatedly called into question the legitimacy of the 2020 election, calling the system rigged on numerous occasions, we expect that people who support Trump will be less likely to report confidence in the integrity of the election.[5]

---

[4] See also Vonnahme and Miller (2013).
[5] Recent research examining the 2020 election shows that Republicans are less likely than Democrats to have confidence in the outcome of the election (e.g., Arceneaux and Truex, 2022).

We also expect people's choice of news to influence attitudes about the integrity of the election. People who consume news emanating from right-leaning sources will be more likely to be exposed to Trump's claims about a rigged election, with these claims facing less scrutiny. To illustrate, the following are just some of the headlines published on Fox News during the 2020 campaign: "New report finds string of ballot mishaps confirms fears of large-scale mail voting," "Texas mayoral candidate arrested for mail-in ballot fraud," "More than 1,600 uncounted NJ primary ballots found in random bin at county elections board," "West Virginia mail carrier admits attempted election fraud."[6]

In contrast, people paying attention to left-leaning sources are less likely to hear Trump's assertions about election fraud and more likely to be exposed to fact-checks of these claims. For example, a story with the headline "Fact Check: Almost Every Single One of Trump's Debate Claims about Mail-in Voting was Wrong" was published by CNN after the first presidential debate.[7] The news story begins by saying that Trump "was especially dishonest on the subject of voting by mail. Almost every single claim Trump made during the debate segment about the integrity of the election was inaccurate in whole or in part. His Tuesday performance was just the latest component of a systematic, months-long disinformation campaign he has waged to try to undermine confidence in mail-in voting." The article continues by fact-checking each of Trump's eleven claims about mail voting fraud. These examples from Fox News and CNN exemplify partisan differences in news coverage, leading us to expect that people's partisan news diet is likely to lead to significant differences in people's trust in US elections.[8]

In addition, people who have a greater connection to the political system are more likely to express confidence in election results. In particular, level of trust in government is positively associated with confidence

---

[6] The news stories can be found here: www.foxnews.com/politics/new-report-finds-string-of-ballot-mishaps-confirms-fears-of-large-scale-mail-in-voting;
  www.foxnews.com/politics/texas-mayoral-candidate-arrested-for-mail-in-ballot-fraud;
  www.foxnews.com/politics/new-jersey-residents-ballots-out-of-state-voters-dead-people-election-anti-fraud;
  www.foxnews.com/us/west-virginia-mail-carrier-admits-attempted-election-fraud
[7] www.cnn.com/2020/09/30/politics/fact-check-trump-first-debate-mail-voting-fraud/index.html
[8] Scholars have shown differences in the types of electoral conspiracies that Democrats and Republicans believe, suggesting that specific electoral conspiracies (e.g., mail-in votes are fraudulent) appear to follow elite communication (see Edelson et al., 2017; Enders et al., 2021).

in the integrity of elections (Atkeson, Alvarez, and Hall, 2015; Norris, Garnett, and Grömping, 2020; Papaioannou, Pantazi, and van Prooijen, 2023).[9] Similarly, people who are more politically engaged and politically active may display more confidence in election results. Furthermore, researchers have shown that people with higher levels of information about politics are less likely to have concerns about the integrity of the election (Norris, Garnett, and Grömping, 2020). These individuals are more likely to know that widespread voter fraud is unlikely in contemporary US elections.

Turning to psychological predispositions, we argue that only one psychological predisposition – conspiracy thinking – is likely to influence confidence in the integrity of the election. In particular, people who are more likely to believe in conspiracies are more likely to believe that election irregularities are not random but are being perpetuated by corrupt officials inside or outside of government (Norris, Garnett, and Grömping, 2020; Papaioannou, Pantazi, and van Prooijen, 2023). Put simply, people high in conspiracy thinking are likely to see conspiracies everywhere, including the tainting of the electoral process.[10]

A series of demographic characteristics have also been associated with confidence in the integrity of elections. First, racial and ethnic minorities show lower levels of confidence in elections (e.g., Norris, Garnett, and Grömping, 2020). The distrust of elections by minority voters may be driven by personal experiences of discrimination or by the long history of impediments to participation in US elections (Alvarez, Hall, and Llewellyn, 2008; Bullock, Hood, and Clark, 2005). Therefore, we expect minorities to be more suspicious of the electoral system than whites.

Studies have demonstrated that education and age are positively related to confidence in the integrity of the election (Edelson et al., 2017; Norris, Garnett and Grömping, 2020), likely reflecting the greater integration into the political system of older and more educated voters. Similarly, educated voters, like the political knowledgeable, might be more acquainted with the evidence demonstrating the lack of corruption in US elections.[11] Finally, both Beaulieu (2014) and Norris, Garnett, and

---

[9] Atkeson et al. (2015) show that voter confidence in elections is unique from trust in government.
[10] While we do not expect the remaining psychological predispositions to systematically alter people's views about the integrity of the election, we continue to include these factors in the model estimated in Table 5.1.
[11] See www.brennancenter.org/our-work/research-reports/its-official-election-was-secure for a report on the integrity of the 2020 election.

Grömping (2020) find that women report less confidence in the integrity of elections compared to men. Norris, Garnett, and Grömping speculate that women may have less confidence in elections because they feel less integrated into the US political system.

## EXPLAINING THE DETERMINANTS OF CITIZENS' CONFIDENCE IN THE INTEGRITY OF THE ELECTION

We begin our examination of people's confidence in the integrity of the election by looking at differences in confidence levels between people who intend to vote for Trump and people who intend to vote for Biden.[12] The findings in Figure 5.3 illustrate that people intending to vote for Biden express significantly more confidence in the election than those who intend to vote for Trump. More than eight out of ten Biden supporters are either "very confident" or "somewhat confident" in the integrity of the election compared to only about six out of ten Trump supporters.[13] Similarly, more than twice as many Trump supporters say they are not confident that the election results will be accurately counted compared to Biden supporters (i.e., 38 percent of Trump supporters are not

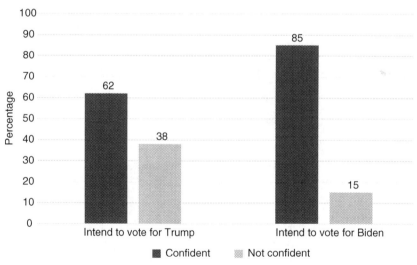

FIGURE 5.3 Difference in confidence in the election by vote intention

[12] In this analysis, we look at vote intention in September and confidence in the election in October.
[13] This difference is statistically significant at $p < .01$, based on the lambda statistic.

confident, compared to 15 percent of Biden supporters). These results are consistent with the "winner's effect." People supporting the likely winner (Biden based on preelection polls) express a great deal more confidence in the integrity of the election than supporters of the likely loser.

While people supporting the leading candidate are significantly more confident about the integrity of the election than people who are supporting the candidate trailing in the polls, we look beyond candidate preference to fully explain people's level of confidence in the election. We rely on the existing literature to generate three sets of possible explanations: political forces (i.e., vote intention, partisan news diet, likelihood of voting, trust in government, political knowledge), psychological predispositions (e.g., conspiracy thinking), and demographic characteristics of citizens (i.e., race and ethnicity, gender, age, education).[14] We present the results of the analysis in Table 5.1.[15]

First, vote intention in September powerfully predicts confidence in the election in October.[16] We also see that partisan news diet is significantly related to confidence in the election. In fact, according to the standardized coefficients, partisan news and vote intention are the most influential variables in the model. And the unstandardized coefficient (i.e., .18) for partisan news indicates that when people move from

---

[14] The independent variables are measured during the September wave of the panel survey. Vote intention is based on the following question: "If the election was held today, who would you vote for president?" with 1 = Biden, 0 = Trump (with remaining respondents excluded from the analysis). Trust in government is measured with the following question: "How often can you trust the federal government in Washington to do what is right?" with options ranging from never (1) to always (4). The political knowledge index is based on people correctly answering five open-ended questions about current political figures as well as basic government questions. The following are the open-ended knowledge questions: What position or office does Elena Kagan hold today? Do you happen to know which party has the most members in the US Senate in Washington, DC, today? Who determines if a federal law is constitutional or not? Who is currently the US secretary of state? How long is the term of a US senator? The political knowledge index ranges from 0 to 5. The remaining variables have been introduced in earlier analysis.

[15] The dependent variable is ordinal, ranging from 1 to 4. We estimate the equation in Table 5.1 with ordinal regression and with OLS regression. The results are substantively similar with both techniques and we choose to present the OLS results in Table 5.1 because of the greater ease of interpretation.

[16] Given the literature documenting the relationship between support for the winner versus the loser and confidence in the election results, we rely on vote preference in this model instead of party identification. When we include party identification in the model in Table 5.1, party identification fails to reach statistical significance. As one would expect, the relationship between party identification and vote intention is strong (i.e., the point biserial; correlation between the two variables is $-.72$, $p < .01$) and including both variables in the model may cause issues of multicollinearity.

TABLE 5.1 *Understanding people's confidence in the integrity of the election*[1]

|  | Confidence in the integrity of the election |  |
|---|---|---|
| *Political forces* |  |  |
| Attention to news | .01 (.01) | .01 |
| Likelihood of voting | .07 (.02)** | .07 |
| Partisan news | .18 (.02)** | .17 |
| Political knowledge | .02 (.01)* | .05 |
| Trust in government | .12 (.02)** | .15 |
| Vote intention | .20 (.04)** | .14 |
| *Psychological predispositions* |  |  |
| Authoritarianism | .003 (.031) | .01 |
| Conflict avoidance | .005 (.005) | .02 |
| Conspiracy thinking | −.010 (.002)** | −.09 |
| Hostile sexism | −.015 (.007)* | −.05 |
| Racial resentment | −.007 (.004) | −.04 |
| *Demographic characteristics* |  |  |
| Age | .004 (.001)** | .08 |
| White | .01 (.03) | .01 |
| Education | .03 (.01)** | .07 |
| Gender | −.09 (.03)** | −.06 |
| Constant |  | 2.26 (.15)** |
| $R^2$ |  | .16 |
| Number of respondents | 2,312 |  |

*Note:* The exact question wording for the dependent variable is "How confident are you that the results of the 2020 presidential election will be counted accurately?" with response categories ranging from "not confident at all" (1) to "very confident" (4). Attention to news ranges from low (1) to high (5). Likelihood of voting ranges from "very unlikely" (1) to "very likely" (4) to vote in the upcoming election in November. Partisan media ranges from −2 (only conservative news) to 3 (only liberal news). Political knowledge ranges from 0 to 5. Trust in government ranges from 1 (low) to 4 (high). Vote intention is based on the following question: "If the election was held today, who would you vote for president," with 1 for Biden and 0 for Trump. Authoritarianism ranges from 0 (low authoritarian thinking) to 4 (high authoritarian thinking). Conflict avoidance ranges from 5 (low conflict avoidance) to 20 (high conflict avoidance). Conspiracy thinking ranges from 0 (low conspiracy thinking) to 30 (high in conspiracy thinking). Hostile sexism ranges from 4 (low sexism) to 16 (high sexism). Racial resentment ranges from 4 (low racial resentment) to 20 (high racial resentment). Age is measured in years. White is 1 for white and 0 for minorities. Education is years of school. Gender is 1 for female and 0 for male. Confidence in the election is measured during the October wave and each of the independent variables is measured during the September wave of the panel survey. For more details about measurement, see the text.

[1] Unstandardized ordinary least squares (OLS) regression coefficients are presented with standard errors (in parentheses), followed by levels of statistical significance, and standardized coefficients.

** $p < .01$
* $p < .05$

paying attention to only liberal news sources to reading and watching only conservative news sources, confidence in the election results declines almost a full point on the four-point confidence scale, controlling for rival explanations.

Additional political forces tapping people's attachment to the political system are also important for understanding people's confidence in the election. As we would expect, people who are more likely to vote in the election have greater confidence in the integrity of the election. Furthermore, people with higher levels of trust in government and people with more knowledge about government and public affairs are more likely to report higher levels of confidence in the election results.

Turning to psychological predispositions, we find that people's propensity to engage in conspiracy thinking is linked to confidence in the integrity of the election. People who score higher in conspiracy thinking are significantly less likely to express confidence in the veracity of the election results. Conspiracy thinking is the most important psychological predisposition explaining confidence in the election based on the level of statistical significance and the size of the standardized coefficients.[17]

Finally, people with more education and older respondents are more likely to express confidence in the integrity of the election, signaling their greater attachment to the political system. In contrast, women are significantly less likely than men to express confidence in the integrity of the election. Although we expected minorities to exhibit less trust in the security of the election, we find no significant difference between whites and minorities in the model in Table 5.1.

Our findings are consistent with the existing literature, illustrating that people with more positive experiences with elections and people with a greater attachment to the political system are more confident that the results of the 2020 presidential election will be counted accurately. Consistent with the citizen-centered theory of campaigns, we find that conspiracy thinking undermines confidence in the election results. Further, we demonstrate that the specifics of the 2020 campaign significantly alter confidence in the election results, with Trump supporters and conservative news consumers displaying much less confidence in the election compared to both Biden supporters and people who pay attention to liberal news sources.

---

[17] We examine whether the impact of conspiracy thinking on confidence in the election is moderated by partisan news attention and we find the interaction coefficient is insignificant (.003 with a standard error of .002).

## CONFIDENCE IN CANDIDATES' ABILITY TO ENSURE THE INTEGRITY OF US ELECTIONS

In the 2020 presidential campaign, only one of the candidates was sowing doubt regarding the integrity of the election. Examining the *Washington Post* database of false claims made by Trump during the length of the campaign, we identify 367 instances between April 2 and Election Day where he raised questions about the legitimacy of the election. Given the asymmetrical attack on the integrity of the presidential election, we ask respondents in September and October to rate their confidence in Biden's and Trump's ability to ensure the integrity of the election.[18]

As in the earlier analysis, we first examine political factors. We expect that vote preference will alter people's ratings of each candidate's ability to ensure the integrity of the election. Second, we expect that partisan news consumption will influence how people rate the candidates, with people who pay attention to conservative news outlets rating Trump more positively than Biden and vice versa. Third, we expect variables measuring attachment to the political system (e.g., political trust) to enhance confidence in each candidate's ability to maintain election integrity.[19]

With regard to citizens' psychological predispositions, we hypothesize that people who are conspiratorial in their perspective will be more likely to think that Trump can ensure the fairness of the election. Trump pushed a variety of different conspiracies before and during the 2020 election, including conspiracies about a "rigged election." According to a CNN news report in September 2020, he actively pushed *nine* conspiracies during the fall campaign (Dale, 2020). Given Trump's penchant for conspiracies, we think others who are high in conspiracy thinking will view him as particularly well-equipped for watching out for obstacles to a fair election.[20]

---

[18] The exact question wording is "How confident are you that Donald Trump/Joe Biden can ensure the integrity of US elections?" with response categories ranging from "not at all confident" (1) to "very confident" (4). These questions are asked in September for all respondents. In October, the question about Trump is asked for all panel respondents and all new respondents. However, because of a mistake in the October survey, the question about Biden is asked only for new respondents in October and not panel respondents (i.e., respondents interviewed in September and October).

[19] We do not include political knowledge in the models in Table 5.2 because it did not achieve statistical significance in the models.

[20] In the present analysis, we do not include demographic variables because we do not have expectations that demographic characteristics will differentially influence people's views of Biden's and Trump's ability to maintain fair elections, once we control for attitudinal variables. When we do include demographic variables, we find that education, race, and

In addition, since views about the candidate's ability to deal with an issue (i.e., maintaining election integrity) is likely to be related to general views of the candidate, we draw on earlier discussions when speculating about how the remaining psychological predispositions will influence assessments of the candidate's ability to ensure election integrity. In Chapter 2, we described Trump's rhetorical style as confrontational and pugnacious, especially compared to Biden. Therefore, we expect that people who are more conflict avoidant will develop less favorable views of Trump, including his ability to deal with issues of election integrity. For Biden, we hypothesize a positive or insignificant relationship between conflict avoidance and assessment of his ability to maintain election integrity.

We have also speculated in earlier chapters that the impact of racist and sexist stereotypes will differentially impact views of Trump and Biden. In the current analysis, we hypothesize that given Trump's history of making racist and sexist remarks, we expect that people scoring higher on racial resentment and hostile sexism will develop more positive views of his ability to deal with issues, including the issue of election integrity. We expect the opposite relationship for Biden; levels of racism and sexism will be negatively related to views of his ability to maintain the integrity of the election. Similarly, we have argued that Trump's authoritarian rhetoric (e.g., "us versus them," cultivating fear of the "other") will resonate with people who score higher on the authoritarianism scale. Therefore, we expect a positive relationship between authoritarianism and assessment of Trump's ability to maintain election integrity and a negative relationship between authoritarianism and assessment of Biden's ability to ensure a fair election.

We predict people's ratings of Biden's and Trump's ability to safeguard election integrity in September and October. The results are presented in Table 5.2.[21] Consistent with our earlier findings, we see that people's candidate preference strongly alters confidence in the candidate's ability to protect the veracity of the election. In the September models, people who say they intend to vote for Trump are estimated to rate him 1.29

---

ethnicity do not influence confidence in either candidate's ability to maintain election integrity. For Trump, we find a negative and significant relationship between age and ratings of his ability to ensure election integrity. For Biden, we find women rate his ability to ensure election integrity significantly lower than men. Omitting the demographic variables does not change the results of models presented in Table 5.2.

[21] The dependent variables in Table 5.2 are ordinal, ranging from 1 to 4. As before, we estimate each of the equations in Table 5.2 with ordinal regression and with OLS regression. The results are substantively similar with both techniques and we choose to present the OLS results in Table 5.2 because of the greater ease of interpretation.

|  | September | | | October | | |
| --- | --- | --- | --- | --- | --- | --- |
|  | Confidence in Trump | Confidence in Biden | | Confidence in Trump | Confidence in Biden | |
| *Political forces* | | | | | | |
| Attention to news | −.01 (.02) | .11 (.02)** | .11 | .02 (.02) | .08 (.03)** | .07 |
| Likelihood of voting | .09 (.03)** | .13 (.03)** | .07 | .12 (.02)** | .11 (.03)** | .09 |
| Partisan news | −.17 (.03)** | .21 (.03)** | .13 | −.08 (.02)** | .17 (.03)** | .14 |
| Trust in government | .28 (.02)** | .19 (.02)** | .15 | .30 (.02)** | .21 (.03)** | .16 |
| Vote intention | −1.29 (.04)** | .94 (.05)** | .40 | −1.25 (.04)** | 1.23 (.07)** | .51 |
| *Psychological predispositions* | | | | | | |
| Authoritarianism | −.015 (.015) | .054 (.017)** | .05 | −.025 (.014) | .028 (.025) | .03 |
| Conflict avoidance | −.012 (.006)* | −.006 (.006) | −.02 | −.022 (.005)** | .025 (.009)* | .06 |
| Conspiracy thinking | .017 (.003)** | .001 (.003) | .01 | .016 (.002)** | .007 (.004) | .05 |
| Hostile sexism | .024 (.008)** | −.021 (.009)* | −.05 | .043 (.007)** | −.031 (.014)* | −.07 |
| Racial resentment | .030 (.005)** | −.067 (.005)** | −.26 | .035 (.004)** | −.037 (.008)** | −.14 |
| Constant | 1.50 (.17)** | 1.69 (.19)** |  | 1.11 (.14)** | .92 (.23)** |  |
| $R^2$ | .58 | .46 |  | .62 | .55 |  |
| Number of respondents | 2,235 | 2,210 |  | 2,304 | 855 |  |

*Note:* The dependent variable is "How confident are you that Donald Trump/Joe Biden can ensure the integrity of US elections?" with response categories ranging from "not at all confident" (1) to "very confident" (4). Attention to news ranges from low (1) to high (5). Likelihood of voting ranges from "very unlikely" (1) to "very likely" (4) to vote in the upcoming election in November. Partisan media ranges from −2 (only conservative news) to 3 (only liberal news). Trust in government ranges from 1 (low) to 4 (high). Vote intention is based on the following question: "If the election was held today, who would you vote for president?" with 1 for Biden and 0 for Trump. Authoritarianism ranges from 0 (low authoritarian thinking) to 4 (high authoritarian thinking). Conflict avoidance ranges from 5 (low conflict avoidance) to 20 (high conflict avoidance). Conspiracy thinking ranges from 0 (low conspiracy thinking) to 30 (high in conspiracy thinking). Hostile sexism ranges from 4 (low sexism) to 16 (high sexism). Racial resentment ranges from 4 (low racial resentment) to 20 (high racial resentment). All variables are measured in September for the September models and all variables are measured in October for the October models.

[1] Unstandardized OLS regression coefficients are presented with standard errors in parentheses, followed by levels of statistical significance, and standardized coefficients.

** $p < .01$
* $p < .05$

136    *The Impact of Election Integrity on the Campaign*

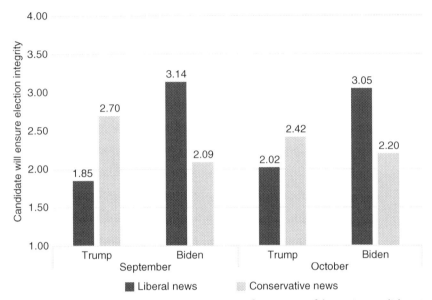

FIGURE 5.4 How partisan news attention influences confidence in candidates' ability to ensure the integrity of US elections

points higher on the four-point election integrity measure compared to people who say they will be voting for Biden. In the Biden model, we see that people planning to vote for Biden are expected to rate him almost a point (i.e., .94) higher than people who are voting for Trump. We find the same significant relationship in the October models where Trump and Biden receive approximately the same benefit from their supporters (i.e., the unstandardized coefficient for vote intention is −1.25 in the Trump model and 1.23 in the Biden model).

We continue to see the importance of people's partisan media diet as it significantly influences confidence in the election. We can estimate the impact of partisan media exposure by calculating the predicted values of the dependent variable (i.e., ability of Trump and Biden to protect the integrity of the election) while varying people's partisan media attention. We display the results in Figure 5.4. When people are looking only at liberal sources, they are confident that Biden can ensure the integrity of the election. However, when people rely on conservative news sources, their confidence in Biden declines, with expected ratings falling more than 1 point on the four-point scale. For Trump, we again see that the partisan nature of news coverage alters perceptions of his ability to ensure the integrity of the election. Nevertheless, regardless of partisan news diet, the findings in Figure 5.4

show that people have more confidence in Biden's ability to guarantee the integrity of the election results. For example, looking at like-minded media sources (i.e., liberal media sources for Biden, conservative news for Trump), on the four-point scale Biden receives a 3.14 in September and a 3.05 (slightly above "somewhat confident") in October. Trump, in contrast, receives a 2.70 in September and a 2.42 (closer to "not too confident") in October from people exposed to like-minded (i.e., conservative) news outlets.

When we look at how often people pay attention to news about politics and government affairs in a typical week, we find that news attention positively and significantly enhances people's views about Biden's ability to maintain the integrity of the election in September and October. In contrast, attention to the news does not influence views of Trump's ability to ensure the accuracy of the election in either time period. These findings show that people who follow news about politics and government are more confident in Biden's ability to ensure the accuracy of the election. We continue to see that people who are more attached to the political system (i.e., more trusting of government, more likely to vote in the election) are more confident in Trump's and Biden's ability to guarantee a safe and secure election.

In addition to political characteristics, we find that people's psychological predispositions influence confidence in the ability of Trump and Biden to safeguard the election. Conspiracy thinking, while negatively related to general views about the integrity of the election (see Table 5.1), is positively and significantly related to confidence in Trump's ability to secure the election. According to the unstandardized coefficient in the September and October models for Trump, we expect people who score at the maximum on the conspiracy thinking measure to rate him about a half point higher on the four-point confidence scale compared to people who score at the minimum on the conspiracy measure. For Biden, people's propensity for conspiracy thinking is not related to confidence in his ability to safeguard the election.[22]

Hostile sexism and racial resentment also consistently influence views of Trump and Biden in September and October. As racial resentment and hostile sexism increases, people's confidence in Trump's ability to maintain the integrity of the election escalates significantly, while their confidence in Biden declines. To illustrate, the unstandardized coefficient for racial resentment in the Trump model for September indicates that as we move from the low point to the high point on the racial resentment scale,

---

[22] We do not find a statistically significant conditional effect between conspiracy thinking and partisan news consumption for either candidate in September or October.

people's confidence in Trump increases by a half point on the four-point scale. For Biden in September, the importance of racial resentment is even more consequential, with confidence in Biden falling more than 1 point as we move from the low point to the high point on the racism measure. In fact, in the Biden model for September, racial resentment is among the most important variables explaining people's level of confidence in his ability to maintain the integrity of the election.[23]

We speculated that attitudes toward conflict would negatively influence assessments of Trump's ability to ensure the election results. We find support for our expectation in the September and October models. In both models, we find that as conflict avoidance increases, people's confidence in Trump declines significantly. For Biden, we find a positive relationship between conflict avoidance and confidence in Biden in October. However, in the September model, conflict avoidance is not related to confidence in Biden.[24]

Finally, we hypothesized that people higher in authoritarian thinking would develop more favorable views of Trump's ability to ensure the accuracy of the election. However, we do not find support for our expectation.[25] Authoritarianism is not related to views of Trump in

---

[23] We find that people's partisan news attention moderates the impact of racial attitudes on confidence in Biden's and Trump's ability to ensure a fair election in September and October. The interaction coefficient predicting Biden's ratings in September is .04 with a standard error of .01, and the interaction coefficient predicting Biden's ratings in October is .02 with a standard error of .01. For Trump, the interaction coefficient between racial resentment and partisan news attention is -.03 with a standard error of .01 in September and -.015 with a standard error of .003 in October. Interpreting the interaction coefficients, as people's consumption of conservative news increases, people with higher levels of racial resentment become more confident in Trump's ability to secure the election and less confident in Biden's ability to safeguard the election. We see a similar conditional relationship between people's partisan news diet and sexist attitudes on the assessment of Biden's ability to secure the election in September (the interaction coefficient is .03 with a standard error of .01) as well as assessments of Trump's ability to guarantee a fair election in September (the interaction coefficient is -.03 with a standard error of .01) and October (the interaction coefficient is .01 with a standard error of .005).

[24] We do not find a statistically significant conditional effect between conflict avoidance and partisan news consumption for either candidate in September or October.

[25] We do find a significant and negative conditional relationship between authoritarianism and partisan news diet for views about Trump in September (the interaction coefficient is -.06 with a standard error of .02). Calculating conditional slopes, for people who pay more attention to conservative news than liberal news (i.e., -1 on the partisan news index), the impact of authoritarianism on beliefs about Trump's ability to secure the election is positive and significant. However, among people paying attention to nonpartisan news, a balanced mix of liberal or conservative news, or liberal news, authoritarianism has no impact on people's assessments of Trump's ability to ensure a fair election.

September and October, and it is positively related to confidence in Biden in September (but not in October).[26] Overall, we find that four of the five psychological predispositions consistently and predictably influence people's confidence in the candidates' ability to ensure the integrity of the election.

## HOW CONFIDENCE IN THE ELECTION INFLUENCES OVERALL EVALUATIONS OF BIDEN AND TRUMP

We turn to exploring the electoral consequences of the issue of election integrity. As we have done in previous chapters, we develop models predicting overall evaluations of Trump and Biden: one estimating September feeling thermometer ratings and one estimating *changes* in feeling thermometer ratings from September to October. The main independent variables of interest in our models are (1) confidence in the integrity of the election and (2) assessments of each candidate's ability to ensure the integrity of the election.[27] In assessing the impact of election integrity on evaluations of the presidential candidates, we need to control for rival factors that are likely to influence views of the candidates. Therefore, as we have done in previous chapters, we control for people's partisan attachment, assessments of the candidates' personality traits, and retrospective evaluations of the nation's economy.[28]

The models predicting thermometer ratings of the presidential candidates are presented in Table 5.3. We begin with the September models. For both Trump and Biden, people's confidence in the candidate's ability to maintain the integrity of the election significantly influences overall candidate evaluations. For Trump, every one-point movement on the four-point integrity measure is associated with almost a seven-point movement on the feeling thermometer. Even after controlling for rival factors known to influence evaluations of Trump (e.g., partisanship, trait

---

[26] In September, we find a significant and positive conditional relationship between authoritarianism and partisan news diet for Biden (the interaction coefficient is .05 with a standard error of .02). An examination of the conditional slopes suggests a positive and significant association between authoritarianism and Biden's ability to ensure a fair election among people who watch more liberal news than conservative news (i.e., 1 on the partisan news index).

[27] All of the independent variables included in the models in Table 5.3, with the exception of confidence in the integrity of the election, are measured during the September wave. Confidence in the integrity of the election is asked only in the October wave of the panel so it is included only in the change model.

[28] We have introduced the measurement of each of these variables in earlier chapters.

TABLE 5.3 *Impact of the integrity of the election on overall evaluations of the presidential candidates*

|  | September thermometer ratings[1] | |
| --- | --- | --- |
|  | Donald Trump | Joe Biden |
| *Integrity of the election* | | |
| Ability to ensure integrity of the election | 6.76 (.55)** | 5.96 (.52) |
| *Rival factors* | | |
| General economic assessment | 2.24 (.33)** | .60 (.29) |
| Party identification | 3.71 (.21)** | −3.57 (.21)** |
| Trait assessment | 3.26 (.11)** | 3.23 (.11)** |
| Constant | −34.04 (.95)** | −.39 (1.93) |
| $R^2$ | .80 | .75 |
| Number of respondents | 2,385 | 2,304 |

|  | Changes in thermometer ratings from September to October[2] | |
| --- | --- | --- |
|  | Donald Trump | Joe Biden |
| *Integrity of the election* | | |
| Ability to ensure integrity of the election | 6.09 (52)** | 5.30 (.50)** |
| Confidence in integrity of the election | −1.98 (.42)** | 1.59 (.45)** |
| *Rival factors* | | |
| General economic assessment | 1.54 (.30)** | 0.49 (.27) |
| Party identification | 3.59 (.19)** | −3.88 (.19)** |

| | | |
|---|---|---|
| Trait assessment | 3.36 (.10)** | 3.21 (.10)** |
| Intercept | −27.38 (1.52)** | −1.48 (1.98) |
| Random effects | | |
| Variance of intercept | 204.18 (8.14)** | 202.28 (8.78)** |
| Variance of repeated measures (time) | 103.37 (3.61)** | 124.15 (4.45)** |
| Model fit | | |
| Akaike information criterion | 34,907.59 | 33,515.29 |
| Log likelihood | 34,891.59 | 33,499.29 |
| Number of respondents | 2,403 | 2,376 |

*Note:* The dependent variable is the feeling thermometer for each candidate, which ranges from 0 (very cold feelings for the candidate) to 100 (very warm feelings for the candidate). Confidence in integrity of the election ranges from 1 (not at all confident) to 4 (very confident). General economic assessment ranges from 1 (the economy has gotten much worse) to 5 (the economy has gotten much better). Party identification ranges from 1 (strong Democrat) to 7 (strong Republican). Trait assessment ranges from 6 (most negative) to 24 (most positive). Each of the independent variables is measured in the September wave of the panel with the exception of confidence in integrity of the election, which is measured only in October. For more details about measurement, see the text.

[1] Unstandardized regression coefficients are presented with standard errors (in parentheses), followed by levels of statistical significance, and standardized coefficients.

[2] Estimated parameters of multilevel modeling are presented with standard errors (in parentheses), followed by levels of statistical significance. In the MLM model, attitudes about the integrity of the election and the rival factors are fixed effects.

** $p < .01$
* $p < .05$

assessments), we see that people's views about his ability to safeguard the election significantly alter views of the incumbent president. Further, the standardized coefficients in the September model indicate that assessments about Trump's ability to secure the election are more consequential than partisanship and general economic assessment.

Turning to Biden, confidence in his ability to ensure a fair election is consequential for predicting overall impressions of Biden in September. The unstandardized coefficient suggests that every one-point movement on the confidence scale is associated with about a six-point change on the Biden feeling thermometer. While election integrity assessments are important for both Biden and Trump in September, the magnitude of the impact is somewhat greater for Trump. Perhaps because Trump focused much more heavily on questioning the integrity of the election than Biden, overall assessments of Trump are more closely tied to the issue of election integrity.

In the bottom half of Table 5.3, we estimate changes in feeling thermometer ratings from September to October. In these models, we include people's confidence in the integrity of the election as well as assessments of how well Trump and Biden can safeguard the election. We find that confidence in the election results produces important changes in feelings for Trump and Biden from September to October. People who are more confident about the security of the election become more negative in their views of Trump over the course of the campaign, while people with less confidence in the accuracy of the election develop more favorable views of Trump. Biden, in contrast, is advantaged by optimistic views about the integrity of the election; increases in confidence in the election are associated with increases in feeling thermometer ratings from September to October.

The change model in Table 5.3. also shows that people's assessments of Biden's and Trump's ability to secure the election have consequences. For both candidates, we find that people who have more confidence in the candidate's ability to ensure the integrity of the election become significantly more favorable to the candidate from September to October. Consistent with the static model, assessments of the candidate's ability to secure the election have a somewhat larger impact on changes in evaluations for Trump compared to Biden (i.e., the parameter estimate is 6.09 in the Trump model and 5.30 in the Biden model).

To summarize, Trump made the integrity of the election central to the 2020 election. For the months leading up to the Election Day, he repeatedly questioned the security of the election, especially the integrity of mail-in ballots. Our results show that highlighting questions about election integrity is a double-edged sword for Trump, producing more favorable views of Trump among people who have worries about the integrity of the election and for people who view him as being able to secure the veracity of the election results. However, Trump receives more negative assessments for people who question his ability to maintain the integrity of the election and for people who have more faith in the electoral system.

Biden, in contrast, did not question the integrity of the electoral process. Consequently, we find that people with more confidence in the accuracy of the electoral count become more positive in their evaluations of Biden in the months preceding the election. Further, while both candidates benefit from positive assessments of their ability to ensure the integrity of the election, people express greater confidence in Biden's ability to secure the election compared to Trump's.[29] These differences are noticeable among independents, with Biden scoring about a half of a point higher than Trump on the election integrity measure in September and October.[30] Finally, people's assessments of Trump's ability to secure the election decline from September to October, while people's confidence in Biden's ability to ensure the integrity is static across the campaign. These trends in election integrity assessments benefit Biden more than Trump.

## CONCLUSION AND IMPLICATIONS

In this chapter, we began by showing how public confidence in the integrity of the election is strongly related to candidate preference, with Trump supporters showing less confidence than Biden supporters. In addition, a propensity to believe in conspiracy theories fuels doubts about the integrity of the election. Furthermore, paying attention to the conservative media produces less trust in the voting process. We also show that people's assessments of the candidates' abilities to ensure election integrity

---

[29] In September, the average confidence assessment for Trump was 2.27 (with a standard error of .02), compared to 2.53 (with a standard error of .02) for Biden. In October, the average confidence assessment for Trump was 2.14 (with a standard error of .02), compared to 2.54 (with a standard error of .04) for Biden.

[30] Among independents in September, Trump receives an average score of 1.96 (with a standard error of .05) on the election integrity scale compared to an average score of 2.40 (with a standard error of .06) for Biden. In October, independents rate Trump at 1.95 (with a standard error of .05) on the election integrity measure compared to an average score of 2.50 (with a standard error of .09) for Biden.

are influenced by candidate preference, partisan news diet, trust in government, and political engagement. Finally, we show that a number of psychological predispositions consistently influence people's views of Biden's and Trump's ability to safeguard the election, including people's level of racial resentment and level of hostile sexism.

Trump's repeated claims of voter fraud, accelerating after the election, likely heightened copartisans' concerns about the election results. Between Election Day and January 6, 2021, Trump made 614 false claims about election fraud, averaging about 10 false claims per day.[31] These assertions were often amplified by right-leaning news sources, creating a perfect storm of supporters who were angry, disgusted, and contemptuous of the election results and potentially primed for action.

In the weeks leading up to January 6, Trump heavily promoted the "Stop the Steal" rally to be held hours before Congress's scheduled certification of the presidential election results.[32] On Facebook, Twitter, and Google, mentions of "Stop the Steal" and the #StopTheSteal peaked on November 5 during the effort to stop vote counting and spiked again in the days before January 6. Trump promoted the January 6 rally on Twitter. On December 19, he promised a "big protest in D.C. on January 6th. Be there, will be wild!" He mentioned the rally again on Twitter on December 27, December 30, and January 1 (Barry and Frenkel, 2021).

At the rally on January 6, Trump reiterated false claims that the election had been stolen. At the end of his speech, he told his followers,

> So we're going to, we're going to walk down Pennsylvania Avenue. And we're going to the Capitol... We're going to try and give our Republicans, the weak ones because the strong ones don't need any of our help. We' going to try and give them the kind of pride and boldness that they need to take back our country. So let's walk down Pennsylvania Avenue.[33]

Following Trump's speech, a violent mob loyal to Trump stormed the US Capitol in an attempt to overturn the results of the US presidential election and keep him in the White House. These insurrectionists, some of whom were armed, overwhelmed the US Capitol and DC police and sent lawmakers into hiding. More than 100 police officers were injured in the melee, with head injuries, cracked ribs, and smashed spinal discs, and

---

[31] We relied on data available via www.washingtonpost.com/graphics/politics/trump-claims-database/ to analyze the number of false claims about the election results.

[32] The "Stop the Steal" rally was held at the Ellipse, just south of the White House and two miles from Capitol Hill.

[33] See text of speech here: www.npr.org/2021/02/10/966396848/read-trumps-jan-6-speech-a-key-part-of-impeachment-trial

several officers died in the days and weeks following the attack (Jackman, 2021; Jackson, 2021).

Representative Liz Cheney (Republican), vice chair of the House Select Committee investigating the January 6 insurrection, blamed Trump for the violence at the Capitol. In her opening statement on June 9, 2022, Cheney said:

> Those who invaded our Capitol and battled law enforcement for hours were motivated by what President Trump had told them: that the election was stolen, and that he was the rightful President. President Trump summoned the mob, assembled the mob and lit the flame of this attack...You will see that Donald Trump and his advisors knew that he had, in fact, lost the election. But, despite this, President Trump engaged in a massive effort to spread false and fraudulent information – to convince huge portions of the U.S. population that fraud had stolen the election from him. This was not true.[34]

While Trump's persistent lies about a "rigged election" contributed to the deadly violence on January 6, these falsehoods continue to undermine people's belief about the legitimacy of the election. Many worry that the "big lie" of a stolen election has grown more entrenched and more dangerous. According to election law expert Rick Hasen, codirector of the Fair Elections and Free Speech Center at the University of California, Irvine, "I've never been more scared about American democracy than I am right now, because of the metastasizing of the 'big lie.'" Hasen has reason to be scared; doubts about the accuracy of elections reduces confidence in democratic institutions (Bowler et al., 2015).

More than two years after Election Day 2020, Trump continues to peddle conspiracy theories about the 2020 election. In a speech delivered on July 27, 2022, he said, "I won a second time, did much better a second time. Did a lot better. Did a lot better. Very corrupt. I always said I ran the first time and I won. And then I ran a second time, and I did much better. What a disgrace it was."[35] Moreover, a number of people who espoused the "big lie" about the 2020 election ran for statewide office as governor, secretary of state, and attorney general in 2022. These office holders are the "referees of our democracy" because they implement elections, supervise the vote counts, and certify election results.[36] More than half (60 percent) of secretary of state contests and more than one-third (40 percent) of governor and attorney general races included a candidate

---

[34] See www.politico.com/news/2022/06/09/liz-cheney-jan-6-committee-full-statement-00038730 for the text of Cheney's opening statement.
[35] See www.cnn.com/2022/07/26/politics/trump-dc-speech/index.html
[36] statesuniteddemocracy.org/resources/replacingtherefs/

who claimed Trump won the 2020 election. Finally, perceptions of election fraud are being used to justify changes in electoral laws, often making voting more difficult and disenfranchising large swaths of citizens. According to the Brennan Center for Justice, lawmakers introduced at least 389 restrictive bills in 48 states in the 2021 legislative sessions.[37] In the 2022 legislative session, lawmakers in 39 states have considered at least 393 restrictive bills.[38] These bills make in-person voting (e.g., limiting the hours and locations of polling places, harsher voter identification requirements) and mail-in voting (e.g., shortening the time frame for requesting ballots, limiting the availability of drop boxes) more difficult.

Widespread perceptions of voter fraud as well as restrictive voting laws could discourage people from participating in elections, thereby making elections less representative of the citizenry (Ansolabehere and Persily, 2007). However, our results also hold some hopeful signs. We show that people who are more likely to participate in elections, people who are more trustful of government, and people with more knowledge about politics are more likely to have confidence in the integrity of elections. Therefore, political education can serve as a bulwark, shielding citizens from harmful rhetoric about the insecurities of the US electoral system.

We turn next to building a comprehensive model where we show how the major events and important issues of the 2020 campaign influence overall evaluations of the rival candidates. Thus far, we have provided evidence for the citizen-centered theory of campaigns, demonstrating that psychological predispositions systematically alter people's views of the first presidential debate, the evolving coronavirus pandemic, issues of race and policing, and views about the integrity of the election. Further, we have shown that these issues and events influence impressions of the candidates in September and changes in evaluations from September to October. In Chapter 6, we examine how all of these issues and events produce changes in the evaluations of Trump and Biden from September to November. We demonstrate that certain campaign events and issues motivate people to change their vote intention over the course of the general election campaign period.

---

[37] www.brennancenter.org/our-work/research-reports/voting-laws-roundup-may-2021
[38] www.brennancenter.org/our-work/research-reports/voting-laws-roundup-december-2022

# 6

## How the Campaign Shapes Voters' Decisions about the Candidates

In a postmortem of the 2020 presidential election, four *Washington Post* reporters relied on interviews with sixty-five Trump and Biden aides, advisers, confidants, lawmakers, and political operatives to explain the outcome of the presidential campaign.[1] The reporters describe Trump as an unpopular president who was divisive and alienating and rarely sought to reach out to the middle of the electorate.

But the president finally lost, aides and allies said, because of how he mismanaged the virus. He lost ... when the virus didn't go away as he promised; when racial unrest roiled the nation in the wake of George Floyd's death and protesters ran rampant through the streets; and when federal and local authorities gassed largely peaceful demonstrators in Lafayette Square across from the White House so Trump could stage a photo op. And he lost, they said, during a roughly three-week stretch from late September to mid-October, when an angry and brooding Trump heckled and interrupted his way through the first debate and then, several days later, announced he had tested positive for the coronavirus.

Late in the campaign, Trump's advisors "grew increasingly concerned about Trump's repeatedly unsubstantiated claims that voting by mail was rife with fraud .... Advisers worried that the president's outlandish rhetoric might push his own supporters away from voting by mail, and convened several meetings to discuss preventing that outcome." Then, late on Election night,

Trump falsely declared victory from the White House's East Room – 'Frankly, we did win this election,' he said – and followed up several hours later with tweets

---

[1] We draw on the following *Washington Post* article: www.washingtonpost.com/elections/interactive/2020/trump-pandemic-coronavirus-election/

baselessly accusing Democrats of "trying to STEAL the Election" and claiming victories in several states he had not won. The 2020 race...remained the rare challenge that Trump could not simply negotiate or spin to his will; Biden was the winner – and the next president of the United States.

In the previous empirical chapters, we validated many of the conclusions made by the *Washington Post* reporters. The candidates' performances in the first debate, Trump's handling of the COVID-19 pandemic, people's reactions to the social justice protests against police brutality, and concerns about the integrity of the election all produce important changes in evaluations of the candidates during the course of the campaign. In each of these chapters, we have explored the impact of a single issue or event on views of the presidential candidates in October. In this chapter, we examine these elements of the campaign simultaneously in order to determine how they influence people's views of the candidates and their vote preference in November. By estimating a multivariate model examining the various aspects of the campaign, we can identify those events and issues that continue to alter citizens' assessments of the candidates at the end of campaign.

More specifically, we estimate three models in the remaining pages of this chapter. First, we look at how the campaign events (i.e., the first presidential debate) and issues (e.g., COVID-19, racial justice protests and policing, election integrity) influence people's feeling thermometer ratings of the candidates in November. Second, we estimate a change model to examine how these same aspects of the campaign produce changes in people's evaluations of the candidates from September to November. Finally, we examine how these events and issues produce changes in vote preference from September to November.

THE IMPACT OF THE CAMPAIGN ON PEOPLE'S
EVALUATIONS OF THE CANDIDATES IN NOVEMBER

We begin by looking at how the various campaign forces influence people's feeling thermometer ratings of the candidates in November. As we have done in previous models predicting overall evaluations of the candidates, we control for party identification, assessments of the economy, and people's impressions of the candidates' personal traits. With this model in hand, we can see how these elements of the campaign, controlling for rival factors, influence people's impressions of the candidates in November.

## First Presidential Debate

We explore whether people's ratings of Trump's and Biden's performance in the first debate alter evaluations of the candidates in November. While our earlier analysis in Chapter 2 shows that views about the September debate influence views of the candidates in October, we want to explore the lasting impact of the first presidential debate on people's impressions of the candidates in November. We expect that people who score the candidates favorably on the debate performance measures will develop more positive overall evaluations of the candidates in November. We also investigate whether people's assessment of who won the September debate impacts November impressions of the candidates.[2] We expect that people are likely to develop more positive views of candidates they believe won the first presidential debate.

## Campaign Issues

We show in Chapter 3 that people's views about COVID-19 influence their assessments of Trump in September and October. It is now time to see if these assessments are also important for understanding overall evaluations of both candidates in November. We measure worries about COVID-19 during the October wave of the panel survey.[3]

Second, expanding our findings from Chapter 4, we explore whether people's attitudes toward the social justice movement and their support of police in October influence evaluations of the candidates in November.[4] We expect that people who are more supportive of social justice protests will have more favorable views of Joe Biden and less favorable attitudes toward Donald Trump. Conversely, we expect people who are more supportive of police may have more positive assessments of Trump and less favorable views of Biden.

Third, concerns about the integrity of the election may influence people's overall views of the candidates in November. More specifically, given Trump's relentless attack on election vulnerabilities during the length of the campaign, we expect that people who are less confident of the integrity of the election (e.g., people who are more likely to agree with the rhetoric regarding electoral fraud) will have more favorable

---

[2] We utilize the debate measures introduced in Chapter 2.
[3] We rely on the COVID-19 worry index developed in Chapter 3.
[4] We utilize the support for social justice protests index and the support for police index introduced in Chapter 4.

views of Trump. In contrast, Biden highlighted the security of the election apparatus during the campaign, and therefore, we expect that people with more confidence in the integrity of the election will develop more positive evaluations of Biden.[5]

## Rival Factors

We examine whether people's views about the state of the economy influence overall impressions of the presidential rivals. During the fall campaign season, more than 55 percent of the respondents in each wave of the survey indicated that the nation's economy had gotten worse over the past year, with about 30 percent of the respondents saying the economy had gotten much worse. And a wealth of literature has demonstrated a strong relationship between assessments of the national economy and support for the incumbent president (e.g., Fiorina, 1981; Vavreck, 2009). We expect that negative views about the nation's economy will translate into less favorable evaluations of the incumbent president.[6] We do not expect economic assessment to influence evaluations of the Democratic challenger. In addition, trait assessments of the candidates are likely to influence overall evaluations of the candidates. A long line of research has shown that people's views of the personality of presidential candidates consistently influence overall impressions of the candidates (e.g., Christenson and Weisberg, 2019; Laustsen and Bor, 2017). Finally, when predicting people's views of the candidates, we need to consider people's party attachment. We have known for more than sixty years that party identification strongly colors people's views of candidates (e.g., Campbell et al., 1960). And in today's highly polarized climate, the impact of party identification on views of the rival presidential candidates has intensified (e.g., Sides, Tausanovitch, and Vavreck, 2022).[7]

---

[5] We measure confidence in the integrity of the election with the following question: "How confident are you that the results of the 2020 presidential election will be counted accurately?" with response options varying from "not at all confident" to "very confident."

[6] We measure economic assessments with the following question: "Now thinking about the economy in the country as a whole, would you say that over the past year the nation's economy has gotten better, stayed about the same, or gotten worse?" with response categories ranging from "much worse" (1) to "much better" (5).

[7] According to the candidate-centered theory of campaigns, we do not expect psychological predispositions to directly influence people's evaluations of the presidential candidates. Instead, we theorize that psychological predispositions, by influencing the acquisition and interpretation of information, will influence people's assessments of campaign events and campaign issues. Nevertheless, we replicate the model in Table 6.1 including the five psychological predispositions as independent variables. We discuss the results of this analysis in the next section.

We turn now to discussing the results of the comprehensive model predicting evaluations of Trump and Biden in November.

## EXPLAINING EVALUATIONS OF THE CANDIDATES IN NOVEMBER

We rely on the November feeling thermometer measure to estimate overall evaluations of Trump and Biden. All of the political and campaign variables (i.e., independent variables) are measured in October. With time-order set, we have more confidence that the independent variables in the model are influencing people's views of the presidential candidates in November. We present the results of our analysis in Table 6.1. In the Trump model, each of the variables reach statistical significance ($p < .05$). In the model predicting feeling thermometer scores for Biden, we find six of the nine variables reach statistical significance ($p < .05$). In both models, the high $R^2$ (i.e., 87 percent of the variance is explained in the Trump model, and 83 percent of the variance is explained in the Biden model) indicates that much of the variance in the feeling thermometer scores are explained by the variables included in the models.

We start by looking at the importance of the first presidential debate on people's evaluations of the candidates. We find that people's views of the candidates' performances in the debate as well as assessments of who won the debate significantly influence evaluations of Trump and Biden. More specifically, we see that evaluations of Trump's performance recorded in the days following the September debate powerfully predict November feeling thermometer ratings for Trump. Even controlling for a host of rival factors, including partisanship, we find every one-point increase in people's views of Trump's performance in the debate translates into almost a four-point increase in feeling thermometer scores.[8] And since views of Trump's performance were negative (Trump's debate performance received an average score of 4.6 on the ten-point scale among viewers of the first presidential debate), the long-term consequences of the September debate almost certainly hurt Trump's electoral prospects.

We also see that views about who won the debate, measured in October, alter impressions of Trump in November. According to the unstandardized regression coefficient, people who say Trump lost the

[8] From our analysis in Chapter 2, we know that assessments of Trump's performance in the debate are not solely driven by partisanship. In particular, we show that news habits, conflict avoidance, conspiracy thinking, racial resentment, and partisanship each influence assessments of his debate performance.

debate rate him, on average, more than 10 points lower than people who view him as the winner of the debate. More specifically, Trump's estimated feeling thermometer scores for people who viewed him as the winner of the debate is 51.4, but these assessments drop to 40.5 for people viewing him as the loser. Moreover, because more than half (52 percent) of the respondents in our survey rate Trump as the loser, with 32 percent classifying him as the winner and 16 percent of the respondents calling the debate a tie, the impact of people's debate assessments is harmful for Trump's overall evaluations in November.

The first presidential debate between the candidates is also consequential for assessments of Biden. We find that people's ratings of Biden's performance in the debate are strongly connected to his feeling thermometer scores. The unstandardized coefficient indicates that every one-point change in debate performance ratings is associated with a two-point change in the feeling thermometer. And, unlike Trump, the impact of debate performance ratings may be more beneficial for Biden who was viewed more favorably; his average performance rating was 5.9 (with a standard error of .06). Further, people's assessment of who won the debate is significant for Biden. Looking at the unstandardized regression coefficient, we find that people who think Biden lost the first debate give him an average rating of 47.9 on the feeling thermometer, holding all remaining variables at their means. However, among people who view Biden as the debate winner, he receives, on average, a 58.6 on the feeling thermometer, an increase of almost 11 points. Biden is likely to benefit from people's assessment of who won the debate since more than half of the respondents view him as the winner. Overall, these results show that Trump's dismal performance in the first presidential debate had lasting effects on people's views of both candidates, producing important alterations in evaluations of the competing candidates in November.

We next look at the major issues of the campaign. As we discussed in Chapter 3, COVID-19 is viewed as the most important issue of the campaign, with 35 percent of respondents in October naming the coronavirus pandemic as the most important issue facing the country. Further, when respondents are queried about their concern about the coronavirus, 61 percent of people say they are "extremely concerned" or "very concerned" in October while only 17 percent of respondents say they are "not very" or "not at all" concerned, and 23 percent of respondents indicate they are "somewhat concerned."

The findings in Table 6.1 confirm that people's anxiety about COVID-19 influences overall evaluations of both Trump and Biden in November. To illustrate the impact of worries about the pandemic on views of Trump

TABLE 6.1 *Ordinary least squares regression predicting overall evaluations of the presidential candidates in November*[1]

|  | Trump |  | Biden |  |
|---|---|---|---|---|
| **Campaign events and issues** |  |  |  |  |
| *Debate* |  |  |  |  |
| Candidate's debate performance | 3.85 (.33)** | .30 | 2.00 (.32)** | .14 |
| Who won the debate | −5.43 (1.08)** | −.11 | 5.34 (1.01)** | .12 |
| *COVID-19 pandemic* |  |  |  |  |
| Worries about COVID-19 | −.92 (.39)** | −.03 | 1.34 (.40)** | .05 |
| *Election integrity* |  |  |  |  |
| Confidence in election integrity | −1.92 (.65)** | −.04 | .92 (.70) | .02 |
| *Social justice protests* |  |  |  |  |
| Support for social justice protests | −.79 (.24)** | −.05 | 1.58 (.29)** | .12 |
| Support for police | .41 (.39) | .01 | .04 (.40) | .01 |
| **Rival factors** |  |  |  |  |
| General economic assessment | 1.14 (.53)* | .03 | .27 (.49) | .01 |
| Party identification | 1.26 (.31)** | .07 | −3.46 (.33)** | −.21 |
| Trait assessments | 2.54 (.17)** | .42 | 2.48 (.17)** | .41 |
| Constant | −5.17 (3.70) |  | 1.15 (3.80) |  |
| $R^2$ | .87 |  | .83 |  |
| Number of respondents | 914 |  | 900 |  |

*Note:* The dependent variable is the November feeling thermometer for each candidate, which ranges from 0 (very cold feelings for the candidate) to 100 (very warm feelings for the candidate). For information about the coding of the independent variables, see the text. All of the independent variables are measured in October.

[1] Unstandardized regression coefficients are presented with standard errors (in parentheses), followed by levels of statistical significance, and standardized coefficients.
** $p < .01$
* $p < .05$

and Biden in November, we vary concern about COVID-19 (from the minimum to the maximum value) and estimate people's placement of Trump and Biden on the feeling thermometer. We display the point estimates in Figure 6.1. The data illustrate that when people are not at all worried about the coronavirus pandemic (i.e., the minimum score on the COVID-19 worry index), they rate Biden 3 points higher on the feeling thermometer than Trump (i.e., 50.5 for Biden, 47.5 for Trump).

154     The Campaign Effect on Voters' Decisions

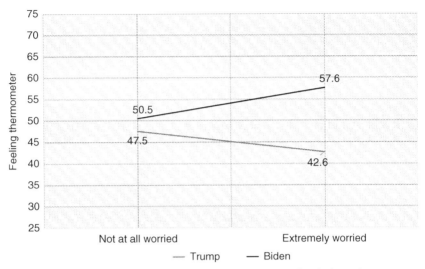

FIGURE 6.1 Impact of worries about COVID-19 on the feeling thermometer ratings of Trump and Biden in November

However, when people's worries about the coronavirus increase, Trump's evaluations *decrease* by about 5 points while Biden's score on feeling thermometer *increases* by 7 points. Hence, among people most worried about COVID-19, Biden has an advantage of more than 15 points. Given that most people classified themselves as concerned about the pandemic in October, the issue of COVID-19 likely produced electoral dividends for Biden while damaging Trump's prospects for reelection.

In addition to COVID-19, the issue of election integrity dominated the campaign during the final months of the election. The results in Table 6.1 show that concerns about the integrity of the presidential election alter views of Trump but not of Biden. As people's confidence in the accuracy of the election declines, people's evaluations of Trump increase significantly. So even after taking into account a host of rival factors, we continue to see that people who are less confident about a secure election view Trump more favorably in November. The unstandardized coefficient in the model estimating Trump's feeling thermometer score in November indicates that every one-point decrease in confidence in the election is associated with almost a two-point increase in evaluations of Trump. Similarly, as people move from being less confident to more confident in the security of the election, Trump's feeling thermometer score declines significantly.

*Explaining Views of the Candidates in November*

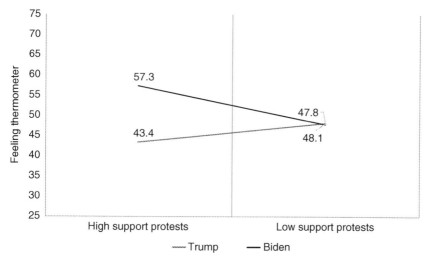

FIGURE 6.2 Impact of support for social justice protests on the feeling thermometer ratings of Trump and Biden in November

We also see that people's support for social justice protests influence evaluations of Biden and Trump in November. However, people's confidence in law enforcement is not linked to their assessments of Trump or Biden. While Trump and his surrogates allocated significant campaign resources trying to paint Biden as an enemy of law enforcement, people's attitudes toward the police did not significantly alter views of either candidate in November.[9] We illustrate the importance of social justice attitudes on people's views of the competing candidates by varying support for the protests from its nadir to its peak. We present these estimates in Figure 6.2.

Figure 6.2 illustrates how support for protests about police brutality strongly influence evaluations of Trump and Biden in November. When support for protests is high, we estimate Biden's feeling thermometer score to be at almost 60 (i.e., 57.3), 14 points higher than Trump's estimated score of 43.4. In contrast, when support for protests is at its lowest point, Biden's evaluations drop by almost 10 points, while evaluations of Trump increase by less than 5 points.[10] While Trump's evaluations are

---
[9] According to the Google Transparency Project, American First Action, a pro-Trump super political action committee, aired an advertisement ("In Joe Biden's America") more than 2.25 million times. The advertisement portrayed Biden as supportive of defunding the police. See adstransparency.google.com
[10] On average, most people supported the social justice movement, with scores averaging 6.13 (with a standard deviation of 2.35) on the social justice index (which ranges from 2 to 10).

higher when support for protests is lower, Trump and Biden have basically equivalent feeling thermometer scores when support for the social justice protests is at its lowest point. These findings demonstrate that people's attitudes about protests against police brutality are important for understanding views of the candidates in November.[11]

Finally, in the models presented in Table 6.1, we include measures tapping general economic assessment, party identification, and assessments of the candidates' personal characteristics. We find, as expected, that views about the state of the economy alter evaluations of the incumbent president but not the challenger. Party identification, as hypothesized, influences evaluations of both candidates. However, we see that partisanship is more powerful for Biden than Trump, with every one-point change in party identification producing more than a three-point change in assessments of Biden. For Trump, in comparison, changes in party identification are associated with about a one-point change in feeling thermometer scores. Turning to trait assessments, we find that views of the candidates' personality characteristics strongly influence evaluations of Trump and Biden. In both models, trait assessments are by far the most powerful variables, according to the standardized coefficients.[12]

---

[11] We also examine whether campaign events and issues are more powerful for weak partisans and independents than for strong partisans (for a review of the most persuadable voters, see Jacobson, 2015). To do this analysis, we divide the sample of respondents into strong partisans (i.e., strong Republicans and strong Democrats) and people less strongly attached to a party (i.e., weak Republicans, weak Democrats, independents). We then replicate the analysis in Table 6.1 for strong partisans ($n = 478$) and for people with weaker (or no) ties to a party ($n = 434$). We continue to find that the campaign events and issues matter for both groups. In particular, when predicting November feeling thermometer scores for Trump, views about the racial justice protests and assessments of the candidates' performances in the debate are consequential for both sets of respondents. We do find that views about who won the debate, assessments of the integrity of the election, and worries about COVID-19 only significantly influence views of Trump for people less attached to a political party. When predicting November feeling thermometer scores for Biden, we find each of the following factors are statistically significant for both groups of respondents: views about social justice protests, ratings of Biden's debate performance, assessments of who won the first debate, and worries about COVID-19. For evaluations of Trump, we find support for the contention that weak partisans and independents will be more affected by elements of the campaign.

[12] We also replicated the models in Table 6.1 including the psychological predispositions. For the five psychological predispositions across the two models, only three of the ten coefficients achieve statistical significance. We find a positive relationship between hostile sexism and Trump's feeling thermometer score (the unstandardized coefficient is .55 with a standard error of .25, $p < .05$) and a positive relationship between authoritarianism and feeling thermometer scores for Trump (the unstandardized coefficient is 1.55 with a standard error of .44, $p < .01$) and Biden (the unstandardized coefficient is 1.28 with a standard error of .46, $p < .01$). The relationship between authoritarianism and

## EXPLAINING CHANGES IN EVALUATIONS OF THE CANDIDATES FROM SEPTEMBER TO NOVEMBER

The results in Table 6.1 clearly demonstrate the importance of campaign events and campaign issues for understanding evaluations of the competing candidates in November. We turn next to explaining *changes* in feeling thermometer ratings of the candidates from September to November. For Trump, we find that people's ratings of the incumbent president decline slightly over the course of the fall campaign, from an average of 44.3 in September to an average of 41.1 in November. In contrast, feeling thermometer ratings for Biden increase modestly over the same period, from an average of 51.9 in September to 53.1 in November.[13] As we have done in earlier analysis, we rely on MLM to estimate changes in people's attitudes over time.[14] To explain changes in the feeling thermometer scores over the months of the fall campaign, we rely on the same independent variables examined earlier.[15] We present the change models in Table 6.2.

We find that campaign forces continue to be important for explaining changes in ratings of the candidates over time. In fact, in the models explaining changes in people's feeling thermometer ratings, we find that ten of the twelve coefficients measuring aspects of the campaign achieve statistical significance. We see that the September debate is influential; views about the debate powerfully and consistently explain changes in views of both Trump and Biden. In addition, the salient issues of the campaign produce variations in views of the candidates over time. For example, people who are more worried about the coronavirus pandemic become more positive in their views of Biden and more negative in their assessments of Trump from September to November.

Similarly, people's level of support for the social justice protest alters views of each of the candidates, with people who are more supportive of the social protest movement becoming significantly more favorable

---

support for both candidates may reflect authoritarians' greater deference to authority figures (e.g., both candidates may be viewed as leaders and authorities based on their current and former positions of power).

[13] These average differences across time for Trump and Biden do not reach statistical significance at the $p < .05$ level.
[14] We also estimated the change models with regression (ordinary least squares, or OLS); however, the results of the OLS models are substantively different than the MLM models. Given that the standard errors in the OLS analysis may be biased (see Hair and Favero, 2019), we report the MLM results here.
[15] Again, we measure the independent variables in October.

TABLE 6.2 *MLM explaining changes in overall evaluations of the presidential candidates (September to November)*[1]

| Fixed effects | Trump thermometer | Biden thermometer |
|---|---|---|
| **Campaign events and issues** | | |
| *Debate* | | |
| Candidate's debate performance | 3.13 (.25)** | 2.31 (.25)** |
| Who won the debate | −4.29 (.82)** | 4.20 (.81)** |
| *COVID-19 pandemic* | | |
| Worries about COVID-19 | −.90 (.28)** | 1.56 (.31)** |
| *Election integrity* | | |
| Confidence in election integrity | −1.05 (.47)** | 2.29 (.54)** |
| *Social justice protests* | | |
| Support for social justice protests | −1.04 (.18)** | 1.16 (.22)** |
| Support for police | −.14 (.28) | −.26 (.31) |
| **Rival factors** | | |
| General economic assessment | 2.01 (.37)** | −.25 (.38) |
| Party identification | 2.14 (.24)** | −3.30 (.27) |
| Trait assessments | 2.66 (.13)** | 2.41 (.13)** |
| Intercept | −7.19 (2.72)** | .97 (3.03) |
| **Random effects** | | |
| Variance of intercept | 165.22 (8.55)** | 176.79 (11.02)** |
| Variance of repeated measures (time) | 68.18 (3.91)** | 115.06 (6.62)** |
| **Model fit** | | |
| Akaike information criterion | 17,592.47 | 17,825.89 |
| Log likelihood | 17,568.47 | 17,801.89 |
| Number of observations | 1,541 | 1,507 |

*Note:* The dependent variable is changes in thermometer ratings from September to November. For information about the coding of the independent variables, see the text. All of the independent variables are measured in October.

[1] Estimated parameters of multilevel modeling are presented (with standard errors in parentheses), followed by levels of statistical significance.

** $p < .01$
* $p < .05$

toward Biden and more negative toward Trump over the campaign season. Further, as in the static model presented in Table 6.1, Trump does not receive a benefit from people who support the police; people's attitudes toward law enforcement do not lead to changes in evaluations of Trump (or Biden) from September to November.

The issue of election integrity is also important for explaining changes in people's evaluations of the competing candidates over the course of the campaign. Consistent with our findings in Table 6.1, the results in Table 6.2 show a negative relationship between people's confidence in the election and changes in people's evaluations of Trump from September to November. However, and in contrast to the findings in Table 6.1, we see that people's confidence in the integrity of the election significantly alter ratings of Biden over the length of the campaign. As people's trust in the security of the election increases, Biden's evaluations improve significantly from September to November.[16]

Turning to the tried-and-true rival variables in the change model, views about the economy significantly alter attitudes toward Trump, with people who view the economy more negatively becoming more critical in their evaluations of Trump from September to November. People's views of the candidates' personal traits produce predictable changes in people's feeling thermometer scores over the fall campaign. Finally, partisanship significantly influences changes in views of the candidates, with partisans becoming more polarized in their evaluations of the Democratic and Republican rivals across the campaign.[17]

## EXPLAINING CHANGES IN VOTE PREFERENCE FROM SEPTEMBER TO NOVEMBER

We have shown, through the powerful analytical leverage of the panel design, that the major campaign issues and campaign events produce consistent and significant changes in people's feeling thermometer scores for

---

[16] Once again, we replicate the analysis in Table 6.2 for strong partisans and for people with weaker attachments to the political parties. We find fewer differences between the two groups in the change analysis. For changes in evaluations of Trump, we find the following campaign factors are significant for both groups of respondents: attitudes toward racial justice protests, assessments of Trump's debate performance, and views of who won the September debate. For people with strong ties to a political party, we find that worries about COVID-19 produce significant declines in evaluations of Trump over time. We also see that views about the integrity of the election are important for people less attached to a political party, with confidence in the integrity of the election producing more negative views of Trump over the length of the campaign. For changes in evaluations of Biden, we see no differences between the two groups of respondents, with the following campaign factors significantly influencing changes in views of Biden from September to November: attitudes toward the social justice movement, assessments of Biden's debate performance, views of who won the September debate, views about the integrity of the election, and worries about COVID-19.

[17] As we did before, we replicate the models in Table 6.2 including the psychological predispositions. For the five psychological predispositions in the two models, only two of the ten parameter estimates achieve statistical significance. We find a positive relationship between hostile sexism and changes in Trump's feeling thermometer score (the estimated parameter is .38 with a standard error of .18, $p < .05$) and a positive relationship between conspiracy thinking and changes in feeling thermometer scores for Biden (the estimated parameter is .16 with a standard error of .06, $p < .05$).

Trump and Biden over the length of the campaign. We now turn to one final test of veracity of campaign effects: Does the campaign lead people to change their vote preference from September to November?[18] We rely on multilevel logit modeling to estimate changes in vote choice over the course of the campaign and we present the results in Table 6.3.[19]

We see that campaign events and issues matter a great deal for understanding changes in vote preference. First, the chaotic first debate in September significantly alters vote preference, according to the model in Table 6.3. People's assessment of who won the debate is powerfully related to changes in vote preference. Interpreting the odds ratio, for every one-point increase in assessments of who won the first debate (i.e., moving away from Trump and toward Biden), we can expect more than a doubling (i.e., 2.2) of the likelihood of changing one's vote preference from Trump to Biden over the course of the campaign. We also see that people's views of Trump's debate performance are significantly associated with changes in their vote preference.

Among the major campaign issues, we see that support for protests against police brutality is associated with significant changes in vote preference from September to November. The odds ratio of 1.15 indicates that for every one-point increase in support for social protests, the odds of changing vote preference toward Biden increase by 15 percent. The remaining issues are less important for explaining changes in vote preference. Worries about COVID-19 fail to reach statistical significance at $p < .05$ (but achieve statistical significance at the $p < .10$ level), suggesting that there may be a weak relationship between concern about the coronavirus pandemic and changes in vote preference over the course of the fall campaign.[20] Views about the

---

[18] In this analysis, we exclude people who said they were voting for someone other than Trump or Biden in September or November. In September, 4 percent of respondents said they were voting for someone else, and in November, 2 percent of respondents said they voted for someone other than Biden and Trump.

[19] We rely on multilevel logit modeling because the dependent variable is dichotomous and because we are using panel data. Such modeling will produce unbiased standard errors for the coefficients. The results produced by the multilevel logit model are different from the results of the standard logit model. Therefore, we present the multilevel model in Table 6.3.

[20] Research examining the impact of COVID-19 on vote choice in the 2020 election has yielded inconsistent findings. Miller, Woods, and Kalmbach (2022), for instance, find that assessments of Trump's ability to deal with the coronavirus pandemic hurt Trump at the ballot box (see also Clarke, Stewart, and Ho, 2021; Levendusky et al., 2023). In contrast, Algara et al. (2022), looking at aggregate level data, find that Trump gained support in counties with higher COVID-19 deaths while Sides, Tausanovitch, and Vavreck (2022) find no statistically significant relationship between the cumulative number of COVID infections per capita and Trump's share of the vote.

TABLE 6.3 *Multilevel logit modeling explaining changes in vote choice (September to November)*[1]

| Fixed effects | Coefficient (SE) | Odds ratio |
| --- | --- | --- |
| **Campaign events and issues** | | |
| *Debate* | | |
| Biden's debate performance | −.02 (.08) | .98 |
| Trump's debate performance | −.18 (.07)** | 1.01 |
| Who won the debate | .80 (.20)** | 2.23 |
| *COVID-19 pandemic* | | |
| Worries about COVID-19 | .17 (.10) | 1.19 |
| *Election integrity* | | |
| Confidence in election integrity | .01 (.19) | 1.01 |
| *Social justice protests* | | |
| Support for social justice protests | .14 (.06)** | 1.15 |
| Support for police | −.07 (.10) | .93 |
| **Rival factors** | | |
| General economic assessment | .12 (.13) | 1.13 |
| Party identification | −.53 (.07)** | .59 |
| Comparative trait assessments | .23 (.03)** | 1.26 |
| Intercept | 1.88 (1.09) | |
| Random effect | | |
| Intercept | | .57 |
| Residual effect | | |
| Var (Time 1) | 2.10 (.09)** | |
| Var (Time 2) | .77 (.03)** | |
| % correctly predicted | 96 | |
| Number of respondents | 1,982 | |

*Note:* The dependent variable is changes in vote intention from September to November. The exact wording for the vote intention question is: "If the election was held today, who would you vote for president?" Respondents who indicated Joe Biden receive a score of 1, while respondents who indicated Donald Trump receive a score of 0.

For information about the coding of the independent variables, see the text. All of the independent variables are measured in October.

[1] Parameter estimates are presented with standard errors (in parentheses), followed by levels of statistical significance, and the odds ratios.
** $p < .01$
* $p < .05$

integrity of the election, while linked to evaluations of the candidates, fail to produce significant changes in people's vote intention from September to November.[21]

---

[21] We replicate the analysis in Table 6.3 for strong partisans and for people less attached to the political parties. We find that the following campaign factors influence changes in vote preference for both sets of respondents: assessments of each candidate's debate

Finally, we see that comparative assessments of the candidates' personality traits are significantly related to changes in vote preference.[22] The odds ratio of 1.26 indicates that for every one-point increase in trait ratings (i.e., moving from advantaging Trump to advantaging Biden), the odds of changing one's vote preference from Trump to Biden increase by 26 percent. The results in Table 6.3 also indicate that party identification is significantly related to changes in people's vote choice.

SUMMARY AND CONCLUSION

We began this chapter by looking at how each of the major campaign issues and events influences feeling thermometer scores for Biden and Trump in November as well as changes in feeling thermometer scores over the campaign season. These comprehensive models demonstrate that reactions to the September presidential debate measured in October continue to powerfully influence people's views of the candidates in November. Furthermore, the primary issues of the campaign (i.e., election integrity, COVID-19, social justice protests) explain views of the candidates in November as well as changes in views of the candidates from September to November. Finally, we examine whether these elements of the campaign motivated changes in vote preference over the course of the campaign. We find that views of the September debate produce substantial changes in vote preference. Further, major issues of the campaign, such as support for protests against police brutality, significantly predict changes in vote from Trump to Biden. Cumulatively, these findings stress repeatedly that the 2020 campaign had strong effects on how people viewed the candidates and how they cast their ballots.

As we move to the final empirical chapter, we turn from predicting evaluations of the competing candidates – and vote preference – to the decision on whether to vote at all. We look both at turnout and *how* people actually cast their ballots (e.g., mail, in-person). We test the

performance, views on who won the September debate, confidence in the integrity of the election, and concern about COVID-19. We find that views about the social justice movement are significant in the model only for people less attached to the political parties. Across the three sets of analyses in this chapter, we find that both strong partisans and people less attached to the parties are influenced by a variety of different campaign events and issues.

[22] When developing the comparative trait measure, trait ratings for Donald Trump (summing across the six traits) are subtracted from trait ratings for Joe Biden (summing across the six traits) so high comparative trait scores indicate more positive trait ratings for Biden relative to Trump. The resulting comparative trait index ranges from −18 to +18.

citizen-centered theory of campaigns in the context of understanding participation in the 2020 presidential election. We examine how views of campaign events and issues, along with citizens' psychological predispositions, influence the decision to cast a vote in the 2020 election. We also examine how the elements of the campaign and people's psychological predisposition alter how people decide to cast their ballot, by voting early, by mail, or on Election Day.

# 7

# The Impact of Campaign Messages on the Decision to Vote

The COVID-19 pandemic led many states to take steps to protect voters and ensure a safe election process. Twenty-nine states and the District of Columbia expanded voting access in 2020. These changes included expanding eligibility for and access to mail voting, such as making it easier for voters to obtain absentee ballots, making it simpler to cast absentee ballots by including prepaid postage or providing safe ballot drop-off options. Many states also increased the number of early polling locations as well as the hours and days of operation (Sweren-Becker, Glatz, and Campbell, 2020).

More than two-thirds (69 percent) of citizens cast their vote by mail or in person before Election Day, compared to less than half (40 percent) in 2016 and one-third in 2012 (Scherer, 2021). In fact, a record 101.4 million people voted early in the 2020 election, with 65.6 million mail ballots returned and 35.8 million early in-person ballots cast (McDonald, 2020). Mail voting was by far the most popular mode of voting in 2020, with 43 percent of people voting by mail, 31 percent of people voting on Election Day, and 26 percent of people voting utilizing early voting locations.

The 2020 election was remarkable in terms of both the number of people voting and the popularity of convenience voting. Looking over the last 100 years, we can see more clearly the historic nature of the 2020 presidential election. The data in Figure 7.1 show that between 1920 and 1948 turnout fluctuated a great deal, from a low of 49 percent to a high of 62 percent.[1] In the 1950s and 1960s, about six out of ten eligible voters routinely participated in the presidential elections. Turnout began to fall in the

---

[1] The data in Figure 7.1 comes from the United States Election Project www.electproject.org/national-1789-present.

## How Campaign Messages Alter the Decision to Vote

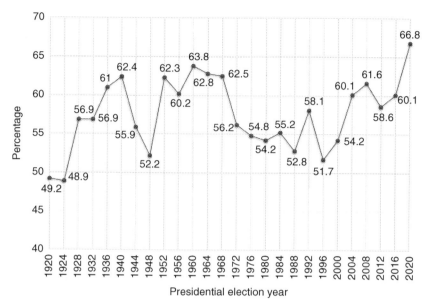

FIGURE 7.1 Turnout rates, 1920–2020

1970s and stayed below 60 percent between 1972 and 2000. Over the last twenty years, we have seen an increase in participation in elections, hovering around 60 percent for presidential elections contested between 2004 and 2016. However, 2020 clearly looks like a watershed election, with turnout exceeding 66 percent of the voting-eligible population in 2020.[2]

We apply the citizen-centered theory of campaigns to understand participation in the 2020 election. We view "Election Day" as the final campaign event of the 2020 electoral season as the campaigns worked tirelessly to drive their supporters to the polls. Therefore, we explore whether people's psychological predispositions help improve our understanding of why certain people choose to vote as well as how people decide to participate (i.e., on Election Day, by mail, in person before Election Day). We also show that different elements of the campaign significantly shape people's participation rates and their preference for convenience voting versus Election Day voting.

According to a rich literature, political characteristics of citizens help explain people's decision to vote. For example, people who are more interested in and more knowledgeable about politics (e.g., Delli Carpini

---

[2] The voting-eligible population includes only people who are eligible to vote (e.g., citizens, nonfelons in certain states).

and Keeter, 1996; Verba, Schlozman, and Brady, 1995) are more likely to vote in elections. However, few scholars have investigated how psychological predispositions influence participation rates in elections.[3] Further, given the rise in convenience voting in 2020, we explore how psychological and political predispositions explain differences in people's preference for different forms of voting (i.e., mail voting, early voting, Election Day voting).

In addition to exploring the impact of people's predispositions on turnout decisions, it is essential to show how campaign issues and events influence both the decision to vote and decisions about how to cast a vote (e.g., on Election day, by mail, in-person early voting). While some scholars have tied elements of political campaigns to levels of political engagement, this research is limited and somewhat inconclusive. For example, researchers have explored the connection between the negativity of campaigns and turnout, but with differing conclusions (e.g., Ansolabehere and Iyengar, 1996; Finkel and Geer, 1998; Fridkin and Kenney, 2019). We seek to improve our understanding of the impact of campaigns on political engagement by exploring how the major issues and events of the 2020 election influence turnout, in general, and modes of voting, in particular. We turn first to examining the classic question of "who votes" and begin by briefly reviewing the extensive turnout literature.

PRIOR RESEARCH EXAMINING VOTER TURNOUT

Scholars have worked diligently to understand why some people cast ballots and others do not. The vast literature has identified four groups of factors that influence participation rates in elections: (1) political profiles of citizens; (2) demographic characteristics of citizens; (3) state laws and regulations regarding voting; and (4) elements of the campaign.

We begin with the political profiles of citizens; strength of partisan attachment (e.g., Cassel and Hill, 1981) and civic duty (e.g., Blais and Achen, 2018) are important determinants of citizens' likelihood of

---

[3] A handful of studies have looked at whether sexism, racism, and authoritarianism condition the impact of ideology and partisanship on turnout. For example, Federico, Fisher, and Deason (2017) find a conditional relationship between ideology and authoritarianism on political engagement. Banda and Cassese (2022) find that racism and sexism demobilize Democrats but do not alter turnout among Republicans in the 2016 presidential election. Kam and Archer (2021) find that Republicans with higher levels of hostile sexism are more likely to turn out in the 2018 midterm election while Democrats with lower levels of hostile sexism turn out at higher levels.

voting. Strong and committed partisans are highly motivated to vote as they believe their lives are better off under one party or another. And civic duty –part of the socialization process taking place in families, communities, and schools – stresses voting as a responsibility in a democratic society. Further, as discussed earlier, people who are more interested in politics and more knowledgeable about politics and government are more likely to participate in elections (e.g., Nie, Junn, and Stehlik-Barry, 1996).

Demographic characteristics of citizens, such as education, age, and income, are positively related to participation in elections (e.g., Brady, Verba, and Schlozman, 1995; Rosenstone and Hansen, 1993; Wolfinger and Rosenstone, 1980). For example, increasing education is associated with a higher likelihood of voting because education lowers the costs associated with bureaucratic hurdles of registering and casting a vote and more schooling is linked to higher levels of interest in politics and civic duty. In addition, analysis of recent elections in the United States suggests that women vote at higher rates than men (e.g., CAWP, 2021); however, this difference might reflect a gender difference in civic duty (Carreras, 2018). With regard to race and ethnicity, turnout is higher among whites than nonwhites in US elections (e.g., Leighley and Nagler, 2013).

In addition to the demographic and political characteristics of citizens, scholars have demonstrated how the legal patchwork of state laws, rules, and regulations influences the likelihood of casting a ballot (e.g., Highton, 2017; Mitchell and Wlezien, 1995; Rosenstone and Wolfinger, 1978). Put simply, easing statewide voter registration laws increases turnout (e.g., Highton, 2017; Mitchell and Wlezien, 1995; Rosenstone and Wolfinger, 1978). A parallel body of research has focused on the impact of convenience voting (e.g., in-person early voting, voting by mail, absentee voting, online voting) on participation rates. These findings are more nuanced than those focused on easing voter registration. Nevertheless, the research indicates that making voting more convenient increases turnout but the impact varies across states and campaigns (e.g., Amlani and Collitt, 2022; Bonica et al., 2021).

Finally, scholars have begun to explore how characteristics of campaigns and candidates influence political engagement. As discussed earlier, they have been unable to reach a consensus regarding the relationship between negative campaigning and political engagement (e.g., Ansolabehere and Iyengar, 1996; Brooks, 2006; Fridkin and Kenney, 2019). In contrast, research has established that mobilization efforts by parties, candidates, and nonpartisan organizations increase turnout (e.g.,

Green and Schwan-Bard, 2015; Malhotra et al., 2011; Mann, 2021).[4] Perhaps because of increases in mobilization efforts in closely contested races, turnout is higher in competitive campaigns than lopsided races (e.g., Gerber et al., 2020; Goldberg, Lanz, and Sciarini, 2019). Furthermore, studies suggest that when candidates and parties are out of step with voters on policy matters, citizens lose interest, show signs of alienation, and are less likely to participate in elections (e.g., Leighley and Nagler, 2013). Additional research suggests that people are mobilized when they have more polarized views of the competing candidates (e.g., Abramowitz and Stone, 2006).

We turn next to developing expectations regarding how elements of the 2020 campaign may alter people's likelihood of participating in the election. By including measures of the campaign in models of turnout, we hope to improve our understanding of participation in elections.

## HOW CAMPAIGN EVENTS AND CAMPAIGN ISSUES INFLUENCE TURNOUT

### The First Presidential Debate

We believe the debate may help explain people's decision to vote. In particular, we expect that people who watched the debate will be more likely to turn out in the 2020 election. Research on debate effects demonstrates that presidential debates can heighten interest in campaigns, increase political knowledge, and encourage greater participation in the campaign, including increasing the likelihood of voting (e.g., McKinney and Chattopadhyay, 2007; Patterson, 2002). We hypothesize that, even controlling for campaign interest and political knowledge, people who watched the September debate will be more likely to vote in the election.[5]

### COVID-19 Pandemic

We examine whether concern about the COVID-19 pandemic alters people's likelihood of voting in the 2020 election. Just as economic issues, like rising unemployment, motivate citizens to go to the polls (e.g., Arceneaux, 2003; Burden and Wichowsky, 2014; Stevens, 2007, we

---

[4] A small set of researchers have linked genetic variation to the likelihood of voting (e.g., Fowler, Baker, and Dawes, 2008; Mondak et al., 2010).

[5] We rely on the survey question asking people if they watched the first presidential debate in the October wave of the survey (1 = yes; 0 = no).

expect that people who are more concerned about the COVID-19 crisis will be more likely to participate in the election.[6]

### Confidence in Election Integrity

We hypothesize that attitudes toward the integrity of the election will influence people's propensity to participate in the election. In particular, we expect that people who have less confidence in the election results will be less likely to vote (Alvarez, Hall, and Llewellyn, 2008).[7]

### Views about the Social Justice Protests

We expect people's support or opposition of the social justice movement to influence people's propensity to vote in the election. Given research showing that "issue polarization energizes the electorate and stimulate participation" (Abramowitz and Stone, 2006: 153), we expect that people with very favorable and very unfavorable views about the racial justice protests will be more likely to vote in the 2020 presidential, compared to people with more ambivalent attitudes toward the protests against police brutality.[8]

We turn now to improving our understanding of "who votes" by discussing how certain psychological predispositions may influence people's likelihood of participating in the 2020 election.

## PSYCHOLOGICAL PREDISPOSITIONS OF CITIZENS AND TURNOUT

Across the five psychological predispositions examined in our study, we develop expectations regarding how two of these predispositions, conflict avoidance and conspiracy thinking, may influence the decision to vote in the 2020 election. We turn first to conflict avoidance.

---

[6] We utilize the COVID-19 worry index introduced in Chapter 3.
[7] We rely on the question measuring people's confidence in the integrity of the election introduced in Chapter 5.
[8] To measure polarized views of the social justice movement, we create an index based on the social protest index introduced in Chapter 4. We recode the original index, which ranges from 2 to 10, so people with the most extreme positive and negative values have the highest score (e.g., people who score at 2 or 10 on the original index are given a score of 5 on the polarization index) and those with the most ambivalent score are given the lowest score on new index (e.g., people who score at 6 on the original index are given a score of 1 on the polarization index).

## Conflict Avoidance

Electoral contests are a conflictual process where competing interests vie for power. And the conflict associated with election campaigns has become more pervasive with the increase in partisan news content, the twenty-four-hour news cycle, and escalating polarization. We expect that people's level of conflict avoidance will alter their propensity to participate in the election. Prior research suggests that people high in conflict avoidance withdraw from public forms of political participation, like participating in protests and attending political rallies because they are uncomfortable with the potential for conflict (e.g., Ulbig and Funk, 1999; Wolak, 2020). However, the relationship between conflict avoidance and voting is inconsistent, with some researchers finding that conflict avoidance is not related to the likelihood of voting (e.g., Ulbig and Funk, 1999), while others report a positive relationship between conflict avoidance and voting (e.g., Blais and St-Vincent, 2011).

In the context of the 2020 election, we develop two rival explanations. First, consistent with the logic described by Ulbig and Funk (1999), we hypothesize an inverse relationship between conflict avoidance and voting since people who dislike conflict are likely to steer clear of the conflict-ridden world of electoral politics. Our rival hypothesis, in contrast, contends that people high in conflict avoidance will be more likely to vote in the 2020 election. During the 2020 campaign (and before), Trump was often described as pugnacious, conflict-seeking, and aggressive (Hochschild, 2020). Biden was rarely, if ever, described in similar terms. Therefore, people who are uncomfortable with conflict may be particularly motivated to vote in 2020 to unseat an incumbent president with a history of bullying behavior.

## Conspiracy Thinking

In addition to conflict avoidance, we expect conspiracy thinking to influence turnout. The literature examining the relationship between conspiracy thinking and participation in electoral campaigns is scant (for an exception, see Kim, 2019). Since conspiracy theories often portray political events as controlled by a small set of powerful elites (Uscinski, Klofstad, and Atkinson, 2016), people who believe in conspiracies are unlikely to believe they can influence these events. If this is the case, then, people high in conspiracy thinking may be disinclined to participate in elections since they see their participation as ineffectual. Given this reasoning, we expect a negative relationship between conspiracy thinking and turnout in the presidential election.

However, the context of the 2020 election leads us to generate a rival explanation regarding conspiracy thinking. The incumbent president and the Republican nominee for president embraced conspiracies and was called the "conspirator-in-chief" by several media outlets.[9] Conspiracy thinkers may see Trump as an ally in their fight against powerful elites, encouraging these individuals to participate in the election and secure Trump's reelection to the presidency. In this scenario, we hypothesize a positive correlation between conspiracy thinking and turnout.[10]

While we expect psychological predispositions and elements of the 2020 campaign to improve our understanding of participation in the election, it is necessary to include rival factors known to influence turnout. We turn to a discussion of these competing characteristics.

## RIVAL FACTORS INFLUENCING TURNOUT

### Additional Campaign Characteristics

We begin by discussing campaign variables known or expected to alter participation rates in elections. We include two types of characteristics: the negativity of the campaign and candidate polarization.[11]

### Negativity of the Campaign

There's a long line of research, beginning with Ansolabehere et al. (1994), exploring the relationship between campaign negativity and political engagement. Some researchers (e.g., Ansolabehere et al., 1994) find that

---

[9] See the following articles: www.salon.com/2017/01/14/conspirator-in-chief-14-fake-news-stories-created-or-publicized-by-donald-trump_partner/www.thenation.com/article/politics/qanon-trump-conspiracy/

[10] While we do not expect the remaining psychological predispositions to influence the decision to vote, we include these predispositions in our turnout model.

[11] We included a variable measuring battleground status. We know mobilization efforts are more extensive in battleground states, often leading to higher levels of turnout, compared to other states (e.g., Bergan et al., 2005; Enos and Fowler, 2018). Further, races where the election outcome is uncertain (i.e., battleground states) generate higher levels of turnout (e.g., Ragsdale and Rusk, 2017). We classify the following states as battleground states based on public opinion polls taken in late summer: Arizona, Florida, Georgia, Iowa, Michigan, North Carolina, Ohio, Pennsylvania, Texas, and Wisconsin. When we include the binary variable measuring battleground status, we find a null effect. More specifically, in the full model presented in Table 7.1, battleground status is not related to turnout.

negativity demobilizes citizens, others find no relationship between negativity and turnout (e.g., Brooks, 2006), and some scholars find that negative campaigning may enhance turnout (e.g., Clinton and Lapinski, 2004; Hillygus, 2005). Based on our research (Fridkin and Kenny, 2019), we expect negative campaigning to initially increase turnout since negative commentary provides valuable information about the costs associated with presidential choices (e.g., Lau, 1982). However, when negativity escalates to very high levels, we hypothesize that people will be turned off and stay home (see also Lau and Pomper, 2004). To assess the impact of negative campaigning, we rely on questions asking respondents to rate the tone of each candidate's presidential campaign.[12] We sum people's scores assessing the tone of Biden and Trump's campaigns, with the resulting measure ranging from 2 to 10.[13]

*Candidate Polarization*
The increasing polarization of the US electorate over the last twenty-five years has been well documented (e.g., Abramowitz and Saunders, 2008, but see Fiorina and Abrams, 2008. The growing polarization among citizens (i.e., affective polarization) has translated into strong positive feelings toward partisans' preferred candidates and sharply negative feelings about the opposing candidates (Iyengar, Sood, and Lelkes, 2012). Affective polarization toward candidates is likely driven by a combination of factors, including policy and ideological differences as well as partisan social identity. Abramowitz and Stone (2006) find that differences in views of the presidential candidates in 2000 and 2004 increased turnout (see also Abramowitz and Saunders, 2008). We explore the relationship between candidate polarization and participation rates in our model of turnout. To measure candidate polarization, we adopt Abramowitz and Stone's (2006) measure and take the absolute value of the difference in feeling thermometer scores for Biden and Trump.[14]

---

[12] Respondents are asked: "Thinking about the ongoing presidential campaign, how would you characterize the tone of Donald Trump's [Joe Biden's] campaign thus far (e.g., his campaign advertisements, his speeches, his tweets)? Would you characterize Trump's [Biden's] campaign as very positive, somewhat positive, a mixture of positive and negative, somewhat negative, very negative?" People who did not rate the tone of the candidates' campaigns are coded to the middle of the scale as not to lose them from the analysis.

[13] Since we expect a curvilinear relationship between the tone of the campaign and turnout, we include the tone of the campaign and the tone of the campaign squared in the turnout model in Table 7.1.

[14] The resulting polarization score ranges from 0 to 100, with 0 meaning that the respondent gave Biden and Trump the same feeling thermometer rating and 100 meaning the

## Political Characteristics of Citizens

We measure four political characteristics of respondents likely to influence the propensity to vote. To begin, we rely on a civic duty measure developed by Blais and Achen (2018) that seeks to lessen the social desirability bias associated with the traditional civic duty question. The exact question wording is:

Different people feel differently about voting. For some, voting is a choice – they feel free to vote or not to vote, depending on how they feel about the candidates and parties. For others, voting is a duty – they feel they should vote in every election no matter how they feel about the candidates and parties. Which of the following comes closest to your view? Very strongly feel voting is a duty (5); Somewhat feel voting is a duty (4); Neither feel voting is a duty nor a choice (3); Somewhat feel voting is a choice (2); Very strongly feel voting is a choice (1).

Second, we create an index to measure people's attention to politics composed of three items: (1) interest in political campaigns, (2) attention to news, and (3) willingness to seek out information about the presidential campaign.[15] Third, we rely on the political knowledge index introduced in Chapter 5 to see whether people with more accurate information about politics and government are more likely to vote in the presidential election. Finally, strength of partisanship is measured with the standard seven-point party identification scale; strong partisans (strong Republicans and strong Democrats) receive the highest score (4), followed by weak partisan (3) and leaning independents (2). Pure independents and people who did not answer the party identification question receive the lowest score (1) on the strength of partisanship scale.[16]

---

respondent rated one of the candidates at 100 and rated the other candidate at 0 on the feeling thermometer. Respondents who did not answer the feeling thermometer question are recoded to 50 so we can include these respondents in the analysis.

[15] The political interest question is "Some people don't pay much attention to political campaigns. How about you? Would you say that you are very much interested (3), somewhat interested (2), or not much interested (1) in political campaigns?" The attention to news question was introduced in Chapter 2. The willingness to seek out campaign information question is "How likely are you to seek out additional information about political candidates running for office" on a scale from "very unlikely" (1) to "very likely" (4). Since these three questions are measured on different scales, we standardize each measure before creating the additive index of political attention.

[16] Based on the literature, we included several demographic variables (i.e., gender, race, age, education, income) when estimating turnout. However, when estimating the full turnout model, none of the demographic variables reach statistical significance. In the interest of parsimony, we do not include these demographic variables in the model presented in Table 7.1.

## State Variation in Voting Access

We examine whether state variation in access to mail voting and early voting enhances turnout.[17] As access to convenience voting increases, we expect turnout in the election will increase.[18] We create a mail voting index based on two state-level measures: (1) ratings of each state's experience with mail voting and (2) ease of mail voting in each state. To measure a state's experience with mail voting, we look at the percentage of mail voting per state in 2018 and classify states into four categories from 1 (less than 5 percent votes cast by mail in 2018) to 4 (more than 80 percent of the votes cast by mail in 2018).[19] Ease of mail voting is measured on a five-point scale ranging from 1 (i.e., the most restrictive rules for mail voting where voters need an excuse beyond COVID-19, such as a physical disability, to qualify for mail voting) to 5 (i.e., states with exclusive mail voting prepandemic). We combine these two measures into an access to mail voting index.[20]

To assess the availability of early voting, we measure the amount of time available in each state for early voting. First, we create a measure based on the number of days available for early voting.[21] Second, each

---

[17] We also look at whether differences in state registration requirements alter turnout. We examine the following variables tapping ease of registration: (1) same day registration, (2) automatic voter registration, (3) online registration, and (4) registration deadline. However, these variables do not influence people's likelihood of voting irrespective of how we included these variables in the models (e.g., separately or composed in an index). The data detailing state registration requirements can be found at NCLS.org.

[18] We also look at additional state-level constraints on voting to see if differences in restrictions across states influence turnout. We do not find a significant relationship between voter identification laws and people's likelihood of voting. We also do not find that states enhancing "felon rights" spur higher turnout compared to other states. Data regarding felon rights and voter identification laws come from NCLS.org. Finally, utilizing the cost of voting index created by Schraufnagel, Pomante, and Li (2020), we find no relationship between the cost of voting index and turnout.

[19] States received a 2 on the scale if more than 10 percent and less than 50 percent of the 2018 votes were cast by mail and states received a score of 3 if more than 50 percent and less than 80 percent of the state's votes were cast by mail in 2018. The data regarding mail voting in 2018 are taken from www.washingtonpost.com/graphics/2020/politics/vote-by-mail-states/

[20] States receive a score of 2 if voters have to seek out their own mail ballot application; states receive a score of 3 if all registered voters are mailed ballot applications; states receive a score of 4 if all registered voters are mailed ballots. The ease of mail voting data come from Vice's "Uncounted: The Voting Access Project," www.vice.com/en/topic/uncounted-the-voting-access-project. In creating the mail voting index, we normalize the mail voting experience measure and ease of mail voting measure before adding the two measures to create the index.

[21] We create a variable based on the number of weeks available for early voting (1 = one week or less, 2 = eight days to two weeks, 3 = fifteen days to three weeks, 4 = twenty-two days to four weeks, 5 = more than four weeks). Data on early voting is available at www.ncsl.org/research/elections-and-campaigns/early-voting-in-state-elections.aspx

state is given a score from 0 to 2 based on whether the state has no early voting on the weekend (0), early voting only on Saturdays (1), or early voting on Saturdays and Sundays (2).[22] We create an early voting index by combining these two aspects of access to early voting.[23] In the next section, we explore how psychological predispositions, campaign events and campaign issues, and a host of rival factors influence people's decision to cast a vote in the 2020 election.

## EXPLAINING TURNOUT IN THE 2020 ELECTION: THE EVIDENCE

We measure turnout with a binary variable: People who voted (irrespective of whether they voted by mail, early, or on Election Day) are coded as 1 and people who did not vote are coded as 0.[24] We ask people if they voted in the presidential election during the November wave of the survey.[25] All attitudinal variables are measured during the October wave of the panel and the psychological predispositions are measured during the respondent's first wave of the panel survey. By establishing time-order, we are more confident that the independent variables are

---

[22] We test the impact of additional measures on people's likelihood of voting. We develop a variable measuring the number of polling places available in each state because research suggests that distance from a polling place can influence turnout (Dyck and Gimpel, 2005; Haspel and Knotts, 2005). We calculate the number of polling places by the voting age population in each state. We also examine whether changes in the number of polling places per state affected turnout. These measures are unrelated to the dependent variable. The data about polling places are from Vice's "Uncounted: The Voting Access Project" and data on voting age population by state come from www.electproject.org/2020g. We examine whether the "signature requirement" on mail-in ballots and the availability of drop boxes influence turnout. These variables did not achieve statistical significance in the turnout model.

[23] Since these two measures are based on different scales, we standardize both measures before creating the additive index.

[24] The dependent variable is based on survey responses given during the November wave of the survey. All attitudinal variables are measured during the October wave of the panel and the psychological predispositions are measured during the respondent's first wave of the panel survey. By establishing time-order, we are more confident that the independent variables are influencing the dependent variable. We recognize that self-reported turnout is significantly higher than actual turnout. Belli, Traugott, and Beckman (2001) explain that overreporting of turnout averages about 10 percentage points in surveys conducted by the American National Election Survey (ANES). However, Verba, Schlozman, and Brady (1995) argue that correlates of turnout are unlikely to be biased when self-reports are used. Further, Berent, Krosnick, and Lupia (2016), examining the ANES 2008–2009 panel study, find actual (validated) and self-reported turnout are nearly identical among respondents matched to government records.

[25] See Appendix A for the exact question wording.

influencing the dependent variable. We begin by looking at how elements of the 2020 campaign influence people's decision to vote.[26]

### The Impact of Campaign Issues and Events on Turnout

First, we look at whether watching the September presidential debate mobilizes people to vote. Based on previous research, we expect watching the general election debate to heighten people's attention and interest in the election, pushing people to the polls. And consistent with our expectations, the results in Table 7.1 show that people who watched the debate are significantly more likely to vote in the election. Interpreting the odds ratio, the likelihood of voting is 41 percent higher for people who watched the debate compared to people who did not watch the debate.

Turning to the major issues of the campaign, we hypothesize that people who are most concerned about the coronavirus pandemic will be mobilized to vote at higher rates than people who are less worried about the health crisis. However, the findings presented in Table 7.1 indicate that concern over COVID-19 does not significantly influence people's probability of turning out to vote.[27]

Next, we look at the connection between people's trust in the integrity of the election and their likelihood of participating in the election. We expect that people who have more confidence in the integrity of the election will be more likely to vote. The results in Table 7.1 support our expectation. The coefficient for confidence in the election is positive and more than three times the size of the standard error. Furthermore, the odds ratio indicates that for every one-point increase in the confidence in the election measure, the odds of voting increase by 44 percent. Or, conversely, for every one-point decrease in confidence in the integrity of the election, the odds of voting decrease by 44 percent.

We also examine whether polarized views of the Black Lives Matter movement mobilize people to cast a vote in the 2020 election. We find that people who are more polarized in their views about the protest

---

[26] Since state-level variables (like the mail voting index) are included in the models in this chapter and respondents are nested within states, we need to utilize multilevel modeling. In particular, we rely on a generalized linear mixed model with a logit link function given the dependent variable is dichotomous. In addition, given the smaller number of cases available for analysis in the November wave of the panel, we rely on *p*-values less than .10 to indicate statistical significance.

[27] We also examine whether retrospective evaluations of the economy affect people's likelihood of voting, but the coefficient for economic assessments is negative and far from statistically significant (−.036 with a standard error of .09).

TABLE 7.1 *Multilevel logit model predicting turnout*

| Fixed effect | Coefficient (SE) | Odds ratio |
|---|---|---|
| *Campaign events and issues* | | |
| Watched debate | .34 (.20)* | 1.41 |
| Worries about COVID-19 | .02 (.06) | 1.02 |
| Confidence in election integrity | .37 (.11)*** | 1.44 |
| Polarized views about social justice protests | .22 (.06)*** | 1.25 |
| *Additional campaign characteristics* | | |
| Tone of campaign | 1.35 (.26)*** | 3.84 |
| Tone of campaign$^2$ | −.096 (.021)*** | .91 |
| Candidate polarization | .005 (.003)* | 1.01 |
| *Psychological predispositions* | | |
| Authoritarianism | .06 (.08) | 1.06 |
| Conflict avoidance | .14 (.03)*** | 1.15 |
| Conspiracy | .01 (.01) | 1.01 |
| Hostile sexism | −.08 (.05) | .93 |
| Racial resentment | −.02 (.02) | .98 |
| *Political characteristics* | | |
| Civic duty | .41 (.07)*** | 1.50 |
| Political attention | .30 (.05)*** | 1.35 |
| Political knowledge | .33 (.08)*** | 1.40 |
| Strength of partisanship | .23 (.08)*** | 1.25 |
| *Access to convenience voting* | | |
| Mail index | .18 (.07)** | 1.19 |
| Early voting index | .14 (.08)* | 1.15 |
| Intercept | −8.38 (1.19)*** | |
| **Random effect** | | |
| Intercept | | .33 (.26) |
| −2 log likelihood | | 9,767.63 |
| % correctly predicted | 90 | |
| Number of states | 46 | |
| Number of respondents | 1,627 | |

*Note:* Parameter estimates are presented with standard errors (in parentheses), followed by levels of statistical significance, and the odds ratios. The dependent variable (measured in the November wave) is voted in the election (1) or did not vote in the election (0). The attitudinal variables are measured in earlier waves. For more information about measurement, see the text.

\* $p < .10$
\*\* $p < .05$
\*\*\* $p < .01$

movement are significantly more likely to participate in the election. Interpreting the odds ratio, every one-point increase in polarization in views about the movement increases the odds of voting by 25 percent.

In addition to issues, we expect people's views of the negative tone of the campaign to alter their likelihood of participating in the election. We hypothesize that people's assessments of the negativity of the campaign will initially enhance engagement since negative information is viewed as interesting and informative. However, when people view the campaign as intensely negative, they are likely to disengage from the election. We estimate the expected curvilinear relationship between the tone of the campaign and turnout by including the tone of the campaign and the tone of the campaign squared in the model. We find support for our expectation: The coefficient for the tone of the campaign is significant and positive, suggesting that turnout increases as the tone of the campaign changes from positive to somewhat negative. However, the negative and significant coefficient for the square of campaign tone indicates that as people view campaigns as intensely negative, their likelihood of voting declines.

Finally, we look at whether people's polarized views of the rival candidates influence turnout. In other words, as people's evaluations of the candidates diverge, are people more motivated to cast a vote in the election? We find a modest relationship between polarization in attitudes toward the rival candidates and people's likelihood of voting. Overall, our analysis shows that several aspects of the 2020 campaign significantly influence turnout, mobilizing people to participate in the election. In particular, people's beliefs about the integrity of the election, polarized views about the social justice protests, and views about the negativity of the campaign powerfully alter people's probability of casting a vote in the 2020 election.

## The Impact of Psychological Predispositions on Turnout

The campaign forces, of course, are not the only reasons people go to the polls. Convenience voting, along with the political, psychological, and demographic characteristics of citizens, is consequential. We turn our attention to people's psychological predispositions. We first look at conflict avoidance. The findings in Table 7.1 demonstrate that the relationship between conflict avoidance and voting is positive and highly significant. Further, the odds ratio of 1.15 suggests that for every one-point increase in conflict avoidance, the odds of voting increase by 15 percent. We reasoned that people high in conflict avoidance may be especially motivated to vote in the 2020 election because the prospect of reelecting Trump, a politician known for his bullying and belittling behavior, was particularly distressing. While conflict avoidance significantly alters people's likelihood of voting, their level of conspiracy thinking does not influence the probability of participating in the election. Lastly, though we do not have clear expectations about how the remaining psychological predispositions (i.e., authoritarianism, hostile sexism, and racial resentment) will influence the likelihood of voting, we include these predispositions in the model presented in Table 7.1. We find that authoritarianism, hostile sexism, and racial resentment do not influence citizens' decisions to cast a ballot in the 2020 election.[28]

## The Impact of Political Predispositions on Turnout

Standard political variables, like civic duty, strength of partisanship, political knowledge, and political attention, each have powerful positive influences on people's likelihood of voting. For example, the odds ratio for civic duty indicates that for every one-unit increase in civic duty, the odds of voting increase by 50 percent. These results reinforce a wealth of work documenting the importance of these political characteristics on people's likelihood of engaging in politics (e.g., Campbell et al., 1960; Delli Carpini and Keeter, 1996; Miller and Shanks, 1996; Prior, 2007).

## The Impact of Convenience Voting on Turnout

We conclude by examining how statewide laws regulating mail voting and early voting influence people's likelihood of voting. We expect that as states ease restrictions, making it easier and more convenient for people to vote, especially during a global pandemic, people will take advantage of these opportunities and will be more likely to vote. As expected, we find the ease of and experience with mail voting to be significantly related to increases in people's likelihood of voting. The odds ratio for the mail index indicates that for every one-unit increase in the mail index, the odds of voting increase by 19 percent. When we look at the accessibility of early voting (i.e., increasing the days for early voting, the availability of weekend voting), we once again

---

[28] Following the lead of Kam and Archer (2021) and Banda and Cassese (2022), we look at whether people's partisanship conditions the impact of hostile sexism and racial resentment on participation rates. We fail to find evidence for a conditioning effect for either hostile sexism or racial resentment. In addition, we examine whether the impact of authoritarianism on political engagement is conditioned by ideology, as Federico, Fisher, and Deason (2017) find. However, the interaction between ideology and authoritarianism in our analysis is far from statistically significant.

see that making early voting easier produces higher levels of turnout. The odds ratio of 1.15 suggests that for every one-unit increase in the accessibility of early voting, the odds of voting increase by 15 percent. These results clearly indicate that making voting easier in 2020 enhanced turnout.

In summary, the model presented in Table 7.1 demonstrates that elements of the campaign shape who decides to vote. How people viewed the competing candidates, the negativity of their campaigns, and views about the integrity of the election each alter people's decision to vote. In addition, the availability of convenience voting increases people's likelihood of voting in the presidential election. Finally, conflict avoidance is associated with an increased likelihood of voting in the election. We turn next to explore how campaign messages, characteristics of citizens (i.e., political, psychological, and demographic characteristics) and access to convenience voting affect *how* people choose to cast their vote in the 2020 election.

## EXPECTATIONS OF HOW THE 2020 CAMPAIGN AFFECTED CONVENIENCE VOTING

The messages from the competing candidates and their camps were diametrically opposed to one another regarding methods of casting ballots. Although both campaigns were urging their supporters to vote, Republicans stressed voting in person on Election Day because it was reliable and secure. For example, during the final segment of the first general election debate, Trump "launched into an extended argument against mail voting, claiming it is ripe for fraud and suggesting mail ballots may be manipulated. 'This is going to be a fraud like you've never seen,' the President said of the massive shift to mail voting prompted by the coronavirus pandemic" (Riccardi, 2020). Democrats, on the other hand, emphasized voting early and voting by mail as safer and accessible options during the COVID-19 pandemic. The candidates, parties, and partisan news outlets preached these contrasting messages to voters repeatedly during the length of the fall campaign. We expect the divergent messages to shape how citizens decide to cast ballots. We outline specific expectations regarding the link between the content of the campaign messages and people's mode of voting.

### Campaign Issues

We hypothesize that people who are more concerned about the pandemic will be less likely to vote on Election Day where lines could be long and the likelihood of contracting the virus could be higher. Instead, we expect that people who are more worried about COVID-19 will choose a safer alternative, either voting by mail or voting early where polling locations were predicted to be less congested than on Election Day.

Trump repeatedly urged his supporters to vote on Election Day while suggesting that early voting, and mail voting in particular, was suspect. Because he specifically challenged the legitimacy of mail voting, we expect that people who are less confident in the integrity of the election will be less likely to utilize mail voting.

## Psychological Predispositions of Citizens

As we have discussed in earlier chapters, Trump's rhetoric all along, before entering politics, as a candidate, and as president, appeals to certain types of individuals more than others – for example, people with more authoritarian attitudes (e.g., Knuckey and Hassan, 2020) and people who are more likely to express views consistent with hostile sexism and racial resentment (Cassese and Barnes, 2019; Schaffner, MacWilliams, and Nteta, 2018). Since these types of individuals may be especially attuned to Trump's campaign messages, we expect that people who score high on scales measuring authoritarianism, racial resentment, and hostile sexism will be more likely to vote on Election Day given Trump's warnings about massive fraud associated with convenience voting.

In addition, people who are more likely to engage in conspiratorial thinking will be more likely to believe Trump's assertions about "rigged" early voting. Put simply, people who tend to believe in conspiracies will be more receptive to Trump's rhetoric about convenience voting being fraught with fraud. Therefore, we expect that people high in conspiracy thinking will be more likely to cast ballots in person on Election Day.

Finally, we expect people high in conflict avoidance to prefer mail voting where people do not need to interact with others when casting their vote. In a campaign season where President Trump urged his supporters "to go into the polls and watch very carefully," election officials and news reports raised concerns about the potential for violence at polling places (Silva, 2020). In a widely publicized example of polling place intimidation, Trump supporters chanted outside an early voting site in Fairfax County, Virginia. While voters were not blocked by Trump supporters, some voters said they felt intimidated by people who waved campaign signs and shouted "Four more years" (Fessler, 2020). Given the chances of encountering a hostile situation at the polls, we expect people high in conflict avoidance to prefer to vote by mail.

## Political Characteristics of Citizens

### Party Differences

Biden, along with Democratic party surrogates, championed the virtues of voting by mail or voting early repeatedly during the course of the campaign, at drive-in events, during the presidential debates, and online via social media. Trump, in comparison, encouraged people to vote on Election Day because of his frequent claims of fraud associated with convenience voting. Given the contrasting messages, we expect stark party differences in the modes of voting favored by Democrats and Republicans. In particular, we expect Democrats to be more likely to take advantage of convenience voting, while we expect Republicans to be more likely to vote on Election Day.[29] To examine whether partisan affiliation influences how people cast their vote, we create two binary variables: one for Democrats (1 = weak or strong Democrat; 0 = other) and one for independents (1 = pure independents, independents who lean toward the Democratic or Republican party; 0 = other).[30] With these binary variables, we can compare convenience voting for Democrats and Republicans (with the Democrat variable) and we can compare convenience voting for independents and Republicans (with the independent variable).

### Political Knowledge

We expect that people with higher levels of political knowledge are more likely to vote early (either in person or via the mail) than on Election Day since these individuals are better equipped to navigate the rules and regulations regarding early voting (e.g., Shino and Smith, 2020).

## Demographic Characteristics of Citizens

Based on previous research on convenience voting, we expect demographic characteristics of citizens to influence decisions about how to cast a ballot. We expect that older voters will be more likely to vote early compared to

---

[29] Atkeson et al. (2022), relying on administrative records from the state of New Mexico, find that Republicans are less likely than Democrats and independents to rely on voting by mail and Republicans are more likely to vote in person early than Democrats or independents.

[30] We rely on the standard seven-point party identification scale to classify respondents as Democrats, independents, and Republicans. The "other" category includes Republicans (weak and strong). We decided to rely on Republicans as the excluded category so we can compare Democrats to Republicans as well as independents to Republicans.

Findings: Convenience Voting in 2020 Election    183

younger voters (e.g., Ashok et al., 2016; Atkeson et al., 2022). Similarly, women may rely on convenience voting more than men, given the greater flexibility inherent in this mode of voting (Southwell, 2007). Based on research by Baringer, Herron, and Smith (2020), we expect that Latinos and Black voters will vote by mail at lower rates than whites.[31] Finally, we expect that in-person early voting will be higher among Black citizens than others (Herron and Smith, 2012; Kaplan and Yuan, 2020; Miller and Chaturvedi, 2018; Walker, Herron, and Smith, 2019).[32]

### Access to Convenience Voting

We expect that people will be more likely to use mail voting when they live in states with more mail voting experience and when obtaining mail-in ballots is easier.[33] In addition, when in-person early voting is not an option, we expect that people will be more likely to choose to vote by mail. Similarly, when people have more opportunities to vote early in person, we expect they will be more likely to go to the polls prior to Election Day.[34] We turn next to examine how campaign forces, psychological and political characteristics, and access to convenience voting influence people's likelihood of voting by mail and voting early (versus voting on Election Day).

## FINDINGS: THE IMPACT OF THE 2020 CAMPAIGN MESSAGES ON CONVENIENCE VOTING

In this section, we present two analyses. First, we predict whether people voted by mail (coded = 1) or voted on Election Day (coded = 0). Second, we predict whether people voted early at their polling place or voting center (coded = 1) or voted on Election Day (coded = 0). The equations predicting people's preference for convenience voting are presented in Table 7.2.

---

[31] Hesitation with mail voting among Black and Latino voters may be explained by that fact that minorities are more likely than whites to have their mail ballots disqualified (e.g., Baringer, Herron, and Smith, 2020).
[32] We expect higher early voting for Black voters because of the nationalization of the "souls to the polls" campaign where the National Association for the Advancement of Colored People, Black church denominations, and get-out-the-vote organizations arrange caravans after Sunday church service prior to Election Day to transport Black congregants to early voting locations (Daniels, 2020).
[33] We rely on the mail index introduced earlier in the chapter.
[34] We utilize the early voting index introduced earlier in the chapter.

TABLE 7.2 *Multilevel logit model predicting convenience voting*

|  | Voting by mail | | Voting early | |
|---|---|---|---|---|
|  | Coefficient (SE) | Odds ratio | Coefficient (SE) | Odds ratio |
| **Fixed effect** | | | | |
| *Campaign events and issues* | | | | |
| Confidence in election | .19 (.09)** | 1.22 | −.14 (.11) | .87 |
| Worries about COVID | −19.18 (.05)*** | 1.20 | .09 (.07) | 1.09 |
| *Psychological predispositions* | | | | |
| Authoritarianism | .05 (.07) | 1.05 | −.05 (.08) | .95 |
| Conflict avoidance | .11 (.03)*** | 1.12 | .01 (.03) | 1.01 |
| Conspiracy | −.03 (.01)** | .97 | −.02 (.01)** | .98 |
| Hostile sexism | −.06 (.03)* | .94 | −.15 (.04)*** | .86 |
| Racial resentment | −.07 (.02)*** | .94 | −.01 (.03) | .99 |
| *Political characteristics* | | | | |
| Democrat | .43 (.19)** | 1.54 | .15 (.24) | 1.16 |
| Independent | .34 (.19)* | 1.40 | .11 (.23) | 1.12 |
| Political knowledge | .17 (.06)*** | 1.19 | .22 (.07)*** | 1.24 |
| *Demographic characteristics* | | | | |
| Age | .04 (.01)*** | 1.04 | .025 (.007)*** | 1.03 |
| Black | −.25 (.34) | .77 | .81 (.36)** | 2.26 |
| White | −.02 (.20) | .98 | .30 (.23) | 1.35 |
| Education | .32 (.06)*** | 1.38 | .01 (.07) | 1.01 |
| Gender | .06 (.17) | 1.06 | .45 (.20)** | 1.57 |

184

| | | | | |
|---|---|---|---|---|
| Income | −.20 (.05)*** | .82 | .05 (.06) | 1.06 |
| *Access to convenience voting* | | | | |
| Early voting available | −1.31 (.56)** | .27 | | |
| Early voting index | | | .35 (.15)** | 1.42 |
| Mail voting index | .34 (.08)*** | 1.41 | | |
| Intercept | −2.96 (.85)*** | | −1.22 (1.00) | |
| **Random effect** | | | | |
| Intercept | .61 (.28)** | | 1.80 (.63)*** | |
| −2 log likelihood | 5,149.67 | | 3,861.38 | |
| % correctly predicted | 77 | | 78 | |
| Number of states | 44 | | 42 | |
| Number of respondents | 1,048 | | 793 | |

*Note:* Parameter estimates are presented followed by standard errors (in parentheses), followed by levels of statistical significance and the odds ratios. The dependent variable in the first model is coded as voting by mail (1) or voting on Election Day (0) and the dependent variable in the second model is coded as voting early (1) or voting on Election Day (0). For additional information about the measurement of the independent variables, see the text.

\* $p < .10$
\*\* $p < .05$
\*\*\* $p < .01$

We begin by examining whether people's worries about the COVID-19 pandemic alter how people decide to cast their vote. We expect that people who are most concerned about the coronavirus will be least likely to vote on Election Day and most likely to vote by mail. We view voting in person before Election Day as a middle option; voting early will likely avoid some of the long lines associated with voting on November 3 but voting in person is not as safe as voting by mail. The results in Table 7.2 demonstrate that concern about COVID-19 significantly increases the probability of utilizing mail voting. As the odds ratio in Table 7.2 indicate, for every one-unit increase in worries about the coronavirus, the odds of voting by mail increase by 20 percent. In contrast, in the early voting model, the coefficient for COVID-19 worries is positive but far from statistically significant. Concern about the coronavirus pushes people to vote by mail (compared to Election Day), but people's worries about contracting COVID-19 does not significantly influence the mode of in-person voting.

Turning to people's views regarding the integrity of the election, we find a significant relationship between people's confidence in the election results and their likelihood of voting by mail. For every one-unit increase in people's confidence in the accurate reporting of the election results, the odds of voting by mail increase by 22 percent. Or, conversely, as confidence in the election decreases, people are significantly more likely to vote on Election Day compared to voting by mail. Confidence in the election results does not influence people's likelihood of voting early, compared to Election Day. These findings suggest Trump's messages regarding "rampant fraud" with mail voting likely affected how people decided to cast their vote.

We turn next to examining whether people's psychological predispositions influence how people cast their vote. People high in conflict avoidance prefer the least conflictual mode of voting: voting by mail. Interpreting the odds ratio for conflict avoidance, we see the odds of voting by mail increase by 12 percent for every unit increase on the conflict avoidance measure. Second, we see that people who are more likely to believe in conspiracies are significantly less likely to utilize both types of convenience voting and prefer to vote on Election Day. In the mail voting model, the odds ratio of .97 indicates that the odds of voting by mail decrease by 3 percent for every one-unit increase in conspiratorial thinking. And in the early voting model, we find a similar relationship; the odds of voting early decrease by 2 percent for each unit increase on the conspiracy scale.

Third, we hypothesized that people high in authoritarianism, racial resentment, and hostile sexism will be receptive to Trump's message about avoiding convenience voting and casting a ballot on Election Day. We find partial support for our expectation: People higher in hostile sexism and racial resentment are less likely to vote by mail and people higher in hostile sexism are less likely to vote early. The odds ratio indicates that the odds of voting by mail decrease by 6 percent for each unit increase on the sexism and racism scales. However, we fail to find a relationship between people's level of authoritarianism and their preference for Election Day voting compared to convenience voting. Overall, the results presented in Table 7.2 demonstrate the importance of psychological predispositions for understanding how people decided to cast their vote in the 2020 election.

The findings regarding partisanship align with the rival candidates' rhetoric. That is, we expect people's partisan attachment to influence preferences for convenience voting. In particular, we expect Republicans to be significantly less likely than others to utilize convenience voting. Furthermore, we expect these party differences to be most dramatic for mail voting. The results in Table 7.2 support our expectation for mail voting. Estimating the marginal means, Republicans have only a .42 probability of voting by mail, while Democrats have a .53 probability of voting by mail.[35] When we compare Republicans with independents, we find a similar relationship: Republicans have a .43 probability of voting by mail, compared to a .52 probability for independents. When looking at the early voting model, we see no partisan differences: Democrats, Republicans, and independent voters do not significantly differ in their preferences for in-person voting.[36]

Beyond partisan differences, we expect people with higher levels of political knowledge to be more likely to engage in convenience voting. Political knowledge is a resource that makes it easier to navigate convenience voting, such as how to request a mail ballot or how to find

---

[35] When estimating the marginal means in the mail voting model, the continuous predictors are fixed at the following values: confidence in elections = 3.1; worries about COVID-19 = .20; authoritarianism = 2.2; conflict avoidance = 14.6; conspiracy thinking = 17.1; hostile sexism = 9.3; racial resentment = 12.5; political knowledge = 2.6; age = 51.8; education = 3.6; income = 4.8; mail index = .57.

[36] Since partisan media outlets were emphasizing different modes of voting highly correlated with the messages disseminated by the Democratic and Republican nominees, we examined whether people's partisan news diet affected people's likelihood of using convenience voting. In both models in Table 7.2, partisan news diet fails to significantly influence mode of voting.

the locations and hours for early voting sites. The results in Table 7.2 indicate that a person's level of political knowledge powerfully increases the likelihood of engaging in both types of convenience voting. In the early voting model, the odds ratio of 1.24 indicates that for every one-unit increase on the political knowledge index, the odds of voting early increase by 24 percent. A similar impact for political knowledge is evident in the mail voting model where every one-unit increase in political knowledge increases the odds of voting by mail by 19 percent.

People's demographic characteristics also influence preferences for convenience voting. We find that as people age they are much more likely to vote by mail and to vote early. In particular, for every one-year increase in age, the odds of voting by mail increase by 4 percent and the odds of voting early increase by 3 percent, compared to voting on Election Day. We also find that women are significantly more likely than men to vote early, compared to voting on Election Day.[37] More specifically, relying on the coefficients from Table 7.2 and estimating the marginal means, we find that men have a .35 probability of voting early while women have a .46 probability of voting early, all other things being equal.[38]

Education and income are less consistently related to convenience voting. Education is strongly and positively related to the probability of voting by mail, but there is no relationship between education and voting early. Also, there is no relationship between income and voting early; more surprisingly, there is a negative relationship between income and the probability of casting a vote by mail. Perhaps because wealthier individuals have more resources at their disposal, it is easier for these individuals to vote on Election Day compared to people with less income who may face constraints, such as the inability to leave work to vote or the lack of transportation to the polls.

Turning to race and ethnicity, we find some support for our expectations. First, Black citizens are significantly more likely than other respondents to prefer to vote early as compared to voting on Election Day.[39]

---

[37] The coefficient for gender in the mail voting model is positive but does not reach statistical significance.

[38] When estimating the marginal means in the in-person voting model, the continuous predictors are fixed at the following values: confidence in elections = 2.9; worries about COVID-19 = .04; authoritarianism = 2.2; conflict avoidance = 14.1; conspiracy thinking = 18.1; hostile sexism = 9.5; racial resentment = 3.2; political knowledge = 2.5; age = 49.3; education = 3.5; income = 4.7; early voting index = −.11.

[39] The coefficient for white respondents is insignificant indicating that whites and non-Black minorities do not differ in their preference for voting early or on Election Day, controlling for rival explanations.

Relying on the coefficients from Table 7.2 and estimating the marginal means, we find Black respondents have a .51 probability of voting early while non-Black respondents have only a .31 probability of voting early, holding all things constant. Second, and contrary to the results from previous studies (e.g., Baringer, Herron, and Smith, 2020), we do not find that minority respondents are less likely to utilize mail voting in the 2020 election.

Finally, we examine whether people's access to convenience voting in their states influences the likelihood of voting by mail or voting early in person. In the model predicting the likelihood of voting by mail, we find that people living in states that score higher on the mail voting index (i.e., states with more experience with mail voting, states that make it easier to vote by mail) are significantly more likely to choose to vote by mail than to vote on Election Day. With an odds ratio of 1.41, we can say that for every one-unit increase on the mail voting index, the odds of voting by mail increase by 41 percent. We also see that the availability of in-person early voting influences people's likelihood of utilizing mail voting. When early voting is not an option, people are significantly more likely to vote by mail. The estimated marginal mean for voting by mail is .63 in states with no in-person early voting, but it dips to .32 in states where people have the option of voting early. These results suggest that when one form of convenience voting is not accessible, people will try alternative options. Finally, the probability of voting early in person is also affected by statewide policies. In particular, we find that in states with more weeks available for early voting and weekend options, people are significantly more likely to show up and vote before Election Day. Interpreting the odds ratio, for every one-unit increase in the availability of early voting, the odds of voting early increase by 42 percent.[40]

In summary, our results show that the messages disseminated during the campaign produce predictable differences in people's preference for convenience voting. For example, we find that people who are most concerned about the coronavirus pandemic are more likely to vote by mail, while people who are most worried about the integrity of the election are less likely to utilize this form of convenience voting. Further, Republicans followed Trump's advice, staying away from mail voting and voting on

---

[40] We test the impact of the following measures on the likelihood of using convenience voting: (1) the number of polling places by voting age population; (2) changes in the number of polling places per state; (3) the "signature requirement" on mail-in ballots; and (4) the availability of drop boxes. These variables did not achieve statistical significance in the relevant convenience models.

Election Day instead. In addition, people's psychological predispositions produce differences in preferences among the mode of voting, with conspiracy thinking, hostile sexism, and racial resentment being associated with less convenience voting. In contrast, people who dislike conflict demonstrate a strong preference for mail voting, compared to voting on Election Day.

### CONCLUSION AND IMPLICATIONS

The citizen-centered theory of campaigns helps explain who voted in the 2020 election and how they decided to cast their vote (e.g., by mail, on Election Day). That is, psychological predispositions, along with political characteristics, influence people's likelihood of casting a vote in 2020. For instance, we find a strong positive relationship between conflict avoidance and turnout, with people who dislike conflict participating at a much higher rate than people who are more tolerant of conflict. Consistent with previous work, we find that political attitudes, such as civic duty, political knowledge, political attention, and strength of partisanship, are strongly related to people's probability of voting in the election.

The results presented in this chapter also demonstrate the significance of the campaign for understanding the decision to cast a vote in the election. We find that people who watched the September presidential debate, people who have higher levels of confidence in the election results, and people who have extreme views of the social justice movement are significantly more likely to vote in the general election. In addition, the perceived negativity of the campaign alters people's decision to turn out as does people's polarized views of the candidates. These findings show that campaign messages shape turnout, even in the face of stiff control variables identified by the vast turnout literature.

Applying the citizen-centered theory of campaigns to decisions about how to vote in the 2020 election also advances our understanding of convenience voting. People who are more sympathetic to Trump (i.e., Republicans, people with more racist and sexist views) are more likely to heed Trump's message of forgoing mail voting and going to the polls on Election Day. In addition, people who are prone to believe in conspiracies appear more likely to believe Trump's conspiracy theory about the "massive fraud" associated with convenience voting and are significantly more likely to vote on November 3. Further, people who dislike conflict are significantly more likely to rely on mail voting, suggesting that the increase in the availability of mail voting in 2020 may have mobilized a set of people who may otherwise stay home on Election Day. Finally, issues dominating the campaign also alter people's decisions regarding the use of convenience voting. In particular, people who are more concerned about the COVID-19 pandemic and people with more confidence in the integrity of the election are more likely to vote by mail than in person on Election Day.

The findings in this chapter suggest that Trump's strategy of questioning the integrity of the 2020 presidential election may have discouraged some of his supporters from going to the polls. While results from the Census Bureau's Current Population Survey show that 2020's voting spiked among white adults without a college degree (Frey, 2021), a group that supported Donald Trump, this group of voters may have achieved even higher turnout rates if they (and other voters) had not been dissuaded by claims about a rigged election. As we discussed earlier, our results indicate that for every one-point decrease in confidence in the election, the odds of voting decrease by more than 42 percent. In other words, Trump's rhetoric challenging the integrity of the election may have cost him votes at the ballot box.

Trump's rhetoric regarding the fraud associated with mail voting may have cost him votes in another way. In particular, discouraging his supporters from voting by mail may have diminished their participation. For example, in the November wave of our survey, we ask people who did not vote "What was the main reason you did not vote?" More than 20 percent of the respondents mention reasons associated with voting on Election Day, especially when compared to mail voting (e.g., bad weather, too busy, out of town, lines too long, did not know where to vote, ill). Specifically, among respondents indicating a preference for Trump, 55 percent mention obstacles associated with in-person voting, like lack of transportation, weather, and long lines. In contrast, among people who did not vote and express a preference for Biden, only 36 percent mention reasons associated with in-person voting. While the number of nonvoting respondents is small, these patterns suggest that by discouraging mail voting, Trump may have hindered his own candidacy.

Since the completion of the 2020 election, a number of states have begun to pass legislation making it more difficult to vote. The vast majority of the state legislation is aiming in one way or another to limit different aspects of convenience voting (e.g., Brennan Center, 2021; Corasaniti and Epstein, 2021). Our analysis comports with a long history of scholarly work showing that erecting complex hurdles for citizens to jump over to cast ballots will limit turnout (e.g., Rosenstone and Wolfinger, 1978). We find that when voting is more accessible, for example, by increasing the number of days of early voting or making it easier to receive a mail ballot, people are significantly more likely to vote and utilize convenient modes of voting. Therefore, the wave of new restrictive voting laws across a wide swath of states is likely to discourage participation in future elections. Reducing participation in elections is problematic since turnout remains a key linchpin for maintaining a representative democracy where citizens feel empowered and government is held accountable. We turn now to our final chapter where we review the key findings supporting the citizen-centered theory of campaigns, offer suggestions on how to study future campaigns, focus on candidate strategies that altered the outcome of the campaign, and discuss challenges that may impinge the functioning of US elections and representative democracy.

# 8

# How Campaign 2020 Matters

The study of whether campaigns matter has preoccupied researchers for more than eighty years, since the first systematic study of campaigns in the 1940 presidential election (Lazarsfeld, Berelson, and Gaudet, 1948). We have shown in the preceding pages how the campaign between Republican Donald Trump and Democrat Joe Biden mattered a great deal in 2020. Because of the wide swath of information available, constantly updated, and continuously disseminated during contemporary campaigns, citizens take an active role in deciding what information they want to acquire and digest and what information they want to ignore or refute. Furthermore, and central to the citizen-centered theory of campaigns, citizens' preexisting values and beliefs drive how they search and assimilate information consistent with their preexisting attitudes. While we have known for decades that people's partisan proclivities influence how components of campaigns are interpreted, we demonstrate the importance of incorporating psychological predispositions into the mix. By looking at both psychological and political characteristics of citizens, we improve our understanding of how people evaluate the major events and issues of campaigns.

In addition, we show that people's assessments of the important issues and events of the campaign influence their views of the candidates as well as produce important changes in their evaluations of the presidential rivals over the course of the campaign. Finally, we connect people's assessments of elements of the campaign with changes in vote preferences from September to Election Day. In other words, we show that campaigns matter, powerfully influencing people's views of the candidates and their vote choice. We also demonstrate that components of the campaign alter people's likelihood of voting in the election as well as influence people's preference for convenience voting versus voting on Election Day.

In our survey panel, a large and representative sample of about 4,500 respondents were interviewed in September, October, and immediately after Election Day in November. The timing of this study provides us with strong analytical leverage to explore how the key events of the campaign influence citizens' attitudes and behavior at various times during the election. Our research shows that four issues and events of the 2020 election affected voters' attitudes and actions. Since elections in a representative democracy are the mechanism whereby citizens hold their leaders accountable for their governing actions, the fact that the 2020 presidential election "mattered" strengthens the legitimacy of elections during these precarious times.

We began our exploration by examining the impact of the first general election debate. We show that people's psychological predispositions, along with partisanship, attention to the news, and partisan news diet, influence their impressions of the candidates' performance in the debate. For example, people who are more likely to engage in conspiracy thinking, people who score higher on the racial resentment scale, and people who are more tolerant of conflict are significantly more likely to view Trump as the winner of the September debate. In addition, we find that assessments of who won the debate are linked to significant changes in people's overall evaluations of the candidates from September to October. Further, evaluations of the candidates' performance in the first presidential debate are persistent, powerfully influencing changes in views of the candidates until Election Day. Perhaps most importantly, people's assessments of the September debate produce changes in vote intention from September to November.

We turn next to a second significant event in the 2020 electoral campaign: Donald Trump's COVID-19 diagnosis in early October, days after the first presidential debate. We began by showing that people's concerns about the COVID-19 crisis are driven by their political and psychological characteristics. Democrats, people who pay more attention to the news, and people who seek out left-leaning news sources are more worried about the coronavirus. In addition, people high in authoritarianism are more concerned about the pandemic over time, supporting an established finding that individuals engaging in authoritarian thinking express more worries about getting sick and dying. In addition, level of conflict avoidance, racial attitudes, and attitudes toward women each significantly influence people's concern about the coronavirus pandemic.

Trump contracted COVID-19 in the days between the September and October wave of our panel survey, allowing us to measure how his diagnosis primed people's worries about the coronavirus. We find that people's concern about COVID-19 increases significantly after Trump contracted the virus and people weighed COVID-19 assessments when evaluating Trump's performance more heavily after he was infected with the virus. Finally, people's concern about the pandemic produces positive changes in overall views of Biden, while leading to significantly more negative impressions of Trump over the length of the campaign.

We also examined people's changing views of race and policing across the campaign and find that psychological predispositions, like conspiracy thinking, authoritarianism, and level of racial resentment, alter views about issues and assessments related to police brutality. For example, level of authoritarianism and racial resentment produce more support for police. And people high in conspiracy thinking become more supportive of social justice protests over the months of the campaign while people intolerant of conflict become less supportive. Finally, attitudes toward the social justice movement alter evaluations of Biden and Trump in November and produce significant changes in vote preferences from September to November.

Next, we looked at people's confidence in the integrity of the election. We show that candidate preference, partisan media usage, and level of conspiracy thinking each influence confidence in the integrity of the election. Views about the integrity of the election are also linked to increases in positive evaluations of Biden from September to October and lead to more critical assessments of Trump. Finally, people's confidence in the integrity of the election produces changes in overall evaluations of the candidates from September to November, with people with more confidence in the security of the election becoming significantly more favorable toward Biden and more negative toward Trump.

We develop a comprehensive model of comparative evaluations of the candidates where we examine how views about the first presidential debate, worries about COVID-19, views about election integrity, and support for the social justice movement and support for police influence views of Trump and Biden in November. We also include additional factors known to be consequential, such as partisanship, views about the economy, and trait assessments of the candidates. We find that each of these elements of the campaign powerfully influences overall evaluations of the candidates in November. In addition, these campaign issues and events produce meaningful changes in views of the candidates from

September to November. In our most conservative test, we find some aspects of the campaign (i.e., views of the debate, support for social justice protests) are associated with significant alterations in people's vote choice from September to November.

Finally, we apply the citizen-centered theory of campaign to the question of "who votes." In the 2020 election, we find that people who are more conflict avoidant are significantly more likely to vote. Further, we find ample evidence that aspects of the campaign influence the likelihood of voting. Watching the first presidential debate, confidence in the integrity of the election, and polarized views of the social justice movement all significantly increase the probability of voting in the 2020 presidential election. In addition, differences in views of the presidential candidates and the perceived negativity of the campaign alter people's decision to turnout.

We also examine the mechanism people utilized to cast their vote in the election. We find people's psychological predispositions are consistently tied to preferences for mail voting versus voting on Election Day. In particular, people who engage in conspiracy thinking and people who score higher on the racism and sexism scales are significantly less likely to vote by mail compared to on Election Day. In contrast, mail voting is significantly higher for people intolerant of conflict, providing these citizens with a nonconfrontational way to exercise their right to vote. We find a similar relationship between conspiracy thinking and hostile sexism scores, on the one hand, and people's likelihood of voting early compared to on Election Day. As conspiracy thinking and hostile sexism increase, people are significantly less likely to rely on early in-person voting to cast a ballot. Campaign issues and messages also influence convenience voting. For example, Democrats and independents are significantly more likely than Republicans to vote by mail when compared to on Election Day. Further, people who are more concerned about COVID-19 and are more confident about the integrity of the election prefer voting by mail.

## SUMMARIZING THE IMPORTANCE OF PSYCHOLOGICAL PREDISPOSITIONS

When we presented the citizen-centered theory of campaigns in Chapter 1, we theorized that people's psychological predispositions will influence how people acquire and interpret information, thereby influencing assessments of the campaign events and issues. In Table 8.1, we summarize the impact of the psychological predispositions on each of the

TABLE 8.1 *Impact of psychological predispositions on assessments of campaign events and issues*

| | \multicolumn{6}{c}{Psychological predispositions} |
| | Authoritarianism | Conflict avoidance | Conspiracy thinking | Hostile sexism | Racial resentment |
|---|---|---|---|---|---|
| Campaign events/issues | | | | | |
| *Debate performance*[1] | | | | | |
| Trump | −.03 | −.18** −.17 | .07** .15 | .04 .03 | .16** .22 |
| Biden | .10 | −.01 −.01 | .03** .07 | −.06* −.06 | −.09** −.15 |
| Debate winner | −.01 | .03** .10 | −.013** −.10 | −.01 −.01 | −.04** −.20 |
| COVID worry | .14** | .04** .09 | −.01 −.01 | −.07** −.12 | −.04** −.11 |
| Support protests | −.01 | .04* .04 | .025** .06 | −.16** −.14 | −.26** −.39 |
| Support police | .14** | −.05** −.08 | −.014** −.06 | .02* .03 | .14** .35 |
| Confidence in election | .003 | .005 .02 | −.010** −.09 | −.015* −.05 | −.007 −.04 |
| *Turnout*[2] | .06 | .14*** 1.15 | .01 1.01 | −.08 .93 | −.02 .98 |
| Mail voting | .05 | .11*** 1.12 | −.03** .97 | −.06* .94 | −.07** .94 |
| Early voting | −.05 | .01 1.01 | −.02** .98 | −.15*** .86 | −.01 .99 |

[1] Cell entries represent the unstandardized coefficients, followed by standardized coefficients (along with statistical significance) from earlier analyses (i.e., Table 2.1, Table 2.2, Table 3.1, Table 4.1, Table 4.2, Table 5.1).

[2] Cell entries represent the multilevel logit parameter estimates, followed by the odds ratios (along with statistical significance) from earlier analyses (i.e., Table 7.1, Table 7.2).

\* $p < .10$
\*\* $p < .05$
\*\*\* $p < .01$

events and issues explored in the preceding chapters.[1] We see that each of the five psychological predispositions significantly influences between two (authoritarianism) and eight (conspiracy thinking) of the ten dependent variables displayed in Table 8.1.

The compilation of our findings shows that the impact of psychological predispositions depends on the campaign event or campaign issue. For example, conspiracy thinking produces *less* confidence in the integrity of the election and *more* support for protests against police brutality and leads people to rely *less* heavily on convenience voting. For conflict avoidance, we find that people high in conflict avoidance develop *more* negative views of Trump's debate performance, are *more* likely to be worried about COVID-19, are *less* supportive of police, and are *more* likely to vote by mail than on Election Day.

These psychological factors do not simply reinforce partisan proclivities. These predispositions offer important and unique explanatory power, enhancing our understanding of how people understand and evaluate presidential campaigns. By including psychological predispositions when predicting assessments of events and issues, we build a more comprehensive and accurate model of what is happening during presidential campaigns. To illustrate, we can replicate the model predicting ratings of Trump's performance in the first debate (see Table 2.1) but exclude the psychological predispositions from the model. As one would expect, the variance explained by the reduced model is .37, significantly lower than the $R^2$ of .46 in the complete model in Table 2.1. Furthermore, the reduced model inflates the impact of partisan news attention (i.e., an unstandardized coefficient of −1.03 in the reduced model, compared to −.69 in the complete model). The impact of party identification is larger in the reduced model as well (i.e., an unstandardized coefficient of .57 in the reduced mode, compared to .44 in the complete model).

Another example, modeling people's support for social justice protests, is also informative. When we remove the psychological predictions from the model presented in the first column of Table 4.1, we find that the unstandardized regression coefficient measuring the impact of partisan news attention more than triples in size from .27 in the complete model to .78 in the reduced model.[2] The unstandardized coefficient for

---

[1] In Table 8.1, we compile the parameter estimates presented in several of the analyses presented in earlier chapters.
[2] The $R^2$ is .54 in the complete model presented in Table 4.1 and .37 for the reduced model.

party identification also increases from −.31 (as seen in Table 4.1) to −.53 in the model without psychological predispositions. These important changes suggest that by excluding psychological predispositions, we present a less comprehensive and less accurate explanation of people's attitudes toward racial justice.

We find ample evidence that campaign events and issues significantly alter how people view the candidates over the course of the 2020 campaign. However, the 2020 election was unique; it was conducted during a deadly pandemic and the incumbent president contracted the virus and was hospitalized while downplaying the seriousness of the COVID-19 outbreak. Further, in the months before the election, the country was rocked by police violence, leading to thousands of protests for racial justice in the streets of big cities and small towns across the country. Finally, the incumbent president repeatedly raised doubts about the integrity of the election and specifically questioned the legitimacy of voting by mail, an option available for nearly 75 percent of Americans in 2020.[3]

While the 2020 election was certainly distinctive in a number of ways, some aspects of the campaign may have worked to suppress "campaign effects." For instance, the electorate has become increasingly polarized and the campaign rhetoric from both sides often reinforces the division between the two parties. In such a polarized environment, we might not expect the campaign to matter as much, with events and issues falling on deaf ears. However, we demonstrate that people are not only polarized by party but they are divided in terms of their attitudes toward race and gender, their tolerance for conflict, their level of authoritarianism, and their tendency to think in terms of conspiracies, and these attitudes shape how people interpret the campaign events and competing candidates.

Since psychological predispositions are not necessarily aligned with party, campaign information can become a powerful agent for changing people's beliefs. For example, we know that support for police is significantly affected by each of the five psychological predispositions, as well as party identification and partisan news attention. Some of these predispositions will reinforce party preferences (e.g., authoritarianism, racial resentment), leading to more favorable views of police. However, levels of conspiracy thinking, weakly related to partisanship,

---

[3] www.nytimes.com/interactive/2020/08/11/us/politics/vote-by-mail-us-states.html

produce less favorable views of police.[4] In addition, conflict avoidance, which is not correlated with partisanship, generates significantly more negative evaluations of policing. In other words, our findings suggest that partisan proclivities compete with psychological characteristics. And paying attention to both sets of factors will improve our understanding of how people interpret and evaluate issues and events during campaigns.

## STUDYING FUTURE CAMPAIGNS

In the 2020 presidential campaign, the nature of candidates and the context of the election privileged certain specific psychological predispositions of citizens over others. However, not all elections will highlight the same configuration of psychological predispositions. A different pair of presidential candidates and a different political landscape (e.g., no pandemic, no candidate questioning the integrity of the election) will likely favor alternative psychological predispositions.

During the contest between Trump and Biden, hostile sexism played a significant and consistent role in explaining people's views of campaign events and issues. For example, we find that people high in hostile sexism are less worried about COVID-19 and have less confidence in the integrity of the US electoral system. We also see that people with low levels of hostile sexism evaluate Biden's debate performance more favorably, view the social justice movement more positively, and develop more negative impressions of police.

As we discussed in Chapter 1, hostile sexism is based on the belief that men are more competent than women; therefore, they are more deserving of power and status (Glick and Fiske, 1996). Further, these beliefs are also associated with a fear that women use their sexuality or their feminist ideology to take power away from men (Becker and Wright, 2011). As Glick (2019: 716) points out when discussing the 2016 election, Trump predominantly communicated a hostile sexist view toward women by "commenting negatively on their appearance, bragging on tape about sexually assaulting women, encouraging 'lock her up' chants at rallies."

The theory of ambivalent sexism identified by Glick and Fiske (1996) includes two dimensions: hostile sexism and benevolent

---

[4] See Table 1.1 for correlations between party identification and the five psychological predispositions.

sexism. Benevolent sexism is associated with protective paternalism (e.g., women need to be protected by men) and complementary gender differentiation (e.g., women are better than men in certain areas). The "positive" view of women implied by benevolent sexism is contingent on women behaving in a stereotypically consistent fashion and is denied to nonconforming women such as feminists (Becker and Wright, 2011). We expect that the particular relevance of hostile sexism and benevolent sexism will vary depending on the electoral context and candidates.

As an illustration, if the 2028 presidential election features Republican Nikki Haley against Democrat Kamala Harris, hostile sexism may play a less pivotal role and benevolent sexism may be more consequential. In such an electoral setting, it is unlikely either general election candidate will make disparaging comments about women or make explicitly sexist remarks or engage in sexually harassing behaviors. Therefore, hostile sexism may not be primed during the campaign. And benevolent sexism may potentially be more significant, especially if Kamala Harris is more likely than Nikki Haley to call herself a feminist and to act in ways that counter common gender stereotypes. In other words, the specific electoral context, altered by the competing candidates, along with the pressing issues of the day, will influence which psychological predispositions are most important for understanding how people process campaign information and how people make decisions about the candidates.

We argued that the electoral context of 2020 highlighted the psychological predispositions of authoritarianism, conspiracy thinking, racism, sexism, and intolerance of conflict. However, these five characteristics do not represent an exhaustive list. Cognitive and personality psychologists have shown that people can differ on a great number of dimensions, including need for cognition (Cacioppo and Petty, 1982), social dominance orientation (Pratto et al., 1994), intolerance of uncertainty (Freeston et al., 1994), and need for affect (Maio and Esses, 2001), to name a few. For example, examining individual differences in people's "need for affect" may help us understand how citizens process campaign messages. According to Maio and Esses (2001), there are systematic differences in people's motivation to seek out emotional stimuli. In other words, certain people prefer to experience emotions more than others. In their research, Maio and Esses find that "need for affect" predicts attitude extremity and they explain that people with a high need for affect may be more inclined to adopt extreme attitudes toward controversial issues because such attitudes may lead to more emotional experiences. Further, people with a greater need for affect may be more likely to react to hyperbolic campaign rhetoric and may prefer political advertisements seeking to arouse emotional reactions. Examining individual differences in need for affect may help explain the effectiveness of campaign messages for different types of citizens.

Overall, we think political psychologists and political scientists need to continue to integrate the advances from psychology into the study of political campaigns. Citizens are people, so understanding how people's psychological predispositions alter how they interpret messages and how these messages influence their attitudes will continue to improve our understanding of campaigns. All the while, these investigations need to consider people's long-standing party attachments, their views of the salient issues of the day, their preexisting views of the candidates, and their consumption of partisan and nonpartisan information. In other words, we are calling for a broader set of explanations to explain people's reactions to complex campaign contests.

### POSTMORTEM ANALYSIS OF THE 2020 PRESIDENTIAL ELECTION

It is easy after the votes are counted to conclude that the losing candidate made some strategic errors during the campaign. Nevertheless, the results reported in the preceding chapters indicate that Donald Trump made a number of mistakes during his campaign. First, our analysis suggests that the first debate hurt evaluations of Trump and these negative impressions lasted until Election Day. Trump's first error was foregoing the second debate because he did not want to take part in a virtual debate with modified rules. In actuality, he needed a second debate desperately to offset his failures in the first debate. His overly aggressive behavior in the first debate could have been offset with a more balanced performance in the planned second debate on October 15, 2020. However, with Trump declining to participate in the second debate, the negative reaction to the first debate became solidified in people's minds, with the final debate taking place more than three weeks (October 22, 2020) after the disastrous first debate. If Trump and Biden had debated on October 15 as originally planned, and if the candidates' performances were more even, we do not think the negative consequences of the first debate would have been as long-lasting.

Second, Trump's approach to the COVID-19 pandemic was to "play it down" and he refused to take precautions advocated by his own health experts (e.g., he held large rallies, he did not routinely wear a mask). So, when he contracted the virus, people became more concerned about the pandemic and subsequently developed more negative impressions of Trump and more positive views of Biden. If Trump's approach to the pandemic had been different (e.g., acknowledging the danger of COVID-19, closely following COVID-19 protocols), when he was sickened by the virus, citizens may have rallied around him. They may have become more sympathetic toward Trump, perhaps developing more positive impressions of the incumbent president.

Third, Trump's relentless rhetoric questioning the legitimacy of the election, and his assault of mail voting, in particular, may have cost him votes in this competitive election. First, confidence in the integrity of the election produced significantly more positive views of Biden and was linked to more critical views of Trump over the months of the fall campaign. Second, and more significantly, people who believed the electoral system was secure were significantly more likely to vote in the 2020 election. Therefore, by attacking the integrity of the election, Trump inadvertently depressed turnout. Third, he clearly pushed his copartisans and supporters away from mail voting. While many of these supporters voted on Election Day, notwithstanding the typical struggles associated with casting a ballot on that day (e.g., locating where to vote, finding time to vote during a workday, realizing registration is not current at the voting booth, showing up to vote at the wrong location), Trump discouraged the easiest mode of voting and may have inadvertently depressed turnout among his supporters. He worked hard to dissuade people from employing the safest way to vote (i.e., mail) in the midst of worldwide pandemic and then reminded everyone of the risks by contracting the disease himself a few weeks ahead of Election Day.

Finally, Trump's confrontational style during the campaign might have hurt his prospects with certain types of voters. As we have discussed, citizens vary in their preference for conflict, and people who prefer to avoid conflict developed significantly less favorable views of Trump's debate performance and they were much more likely to view Trump as the loser of the September debate. People who dislike conflict were also more worried about COVID-19, and concern about the pandemic produced less favorable views of Trump. In addition, Trump disparaged the racial justice movement while defending police, putting Trump at odds with people sensitive to conflict who viewed the Black Lives Matter movement more favorably and police more negatively. Most importantly, people who dislike conflict were significantly more likely to vote in the 2020 election, and given Trump's behavior and his policy views (e.g., opposition to social justice protests), they were far less likely to cast a vote for Trump.

In the end, some of Trump's strategic choices in the 2020 election probably cost him precious votes. Given Trump's history and personality, maybe these decisions were not up for consideration. That is, his behavior in 2020 was reminiscent of his 2016 campaign and did not differ from his presidential governing style. In other words: "Trump was being Trump." However, given the strong evidence discussed in the preceding chapters, Trump's decisions about how to handle COVID-19, his choice to forgo the virtual debate, his aggressive style, and his questioning of the integrity of the election likely hurt him both in terms of who was mobilized to cast a ballot and how people voted during the fall 2020 campaign.

## THE HEALTH OF US ELECTIONS

Campaigns and elections play a fundamental role in representative democracies in the United States and across the globe. The vast majority of citizens influence the selection of leaders and the direction of public policy through casting ballots for candidates and political parties. This seemingly straightforward act of civic participation is the cornerstone for democratic legitimacy and stability, relying on broad citizen feedback every few years. The implementation of democratic elections has always been a contested process related to who is eligible to vote, how are votes cast, and how are results tallied. This is especially true in the US federal system where founding documents placed the responsibility to execute elections with the states. Since the Hawaii and Alaska became states in the late 1950s, the fifty states have implemented elections in different ways across the last sixty years.

There have been sixteen presidential elections from 1960 to 2020. Remarkably, there has been a smooth transfer of power in fifteen of those elections, whereby the competing candidates have accepted the outcome of the electoral process unfolding in precinct by precinct across the nation. This has been true in even the closest of elections across the time frame where reasonable people could worry about outcomes driven by narrow margins. For example, in 1960, Kennedy defeated Nixon by approximately 100,000 votes out of 68 million ballots cast. In 1968, Nixon defeated Humphrey by 510,000 votes out of 73 million cast. And in 2000, Gore defeated Bush by 543,000 out of 101 million total votes but lost in the Electoral College. The election boiled down to the vote in Florida where Bush won by approximately 537 votes out of 6 million cast. To be sure, Gore contested the Florida vote in state and federal courts asking for recounts in certain Florida counties. But he readily accepted the decision by the US Supreme Court to end the counting, thus declaring Bush the winner in Florida. Gore immediately conceded after the Court ruling.

But the 2020 election was different and the pattern of an easy transition of power was broken. The incumbent president began to sow doubt in the integrity of the election early on in the campaign. He repeatedly claimed during the spring, summer, and fall of the 2020 election that the election was rigged. These claims were false (e.g., Brennan Center for Justice, 2020; Yen, Swenson, and Seitz, 2020). For example, an analysis done by MITRE's nonpartisan National Election Security Lab, looking at presidential election results from Arizona, Florida, Georgia, Michigan, North Carolina, Ohio, Pennsylvania, and Wisconsin, finds "no evidence of fraud, manipulation, or uncorrected error," concluding that the presidential race wasn't "stolen" or fraudulent.[5]

Even though Biden was sworn in on January 20, 2021, as the forty-sixth president of the United States, Trump did not attend the inauguration, conceding the election (without naming Biden as the winner) less than two weeks before Inauguration Day.[6] In the weeks following Election Day, Trump intensified his baseless allegations of election fraud, and these allegations were magnified by allies and conservative-leaning media outlets. His legal team launched dozens of lawsuits in states where Biden's margin of victory was the smallest. However, Trump and his legal team were unable to advance their cases in sixty attempts, including at the US Supreme Court.

We have shown that certain types of people were more likely to question the integrity of the 2020 election: people who intended to vote for Trump, people who believe in conspiracies, people who pay attention to right-leaning news sources. The unsubstantiated claims about

[5] www.mitre.org/sites/default/files/publications/pr-21-0431-data-analytics-to-enhance-election-transparency.pdf
[6] www.cnbc.com/2021/01/07/trump-for-first-time-acknowledges-new-administration-will-take-office-jan-20.html

voter fraud had a multitude of consequences that continue to reverberate today. First, more than six months after the 2020 election and four months after Biden's victory was confirmed by Congress, a survey by Reuters/ Ipsos found that 53 percent of Republicans said Trump is the "true president."[7] And a few months later, a survey by Yahoo News/ YouGov found even more support for the "Big Lie," with 66 percent of Republicans continuing to insist "the election was rigged and stolen from Trump."[8]

Questions about the integrity of the 2020 election persist today. In June 2022, a poll conducted by YouGov found that almost one-third of the respondents believed "a lot" of voter fraud occurred in the 2020 election, with predictable partisan differences. Among Republicans, 61 percent of the respondents said "a lot" of voter fraud, compared to 13 percent of Democrats and 30 percent of independents.[9] A few months later, in August 2022, YouGov asked respondents, "Would you say that Joe Biden legitimately won the 2020 election?" About two-thirds of respondents indicated that Biden legitimately won the election, with about one-third of the sample saying Biden did not legitimately win. While almost all of the Democrats (94 percent) believed Biden won, less than one-third of Republicans (31 percent) and a little less than two-thirds of independents (63 percent) agreed that Biden was elected legitimately.[10]

In our analyses examining the determinants of confidence in the integrity of the election, we show that trust in government is an important corrective to doubts about the accuracy of the voting process. People who are more trustful of government are more confident about the integrity of the election. Unfortunately, according to data compiled by PEW, trust in government is near historic lows. In 1958, when the American National Election Study (ANES) began asking respondents whether they trusted the government in Washington to do what is right "just about always" or "most of the time," almost three-quarters of respondents indicated they trusted the government in Washington (PEW Research Center, 2021). However, this number slowly dipped over the next several decades, and during Obama's presidency, the percentage of people saying they trust

---

[7] www.ipsos.com/sites/default/files/ct/news/documents/2021-05/Ipsos%20Reuters%20Topline%20Write%20up-%20The%20Big%20Lie%20-%2017%20May%20thru%2019%20May%202021.pdf
[8] news.yahoo.com/poll-two-thirds-of-republicans-still-think-the-2020-election-was-rigged-165934695.html
[9] See today.yougov.com/topics/politics/survey-results/daily/2022/06/03/73ca6/2
[10] See docs.cdn.yougov.com/d1ik3gw9iw/econTabReport.pdf

the government in Washington to do the right thing was averaging about 20 percent of the electorate. During Trump's first term, political trust was low, averaging between 17 percent and 21 percent of the electorate. During the first fifteen months of Biden's first term, trust in government continues to be at historically low levels, with 20 percent of respondents saying they trust the government in Washington to do what is right "just about always" or "most of the time."[11]

Through the entire period from 1958 to 2021, trust in government has been higher among members of the party that controls the White House (PEW Research Center, 2021). During Trump's term in office, only 15 percent of Democrats said they trusted the government in Washington compared to 27 percent among Republicans. However, after Biden was sworn in as president, trust dropped among Republicans to 9 percent but rebounded to 36 percent among Democrats.[12] Given low levels of trust in government, trust may not be a potent resource to guard against low confidence in election integrity, especially among Republicans. The blend of distrust of government and skepticism regarding our elections creates an obstacle for the effective functioning of our democratic republic.

Not only did Trump's rhetoric about election fraud produce attitudinal changes among his supporters but his charges about a "stolen election" encouraged some of his supporters to attend the January 6 "Stop the Steal" rally where Trump addressed his supporters on the National Mall and said,

All of us here today do not want to see our election victory stolen by emboldened radical-left Democrats, which is what they're doing. And stolen by the fake news media. That's what they've done and what they're doing. We will never give up; we will never concede. It doesn't happen. You don't concede when there's theft involved…We're going to walk down to the Capitol, and we're going to cheer on our brave senators and congressmen and women, and we're probably not going to be cheering so much for some of them. Because you'll never take back our country with weakness. You have to show strength, and you have to be strong.[13]

---

[11] www.pewresearch.org/politics/2022/06/06/public-trust-in-government-1958-2022/

[12] As Biden approaches the half way mark in his first term, trust among Republicans and independents who lean toward the Republican party remains steady, with 9 percent agreeing that they "trust government to do what is right" "about always" or "most of the time." Among Democrats and independents leaning toward the Democratic party, trust has declined to 29 percent. See www.pewresearch.org/politics/2022/06/06/public-trust-in-government-1958-2022/

[13] www.npr.org/2021/02/10/966396848/read-trumps-jan-6-speech-a-key-part-of-impeachment-trial

Even before Trump ended his speech, thousands of protestors began walking to the US Capitol. As protestors arrived at the Capitol, many became violent, clashing with police, breaching multiple barriers, and storming the Capitol to try to disrupt Congress as they convened to certify the results of the 2020 general election.

The riots at the Capitol caused millions of dollars of damage when rioters kicked doors, smashed windows, and sprayed chemical irritants and fire extinguishers, damaging statues and paintings in the Rotunda, the Crypt, and the National Statuary Hall. Far more tragic, five people died during the violent protests (Healy, 2021). In addition, four police officers took their own lives after defending the US Capitol during the January 6 riot. And more than 140 police officers were injured during the insurrection. Gus Papathanasiou, chairman of the executive board for the US Capitol police, explained shortly after the insurrection, "I have officers who were not issued helmets prior to the attack who have sustained head injuries…One officer has two cracked ribs and two smashed spinal discs, and another was stabbed with a metal fence stake, to name some of the injuries" (Jackman, 2021).

Unsubstantiated assertions about a stolen election have not only lowered confidence in the US electoral system and spurred violence on January 6, allegations of voter fraud have also prompted a number of states to make voting more difficult in an effort to make "voting safer." These laws make voting more difficult in a number of ways such as shortening the window to apply for a mail ballot, shortening the deadline to deliver a mail ballot, making it harder to remain on absentee voting lists, imposing stricter signature requirements for mail ballots, imposing harsher voter identification requirements for mail and in-person voting, expanding voter purges, eliminating Election Day registration, reducing the number and hours of polling places, and limiting early voting days and hours.

While state legislatures justify these new voting restrictions as a way to safeguard voting, the push to increase obstacles to voting is a partisan affair. In particular, nearly 90 percent of the restrictive voting laws have been passed by Republican legislatures and these laws are likely to have a greater impact on minority voters who are less likely to support Republican candidates at the polls.[14] This aggressive push by Republican legislatures to pass new voter restriction bills limiting access to the polls prompted Stacey Abrams, a prominent Democratic activist, to call these

---

[14] www.brennancenter.org/our-work/research-reports/voting-laws-roundup-december-2021

new voting laws a "redux of Jim Crow in a suit and tie."[15] These new voting laws are framed in racially neutral terms, but they have significant racist intent and impact.

Further, legislation aimed at reducing voter fraud is targeting a problem that is largely nonexistent. In fact, the top federal agencies in charge of election security issued a joint statement declaring that the November 3 election was "the most secure in American history" and that there was "no evidence that any voting system deleted or lost votes, changed votes, or was in any way compromised" (Brennan Center for Justice, 2020). Similarly, a group of *New York Times* reporters called election officials representing both parties in every state after the 2020 election; these officials said there was no evidence that fraud or other irregularities played a role in the outcome of the presidential race (Corasaniti, Epstein, and Rutenberg, 2021).

So, what can we say about the health of the US electoral system? In some ways, we are in a precarious position given people's suspicions about the safety of our elections, political leaders stoking these fears, and people's trust in government at near record lows. These persistent doubts about the integrity of elections is worrisome for the health of the US democratic system. Citizens' confidence in the electoral process is critical "because elections are the link between citizens and their elected officials. If voters do not have faith in this most fundamental aspect of a democratic society – the outcome of elections and the correct counting of votes – then the legitimacy of representative government might be at risk" (Atkeson, 2010: 3). The Commission on Federal Election Reform (2005: 1) noted the importance of voter confidence when explaining "Democracy is endangered when people believe that their votes do not matter or are not counted correctly."

Representative democracy requires equal access to the ballot box, confidence in the integrity of the election, and support for the electoral system regardless of the outcome. The distinguished political theorist Robert Dahl (1997: 468), reflecting on his many works focusing on democracy in the United States, concluded that democracy was resilient even in times of crisis (e.g., wars, economic collapse, partisan and ideological polarization). Dahl stressed this was true as long as citizens believe in democratic institutions, but it is *essential* that elites believe in these institutions. In 2020, the crisis of confidence in democracy was driven by the incumbent

---

[15] www.cnn.com/2021/03/25/opinions/voting-rights-suppression-is-jim-crow-suit-and-tie-hemmer/index.html

president and echoed by Republican elected officials. Trump and his allies purposely tapped into citizens' low levels of trust and amplified conspiracies held by certain elements of the electorate, intentionally escalating fears and worries about the counting of the ballots.

Political elites are in a powerful position because public opinion responds to the messages delivered by these elites (Zaller, 1992). It is essential that candidates who are unsuccessful at the ballot box explain to their supporters that the American citizens have spoken and each American must support and honor the will of the people. The long-standing tradition of the concession speech in US presidential elections serves an important function, encouraging the peaceful transfer of power by showing supporters that the losing candidate is accepting the results of a free and fair election. After the contested 2000 election between Democrat Al Gore and Republican George W. Bush, Gore conceded after the Supreme Court's ruling in Gore *v.* Bush to end the recount, saying,

Just moments ago, I spoke with George W. Bush and congratulated him on becoming the 43rd president of the United States…I say to President-elect Bush that what remains of partisan rancor must now be put aside, and may God bless his stewardship of this country…For the sake of our unity as a people and the strength of our democracy, I offer my concession…History gives us many examples of contests as hotly debated and as fiercely fought, with their own challenges to the popular will. Other disputes have dragged on for weeks before reaching resolution, and each time, both the victor and the vanquished have accepted the result peacefully and in a spirit of reconciliation. So let it be with us."[16]

In difficult times, after bitter and fiercely contested elections, the public turns to their political leaders to support the outcome of the election; this process helps ensure the peaceful transfer of power, a fragile hallmark of the US democratic republic for more than 200 years.

---

[16] www.washingtonpost.com/history/2020/11/08/presidential-concession-speech-history-trump-gore/
  The survey questions were included in each wave of the survey unless otherwise indicated.

# APPENDIX

# Survey Questionnaire*

Thinking about the United States as a whole, what do you think is the most important problem facing the country today?

Economy
Gap between rich and poor
Race relations/Racism
Unifying the country
Crime/Violence
Healthcare
Coronavirus
Ethics and moral decline
Police brutality
The news media
Immigration
Climate change
Gun control
Election integrity/Obstacles to voting
Other _____

Some people don't pay much attention to political campaigns. How about you? Would you say that you are very much interested, somewhat interested, or not much interested in political campaigns?

Not much interested
Somewhat interested
Very much interested

---

* The survey questions were included in each wave of the survey unless otherwise indicated.

How concerned are you, if at all, about the coronavirus or COVID-19 outbreak?

Extremely concerned
Very concerned
Somewhat concerned
Not very concerned
Not at all concerned

How often do you pay attention to news about politics and government affairs in a typical week?

Every day
A few times a week
About once a week
A few times a month
Less than once a month

If the election was held today, who would you vote for president?

Joe Biden
Donald Trump
Other
Don't know

The following questions assess your views about negative advertisements, in general. Please indicate how much you agree with the following statement:

|  | Agree strongly | Agree somewhat | Disagree somewhat | Disagree strongly |
| --- | --- | --- | --- | --- |
| Some negative advertisements are so nasty that I stop paying attention to what the candidates are saying | | | | |
| Negative advertisements discussing a candidate's personal misbehavior are fair game | | | | |
| Hard-hitting commercials attacking the opponent are not helpful during election campaigns | | | | |
| I find negative political commercials attacking a candidate for conduct occurring long before the candidate entered public life as uninformative | | | | |

Do you approve or disapprove of the way Donald Trump is handling his job as president?

Strongly approve
Somewhat approve
Somewhat disapprove
Strongly disapprove
Don't know

Generally speaking, do you usually think of yourself as a Republican, Democrat, an independent, or what? Where would you place yourself on the following scale?

Strong Democrat
Weak Democrat
Independent, leaning toward the Democratic Party
Independent
Independent, leaning toward the Republican Party
Weak Republican
Strong Republican
Don't know

In 2016, who did you vote for in the presidential election?

Donald Trump
Hillary Clinton
Gary Johnson
Jill Stein
None of the above
Didn't vote in 2016

Thinking about the ongoing presidential campaign, how would you characterize the tone of Donald Trump's campaign thus far (e.g., his campaign advertisements, his speeches, his tweets)? Would you characterize Trump's campaign as very positive, somewhat positive, a mixture of positive and negative, somewhat negative, very negative?

Very positive
Somewhat positive
Mixture of positive and negative
Somewhat negative
Very negative
Don' know

Thinking about the ongoing presidential campaign, how would you characterize the tone of Joe Biden's campaign thus far (e.g., his campaign advertisements, his speeches, his tweets)? Would you characterize Biden's campaign as very positive, somewhat positive, a mixture of positive and negative, somewhat negative, very negative?

Very positive
Somewhat positive
Mixture of positive and negative
Somewhat negative
Very negative
Don't know

Please indicate your degree of agreement or disagreement with the following statements.

|  | Agree strongly | Agree somewhat | Disagree somewhat | Disagree strongly |
| --- | --- | --- | --- | --- |
| I hate arguments | | | | |
| I find conflicts exciting | | | | |
| I feel upset after an argument | | | | |
| I enjoy challenging the opinions of others | | | | |
| Arguments don't bother me | | | | |

Please rate the following political figures on the feeling thermometer. Ratings between 51 degrees and 100 degrees mean that you feel favorable and warm toward the person. Ratings between 0 degrees and 49 degrees mean that you don't feel favorable toward the person and that you don't care too much for that person. You would rate the person at the 50-degree mark if you don't feel particularly warm or cold toward the person. If you come to a person whose name you don't recognize, you don't need to rate that person.

Donald Trump
Joe Biden
Mike Pence
Kamala Harris

Do you approve or disapprove how the police in the United States are doing their job?

Strongly approve
Somewhat approve

Somewhat disapprove
Strongly disapprove
Don't know

Would you support or oppose cutting some funding from police departments in your community and shifting it to social services?

Strongly support
Somewhat support
Somewhat oppose
Strongly oppose
Don't know

Please indicate how likely you will participate in the following activities in the remaining weeks of the campaign

|  | Very likely | Somewhat likely | Somewhat unlikely | Very unlikely |
|---|---|---|---|---|
| Seek out additional information about the political candidates running for office | | | | |
| Attend a campaign rally | | | | |
| Work or volunteer for a political party, candidate, or campaign | | | | |
| Contact an elected official | | | | |
| Contribute money to a candidate running for public office or to a group working to elect a candidate | | | | |
| Attend government meetings (virtually or in person) in your community, such as city or town council meetings | | | | |
| Attend a political protest | | | | |
| Express your opinion about a candidate, elected official or political campaign on Facebook, Twitter, or other social media | | | | |

How much confidence, if any, do you have in each of the following to act in the best interests of the public?

|  | A great deal of confidence | Some confidence | Not too much confidence | No confidence at all | Don't know |
|---|---|---|---|---|---|
| Elected officials | | | | | |
| The news media | | | | | |
| Business leaders | | | | | |
| Police officers | | | | | |

Now thinking about the economy in the country as a whole, would you say that over the past year the nation's economy has gotten better, stayed about the same, or gotten worse?

Much better
Somewhat better
About the same
Somewhat worse
Much worse
Don't know

Do you support or oppose the Black Lives Matter movement?

Strongly support
Somewhat support
Neither support nor oppose
Somewhat oppose
Strongly oppose
Don't know

Thinking about Floyd's death and recent protests. In general, do you approve or disapprove of the recent protests against police violence in response to Floyd's death?

Strongly approve
Somewhat approve
Neither approve nor disapprove
Somewhat disapprove
Strongly disapprove
Don't know

We would like to ask you a few questions about the government in Washington. Many people are too busy to keep up with these topics, so if you don't know the answer, just skip the question. (Please do not look up the answers. We are interested in what you know right now.)
What position or office does Elena Kagan hold today?
Do you happen to know which party has the most members in the US Senate in Washington, DC, today?
Who determines if a federal law is constitutional or not?
Who is currently the US secretary of state?
How long is the term of a US senator?
One way that people talk about politics in the United States is in terms of liberal, conservative, and moderate ideology. The political views people

might hold are often arranged from extremely liberal to extremely conservative. Where would you place yourself on this scale?

Extremely liberal
Liberal
Somewhat liberal
Moderate
Somewhat conservative
Conservative
Very conservative
Don't know

How often can you trust the federal government in Washington to do what is right?

Always
Most of the time
About half the time
Less than half of the time
Never

Are you registered to vote?

Yes
No
Don't know

How likely are you to vote in the upcoming election in November?

Very likely
Somewhat likely
Somewhat unlikely
Very unlikely
Don't know

How confident are you that the results of the 2020 presidential election will be counted accurately?

Very Confident
Somewhat Confident
Not Very Confident
Not Confident at all

On a scale from 0 (0 percent certainty) to 10 (100 percent certainty), please answer the following questions.

I think that many very important things happen in the world which the public is never informed about.
I think that politicians usually do not tell us the true motives for their decisions.
I think that government agencies closely monitor all citizens.
I think that events superficially seem to lack a connection are often the result of secret activities.
I think that there are secret organizations that greatly influence political decisions.

Thinking about DONALD TRUMP'S ability to handle a number of things, how confident are you that Donald Trump can do each of the following?

|  | Very confident | Somewhat confident | Not too confident | Not at all confident | Don't know |
|---|---|---|---|---|---|
| Handle the public health impact of the coronavirus outbreak | | | | | |
| Make good decisions about foreign policy | | | | | |
| Make good decisions about economic policy | | | | | |
| Effectively handle race relations | | | | | |
| Effectively handle issues surrounding law enforcement | | | | | |
| Bring the country together | | | | | |
| Ensure the integrity of US elections | | | | | |

Thinking about JOE BIDEN'S ability to handle a number of things, how confident are you that Joe Biden can do each of the following?

|  | Very confident | Somewhat confident | Not too confident | Not at all confident | Don't know |
|---|---|---|---|---|---|
| Handle the public health impact of the coronavirus outbreak | | | | | |
| Make good decisions about foreign policy | | | | | |
| Make good decisions about economic policy | | | | | |

|  | Very confident | Somewhat confident | Not too confident | Not at all confident | Don't know |
|---|---|---|---|---|---|
| Effectively handle race relations | | | | | |
| Effectively handle issues surrounding law enforcement | | | | | |
| Bring the country together | | | | | |
| Ensure the integrity of US elections | | | | | |

Although there are a number of qualities that people feel that children should have, every person thinks that some are more important than others. Read the following pairs of desirable qualities. Please indicate which one is more important for a child to have.

Respect for Elders or Independence
Respect for Elders
Independence

Obedience or Self-Reliance
Obedience
Self-Reliance

Curiosity or Good manners
Curiosity
Good manners

Being Considerate or Well-Behaved
Being considerate
Being well-behaved

Different people feel differently about voting. For some, voting is a choice – they feel free to vote or not to vote, depending on how they feel about the candidates and parties. For others voting is a duty – they feel they should vote in every election no matter how they feel about the candidates and parties. Which of the following comes closest to your view?

Very strongly feel voting is a duty
Somewhat feel voting is a duty
Neither feel voting is a duty nor a choice
Somewhat feel voting is a choice

Very strongly feel voting is a choice

How well does each of the following describe DONALD TRUMP?

|  | Very well | Fairly well | Not too well | Not well at all | Don't know |
|---|---|---|---|---|---|
| Strong leader | | | | | |
| Cares about people | | | | | |
| Good sense of humor | | | | | |
| Honest | | | | | |
| Hardworking | | | | | |
| Even-Tempered | | | | | |

How well does each of the following describe JOE BIDEN?

|  | Very well | Fairly well | Not too well | Not well at all | Don't Know |
|---|---|---|---|---|---|
| Strong leader | | | | | |
| Cares about people | | | | | |
| Good Sense of humor | | | | | |
| Honest | | | | | |
| Hardworking | | | | | |
| Even-Tempered | | | | | |

How many times have you seen political ads on the following platforms?

|  | Never | Seldom | Sometimes | Often | Don't use this platform |
|---|---|---|---|---|---|
| Facebook | | | | | |
| Twitter | | | | | |
| Snapchat | | | | | |
| Instagram | | | | | |
| Cable News | | | | | |
| Broadcast News | | | | | |
| YouTube | | | | | |
| Video Streaming Services (e.g., Hulu, Sling) | | | | | |

Please indicate how much you agree with the following statements.

Many women are actually seeking special favors, such as hiring policies that favor them over men, under the guise of asking for "equality."

Strongly agree
Somewhat agree

Somewhat disagree
Strongly disagree

Feminists are not seeking for women to have more power than men.
Strongly agree
Somewhat agree
Somewhat disagree
Strongly disagree

Most women interpret innocent remarks or acts as being sexist.
Strongly agree
Somewhat agree
Somewhat disagree
Strongly disagree

Feminists are making entirely reasonable demands of men.
Strongly agree
Somewhat agree
Somewhat disagree
Strongly disagree

For the following statements, indicate whether you agree strongly, agree somewhat, neither agree nor disagree, disagree somewhat, or disagree strongly with this statement.

Irish, Italians, Jewish, and many other minorities overcame prejudice and worked their way up. Blacks should do the same without any special favors.
Agree strongly
Agree somewhat
Neither agree nor disagree
Disagree somewhat
Disagree strongly

Generations of slavery and discrimination have created conditions that make it difficult for Blacks to work their way out of the lower class.
Agree strongly
Agree somewhat
Neither agree nor disagree
Disagree somewhat
Disagree strongly

Over the past few years, Blacks have gotten less than they deserve.

Agree strongly
Agree somewhat
Neither agree nor disagree
Disagree somewhat
Disagree strongly

It's really a matter of some people not trying hard enough; if Blacks would only try harder they could be just as well off as whites.

Agree strongly
Agree somewhat
Neither agree nor disagree
Disagree somewhat
Disagree strongly

When it comes to staying up with the news, which of these news sources, if any, do you watch or consume regularly?
Broadcast network news, such as NBC, ABC, or CBS

Facebook
Twitter
MSNBC
CNN
Fox News
Other conservative news outlets, blogs, or websites
Other progressive or liberal news outlets, blogs, or websites
Other
Don't pay attention to news

Finally, we would like to ask you some questions about yourself.

What is your age?

What is your gender?
Male
Female
Other

What is the highest degree or level of school you have completed?

Less than high school diploma
High school diploma or GED
Some college, but no degree
Associates degree (e.g., AA, AS)

Bachelor's degree (e.g., BA, BS)
Master's degree (e.g., MA, MS)
Professional degree (e.g., MD, DDS, JD)
Doctorate (e.g., PhD, EdD)

What was your total household income before taxes during the past twelve months?

Less than $25,000
$25,000 to $34,999
$35,000 to $49,999
$50,000 to $74,999
$75,000 to $99,999
$100,000 to $149,999
$150,000 to $199,999
$200,000 or more

What is your present religion, if any?

Protestant (e.g., Baptist, Methodist, Lutheran, Pentecostal, Presbyterian, Anglican/Episcopal)
Roman Catholic
Latter-day Saints/ Mormon
Orthodox (i.e., Greek or Russian Orthodox)
Jewish
Muslim
Buddhist
Hindu
Atheist
Agnostic
Another religion, please specify _____

Now think of your own background in racial and ethnic terms. How would you describe your race and ethnicity?

African American
White
Hispanic or Latino
Asian
Native American or American Indian
Other

What is your state of residence?

# References

Abramowitz, Alan I., and Kyle L. Saunders. 2008. Is polarization a myth? *The Journal of Politics*, 70(2): 542–555.
Abramowitz, Alan I., and Walter J. Stone. 2006. The Bush effect: Polarization, turnout, and activism in the 2004 presidential election. *Presidential Studies Quarterly*, 36(2): 141–154.
Abramson, Alana. 2016. How Donald Trump perpetuated the 'Birther' movement for years. *ABC News*. [online]. September 16. abcnews.go.com/Politics/donald-trump-perpetuated-birther-movement-years/story?id=42138176
Aday, Sean. 2010. Chasing the bad news: An analysis of 2005 Iraq and Afghanistan war coverage on NBC and Fox News Channel. *Journal of Communication*, 60(1): 144–164.
Adorno, Theodor. W., Else Frenkel-Brunswik, Daniel Levinson, and Nevitt Sanford. 1950. *The authoritarian personality*. New York: Harper and Row.
Aggarwal, Minali, Jennifer Allen, Alexander Coppock, et al. 2023. A 2 million-person, campaign-wide field experiment shows how digital advertising affects voter turnout. *Nature Human Behaviour*, 7(3): 1–10.
Algara, Carlos, Sharif Amlani, Samuel Collitt, Isaac Hale, and Sara Kazemian. 2022. Nail in the coffin or lifeline? Evaluating the electoral impact of COVID-19 on President Trump in the 2020 election. *Political Behavior*, 1–29. doi.org/10.1007/s11109-022-09826-x
Altemeyer, Bob. 1981. *Right-wing authoritarianism*. Winnipeg: University of Manitoba Press.
Alter, Charlotte. 2020. Inside Joe Biden campaign's plan to get out the vote. *Time Magazine*. [online]. time.com/5906237/inside-joe-biden-campaigns-plan-to-get-out-the-vote-online/
Alvarez, R. Michael. 1998. *Information and elections*. Ann Arbor: University of Michigan Press.
Alvarez, R. Michael, and Garrett Glasgow. 1997. Do voters learn from presidential election campaigns. Social Science Working Paper 1022. [online]. core.ac.uk/download/pdf/216273208.pdf

Alvarez, R. Michael, Thad E. Hall, Ines Levin, and Charles Stewart III. 2011. Voter opinions about election reform: Do they support making voting more convenient? *Election Law Journal*, 10(2): 73–87.

Alvarez, R. Michael, Thad E. Hall, and Morgan Llewellyn. 2008. Are Americans confident their ballots are counted? *The Journal of Politics*, 70(3): 754–766.

Amaya, Ashley, Nick Hatley, and Arnold Lau. 2021. Measuring the risks of panel conditioning in survey research. *PEW Research Center*. [online]. www.pewresearch.org/methods/2021/06/09/measuring-the-risks-of-panel-conditioning-in-survey-research/

Amlani, Sharif, and Samuel Collitt. 2022. The impact of vote-by-mail policy on turnout and vote share in the 2020 election. *Election Law Journal: Rules, Politics, and Policy*, 21(2): 135–149.

Ansolabehere, Stephen, and Shanto Iyengar. 1999. *Going negative: How political advertisements shrink and polarize the electorate*. New York: The Free Press.

Ansolabehere, Stephen, Shanto Iyengar, Adam Simon, and Nicholas Valentino. 1994. Does attack advertising demobilize the electorate? *American Political Science Review*, 88(4): 829–838.

Ansolabehere, Stephen, and Nathaniel Persily. 2007. Vote fraud in the eye of the beholder: The role of public opinion in the challenge to voter identification requirements. *Harvard Law Review*, 121(7): 1737–1774.

Arceneaux, Kevin. 2007. I'm asking for your support: The effects of personally delivered campaign messages on voting decisions and opinion formation. *Quarterly Journal of Political Science*, 2(1): 43–65.

Arceneaux, Kevin. 2010. The benefits of experimental methods for the study of campaign effects. *Political Communication*, 27(2): 199–215.

Arceneaux, Kevin, Timothy B. Gravelle, Mathias Osmundsen, et al. 2021. Some people just want to watch the world burn: The prevalence, psychology, and politics of the "Need for Chaos." *Philosophical Transactions of the Royal Society B*, 376(1822): 20200147.

Arceneaux, Kevin, and Martin Johnson. 2013. *Changing minds or changing channels? Partisan news in an age of choice*. Chicago: University of Chicago Press.

Arceneaux, Kevin, and Rory Truex. 2022. Donald Trump and the lie. *Perspectives on Politics*, 21(3): 1–17.

Aschwanden, Damaris, Jason E. Strickhouser, Amanda A. Sesker, Ji Hyun Lee, Martina Luchetti, Yannick Stephan, Angelina R. Sutin, and Antonio Terracciano. 2021. Psychological and behavioural responses to coronavirus disease 2019: The role of personality. *European Journal of Personality*, 35(1): 51–66.

Asher, Abe. 2022. US police have already killed over 700 people in 2022, on track to break record. *The Independent*. [online]. 4 August. www.independent.co.uk/news/world/americas/police-killing-record-2022-b2137757.html

Ashok, Vivekinan, Daniel Feder, Mary McGrath, and Eitan Hersh. 2016. The dynamic election: Patterns of early voting across time, state, party, and age. *Election Law Journal*, 15(2): 115–128.

Atkeson, Lonna Rae, R. Michael Alvarez, and Thad E. Hall. 2015. Voter confidence: How to measure it and how it differs from government support. *Election Law Journal: Rules, Politics, and Policy*, 14(3): 207–219.

# References

Atkeson, Lonna Rae, Wendy L. Hansen, Maggie Toulouse Oliver, Cherie D. Maestas, and Eric C. Wiemer. 2022. Should I vote-by-mail or in person? The impact of COVID-19 risk factors and partisanship on vote mode decisions in the 2020 presidential election. *Plos one*, 17(9): e0274357.

Atkeson, Lonna Rae, and Kyle L. Saunders. 2007. The effect of election administration on voter confidence: A local matter? *PS: Political Science & Politics*, 40(04): 655–660.

Baker, Peter, and Maggie Haberman. 2020a. Trump tests positive for the coronavirus. The *New York Times*. [online]. 2 October. www.nytimes.com/2020/10/02/us/politics/trump-covid.html.

Baker, Peter, and Maggie Haberman. 2020b. Trump fans strife as unrest roils the U.S. *The New York Times*. [online]. 31 August. www.nytimes.com/2020/08/31/us/politics/trump-kenosha.html

Ball, Molly, and Charlotte Alter. 2020. The first 2020 presidential debate was nasty, brutish and long. *Time Magazine*. [online]. 1 October. time.com/5894588/presidential-debate-analysis-chaos/

Banda, Kevin K., and Erin C. Cassese. 2022. Hostile sexism, racial resentment, and political mobilization. *Political Behavior*, 44: 1317–1335.

Barbaranelli, Claudio, Gian Vittorio Caprara, Michele Vecchione, and Chris R. Fraley. 2007. Voters' personality traits in presidential elections. *Personality and Individual Differences*, 42(7): 1199–1208.

Barnhart, Brent. 2021. Everything you need to know about social media algorithms. *Sprout Social*. [online]. 26 March. sproutsocial.com/insights/social-media-algorithms/

Barrabi, Thomas. 2020. Trump says he's 'medication free,' details COVID-19 recovery in first on-camera interview since diagnosis. *Fox News*. www.foxnews.com/politics/trump-medication-free-covid-19-recovery-tucker-carlson

Barroso, Amanda. 2020. Key takeaways on Americans' views on gender equality a century after U.S. women gained the right to vote. *Pew Research Center*. [online]. 13 August. www.pewresearch.org/fact-tank/2020/08/13/key-takeaways-on-americans-views-on-gender-equality-a-century-after-u-s-women-gained-the-right-to-vote/

Barroso, Amanda, and Anna Brown. 2021. Gender pay gap in U.S. held steady in 2020. *PEW Research Center*. [online]. 25 May. www.pewresearch.org/fact-tank/2021/05/25/gender-pay-gap-facts/

Barry, Dan, and Sheera Frenkel. 2021. Be There. Will Be Wild! Trump all but circled the date. *The New York Times*. [online]. 7 January. www.nytimes.com/2021/01/06/us/politics/capitol-mob-trump-supporters.html

Barsky, Allan E., and Lorinda Wood. 2005. Conflict avoidance in a university context. *Higher Education Research & Development*, 24(3): 249–264.

Bartels, Larry M. 2000. Partisanship and voting behavior, 1952–1996. *American Journal of Political Science*, 44: 35–50.

Bartels, Larry M. 2018. Partisanship in the Trump era. *The Journal of Politics*, 80(4): 1483–1494.

BBC News. 2016. US presidential debate: Trump won't commit to accept election result. 2016. *BBC News*. [online]. 20 October. www.bbc.com/news/election-us-2016-37706499

Beason, Tyrone. 2020. Trump and Biden couldn't be more different on the complicated issue of race. *Los Angeles Times*. [online]. 17 August, updated 3 October. www.latimes.com/politics/story/2020-08-06/trump-biden-race-policy

Beaulieu, Emily. 2014. From voter ID to party ID: How political parties affect perceptions of election fraud in the U.S. *Electoral Studies*, 35: 24–32.

Becker, Julia C., and Stephen C. Wright. 2011. Yet another dark side of chivalry: Benevolent sexism undermines and hostile sexism motivates collective action for social change. *Journal of Personality and Social Psychology*, 101(1): 62–77.

Belli, Robert F., Michael W. Traugott, and Matthew N. Beckmann. 2001. What leads to voting overreports? Contrasts of overreporters to validated voters and admitted nonvoters in the American National Election Studies. *Journal of Official Statistics*, 17(4): 479–498.

Bennett, Anthony J. 2013. *The race for the White House from Reagan to Clinton*. New York: Palgrave Macmillan.

Benoit, William L., Joseph R. Blaney, and Penni M. Pier. 1998. *Campaign '96: A functional analysis of acclaiming, attacking, and defending*. Westport, CT: Praeger.

Benoit, William L., and Glenn J. Hansen. 2004. Presidential debate watching, issue knowledge, character evaluation, and vote choice. *Human Communication Research*, 30(1): 121–144.

Berelson, Bernard R., Paul F. Lazarsfeld, and William N. McPhee. 1954. *Voting: A study of opinion formation in a presidential campaign*. Chicago: University of Chicago Press.

Berent, Matthew K., Jon A. Krosnick, and Arthur Lupia. 2016. Measuring voter registration and turnout in surveys. *Public Opinion Quarterly*, 80(3): 597–621.

Bergan, Daniel E., Alan S. Gerber, Donald P. Green, and Costas Panagopoulos. 2005. Grassroots mobilization and voter turnout in 2004. *Public Opinion Quarterly*, 69(5): 760–777.

Berinsky, Adam J. 2012. Rumors, truths, and reality: A study of political misinformation. Unpublished manuscript. Massachusetts Institute of Technology, Cambridge, MA. citeseerx.ist.psu.edu/viewdoc/download?doi=10.1.1.945.4298&rep=rep1&type=pdf

Berlinski, Nicolas, Margaret Doyle, Andrew M. Guess, Gabrielle Levy, Benjamin Lyons, Jacob M. Montgomery, Brendan Nyhan, and Jason Reifler. 2023. The effects of unsubstantiated claims of voter fraud on confidence in elections. *Journal of Experimental Political Science*, 10(1): 34–49.

Berman, John. 2020. Donald Trump visits Kenosha, Wisconsin; politics of fear; convalescent plasma not recommended to treat COVID-19; New White House Adviser pushing controversial pandemic response. Aired 8-9p ET. *Anderson Cooper 360 [CNN] (USA)*. 1 September. Available from NewsBank: Access World News: infoweb.newsbank.com/apps/news/documentview?p=AWNB&docref=news/17D43177DC0D6968

Bernheim, Bert Douglas, Nina Buchmann, Zach Freitas-Groff, and Sebastián Otero 2020. The effects of large group meetings on the spread of COVID-19: The case of Trump rallies. Stanford Institute for Economic Policy Research (SIEPR) Working Paper 20-043. siepr.stanford.edu/research/publications/effects-large-group-meetingsspread-covid-19-case-trump-rallies

Bierwiaczonek, Kinga, Aleksander B. Gundersen, and Jonas R. Kunst. 2022. The role of conspiracy beliefs for COVID-19 health responses: A meta-analysis. *Current Opinion in Psychology*, 46: 1–4.

Bjarnøe, Camilla, Claes Holger de Vreese, and Erik Albæk. 2020. The effect of being conflict non-avoidant: Linking conflict framing and political participation. *West European Politics*, 43(1): 102–128.

Blais, André, and Simon Labbé St-Vincent. 2011. Personality traits, political attitudes and the propensity to vote. *European Journal of Political Research*, 50(3): 395–417

Blais, André, and Christopher H. Achen. 2018. Civic duty and voter turnout. *Political Behavior*, 41(2): 473–497.

Blitzer, Wolf. 2020. Trump-Biden chaotic presidential debate analysis. Aired 10:30-11p ET. *CNN Live Event Special [CNN] (USA)*. 29 September. Available from NewsBank: Access World News: infoweb-newsbank-com.ezproxy1.lib.asu.edu/apps/news/document-view?p=AWNB&docref=news/17DD6C112D378FC0

Bobo, Lawrence. 1988. Attitudes toward the Black political movement: Trends, meaning, and effects on racial policy preferences. *Social Psychology Quarterly*, 51(4): 287–302.

Boburg, Shawn. 2020. Trump campaign flouted agreement to follow health guidelines at rally, documents show. *Washington Post*. [online]. 24 October. www.washingtonpost.com/investigations/trump-duluth-rally-covid-guidelines/2020/10/23/10c1367c-1317-11eb-82af-864652063d61_story.html

Bogel-Burroughs, Nicholas. 2021. Prosecutors say Derek Chauvin knelt on George Floyd for 9 minutes 29 seconds, longer than initially reported. *New York Times*. [online]. 30 March. www.nytimes.com/2021/03/30/us/derek-chauvin-george-floyd-kneel-9-minutes-29-seconds.html

Boudreau, Cheryl, Scott A. MacKenzie, and Daniel J. Simmons. 2022. Police violence and public opinion after George Floyd: How the Black Lives Matter movement and endorsements affect support for reforms. *Political Research Quarterly*, 75(2): 497–511.

Bowler, Shaun, Thomas Brunell, Todd Donovan, and Paul Gronke. 2015. Election administration and perceptions of fair elections. *Electoral Studies*, 38: 1–9.

Brader, Ted. 2005. Striking a responsive chord: How political ads motivate and persuade voters by appealing to emotions. *American Journal of Political Science*, 49(2): 388–405.

Brady, Henry E., Richard Johnston, and John Sides. 2006. The study of political campaigns. In Henry E. Brady and Richard Johnston (eds.) *Capturing campaign effects*. Ann Arbor: University of Michigan Press, 1–26.

Brady, Henry E., Sydney Verba, and Kay Lehman Schlozman. 1995. Beyond SES: A resource model of political participation. *The American Political Science Review*, 89(2): 271–294.

Brennan Center for Justice. 2020. The myth of voter fraud. *Brennan Center*. [online]. www.brennancenter.org/issues/ensure-every-american-can-vote/vote-suppression/myth-voter-fraud?fbclid=IwAR268babunGm_5OmLwGMgrKMLoyui2rC_mMqsG705maoXvm6TV2kpRoOpac

Bresnahan, Mary Jiang, William A. Donohue, Sachiyo M. Shearman, and Xiaowen Guan. 2009. Research note: Two measures of conflict orientation. *Conflict Resolution Quarterly*, 26(3): 365–379.

Brooks, Deborah J. 2006. The resilient voter: Moving toward closure in the debate over negative campaigning and turnout. *The Journal of Politics*, 68(3): 684–696.

Brown, Ben, and Wm Reed Benedict. 2002. Perceptions of the police: Past findings, methodological issues, conceptual issues and policy implications. *Policing: An International Journal of Police Strategies & Management*, 25(3): 543–580.

Brownstein, Ronald. 2020. The rage unifying boomers and Gen Z. *The Atlantic*. [online]. 18 June. www.theatlantic.com/politics/archive/2020/06/todays-protest-movements-are-as-big-as-the-1960s/613207/

Bruder, Martin, Peter Haffke, Nick Neave, Nina Nouripanah, and Roland Imhoff. 2013. Measuring individual differences in generic beliefs in conspiracy theories across cultures: Conspiracy mentality questionnaire. *Frontiers in Psychology*, 4(225): 1–15

Buchanan, Larry, Quoctrung Bui, and Jugal K. Patel. 2020. Black Lives Matter may be the largest movement in U.S. history. *New York Times*. [online]. 3 July. www.nytimes.com/interactive/2020/07/03/us/george-floyd-protests-crowd-size.html

Bullock, John G. 2009. Partisan bias and the Bayesian ideal in the study of public opinion. *The Journal of Politics*, 71(3): 1109–1124

Bullock III, Charles S., M. V. Hood III, and Richard Clark. 2005. Punch cards, Jim Crow, and Al Gore: Explaining voter trust in the electoral system in Georgia, 2000. *State Politics & Policy Quarterly*, 5(3): 283–294.

Bump, Philip. 2020. Reliable polls show that Biden won the debate – So those aren't what Trump's allies are highlighting. *Washington Post*. [online]. 30 September. www.washingtonpost.com/politics/2020/09/30/reliable-polls-show-that-biden-won-debate-so-those-arent-what-trumps-allies-are-highlighting/

Burden, Barry C., and Amber Wichowsky. 2014 Economic discontent as a mobilizer: Unemployment and voter turnout. *The Journal of Politics*, 76(4): 887–898.

Burns, Alexander. 2020. Joe Biden had close ties with Police Leaders. Will they help him now? *New York Times*. [online]. 24 October. www.nytimes.com/2020/10/24/us/politics/joe-biden-police.html

Burns, Alexander, and Katie Glueck. 2020. Kamala Harris is Biden's choice for Vice President. *New York Times*. [online]. 11 August. www.nytimes.com/2020/08/11/us/politics/kamala-harris-vp-biden.html

Butler, J. Corey. 2013. Authoritarianism and fear responses to pictures: The role of social differences. *International Journal of Psychology*, 48(1): 18–24.

Cacioppo, John T., and Richard E. Petty. 1982. The need for cognition. *Journal of Personality and Social Psychology*, 42(1): 116–131.

Camobreco, John F., and Zhaochen He. 2022. The party-line pandemic: A closer look at the Partisan response to COVID-19. *PS: Political Science & Politics*, 55(1): 13–21.

Campbell, Angus, Philip E. Converse, Warren E. Miller, and Donald E. Stokes. 1960. *The American voter*. New York: John Wiley and Sons, Inc.

Campbell, James E. 2005. Why Bush won the presidential election of 2004: Incumbency, ideology, terrorism and turnout. *Political Science Quarterly*, 120(2): 219–241.
Campbell, James E., 2008. *The American campaign: US presidential campaigns and the national vote*. College Station: Texas A&M University Press.
Campbell, W. Joseph. 2010. *Getting it wrong: Ten of the greatest misreported stories in American journalism*. Berkeley: University of California Press.
Caprara, Gian Vittorio, and Michele Vecchione. 2013. Personality approaches to political behavior. In Leonie Huddy, David O. Sears, and Jack S. Levy (eds.) *The Oxford handbook of political psychology*. New York: Oxford University Press, 23–58.
Carlson, Tucker. 2020a. Coronavirus cover-up in Nashville. *Tucker Carlson Tonight [Fox News] (USA)*. 17 September. Available from NewsBank: Access World News: infoweb-newsbank-com.ezproxy1.lib.asu.edu/apps/news/document-view?p=AWNB&docref=news/17D923A9B2722B58
Carlson, Tucker. 2020b. Political violence is the greatest threat we face. *Tucker Carlson Tonight [FOX News] (USA)*. 1 September. Available from NewsBank: Access World News: infoweb-newsbank-com.ezproxy1.lib.asu.edu/apps/news/document-view?p=AWNB&docref=news/17D3DCCCDF6BEE18
Carreras, Miguel. 2018. Why no gender gap in electoral participation? A civic duty explanation. *Electoral Studies*, 52: 36–45.
Carter, J. Scott, and Mamadi Corra. 2016. Racial resentment and attitudes toward the use of force by police: An over-time trend analysis. *Sociological Inquiry*, 86(4): 492–511.
Cassata, Cathy. 2020. Doctors debunk 9 popular COVID-19 vaccine myths and conspiracy theories. *Healthline*. 22 June. www.healthline.com/health-news/doctors-debunk-9-popular-covid-19-vaccine-myths-and-conspiracy-theories
Cassese, Erin C., and Tiffany D. Barnes. 2019. Reconciling sexism and women's support for Republican candidates: A look at gender, class, and whiteness in the 2012 and 2016 presidential races. *Political Behavior*, 41: 677–700.
Cathey, Libby. 2020. Trump, downplaying virus, has mocked wearing masks for months: He wore one as he headed to the hospital Friday afternoon. *ABC News*. [online]. 2 October. abcnews.go.com/Politics/trump-downplaying-virus-mocked-wearing-masks-months/story?id=73392694
CAWP. 2021. Gender differences in voter turnout. Center for American Women and Politics Eagleton Institute of Politics, Rutgers, The State University of New Jersey. cawp.rutgers.edu/facts/voters/turnout
Chiu, Allyson. 2020. Rush Limbaugh on coronavirus: "The common cold" that's being "weaponized" against Trump. *The Washington Post*. [online]. 25 February. www.washingtonpost.com/nation/2020/02/25/limbaugh-coronavirus-trump/
Choma, Russ. 2020. Donald Trump mingled without a mask at a New Jersey fundraiser. *Mother Jones*. [online]. 2 October. www.motherjones.com/politics/2020/10/donald-trump-mingled-without-a-mask-at-a-new-jersey-fundraiser/
Choma, Becky L., and Yaniv Hanoch. 2017. Cognitive ability and authoritarianism: Understanding support for Trump and Clinton. *Personality and Individual Differences*, 106: 287–291.

Christenson, Dino P., and Herbert F. Weisberg. 2019. Bad characters or just more polarization? The rise of extremely negative feelings for presidential candidates. *Electoral Studies*, 61: 1–12.

Claibourn, Michele P. 2008. Making a connection: Repetition and priming in presidential campaigns. *The Journal of Politics*, 70(4): 1142–1159.

Clarke, Harold, Marianne C. Stewart, and Karl Ho. 2021. Did Covid-19 kill Trump politically? The pandemic and voting in the 2020 presidential election. *Social Science Quarterly*, 102(5): 2194–2209.

Clifton, Derrick. 2020. Trump deploys the 'angry Black woman' trope against Kamala Harris. *NBC News*. [online]. 17 August. www.nbcnews.com/news/nbcblk/trump-deploys-angry-black-woman-trope-against-kamala-harris-n1236975

Clinton, Joshua, Jon Cohen, John Lapinski, and Marc Trussler. 2021. Partisan pandemic: How partisanship and public health concerns affect individuals' social mobility during COVID-19. *Science Advances*, 7(2): eabd7204. doi.org/10.1126/sciadv.abd7204.

Clinton, Joshua D., and John S. Lapinski. 2004. "Targeted" advertising and voter turnout: An experimental study of the 2000 presidential election. *The Journal of Politics*, 66(1): 69–96.

Cohen, Elizabeth. 2020. New CDC guidance says older adults should 'stay at home as much as possible' due to coronavirus. *CNN*. [online]. 6 March. www.cnn.com/2020/03/06/health/coronavirus-older-people-social-distancing/index.html

Collinson, Stephen. 2016. Why Trump's talk of a rigged vote is so dangerous. *CNN*. [online]. 19 October. www.cnn.com/2016/10/18/politics/donald-trump-rigged-election/index.html

Colvin, Jill, and Darlene Superville. 2020. Tear gas, threats for protestors before Trump visits church. *AP News*. [online]. 1 June. apnews.com/article/donald-trump-ap-top-news-dc-wire-religion-politics-15be4e293cdebe72c10304fe0ec668e4

Conover, Pamela Johnston, and Stanley Feldman. 1989. Candidate perception in an ambiguous world: Campaigns, cues, and inference processes. *American Journal of Political Science*, 33(4): 912–94

Converse, Philip E., and Gregory B. Markus. 1979. Plus ca change...: The new CPS election study panel. *The American Political Science Review*, 73(1): 32–49.

Coppock, Alexander. 2023. *Persuasion in parallel: How information changes minds about politics*. Chicago: University of Chicago Press.

Coppock, Alexander, Donald P. Green, and Ethan Porter. 2022. Does digital advertising affect vote choice? Evidence from a randomized field experiment. *Research & Politics*, 9(1): 1–7.

Coppock, Alexander, Seth J. Hill, and Lynn Vavreck. 2020. The small effects of political advertising are small regardless of context, message, sender, or receiver: Evidence from 59 real-time randomized experiments. *Science Advances*, 6(36): 1–6.

Corasaniti, Nick, and Reid J. Epstein. 2021. Florida and Texas join the march as republicans press voting limits. *New York Times*. [online]. 6 May. www.nytimes.com/2021/05/06/us/politics/florida-texas-voting-rights-bills.html

Corasaniti, Nick, Reid J. Epstein, and Jim Rutenberg. 2021. The Times called officials in every state: No evidence of voter fraud. *New York Times*. [online]. 23 September. www.nytimes.com/2020/11/10/us/politics/voting-fraud.html

Cox, Gary W., and Michael C. Munger. 1989. Closeness, expenditures, and turnout in the 1982 US House elections. *American Political Science Review*, 83(1): 217–231.

Crabtree, Kiela, and Nicole Yadon. 2022. Remaining neutral?: White Americans' reactions to police violence and policing. *Political Behavior*, 1–21.

Cramer, Katherine. 2020. Understanding the role of racism in contemporary US public opinion. *Annual Review of Political Science*, 23: 153–169.

Dahl, Robert A. 1997. *Toward democracy – A journey, reflections: 1940–1997*. Berkeley, CA: Institute Government Study Press.

Dalager, Jon K. 1996. Voters, issues, and elections: Are the candidates' messages getting through? *The Journal of Politics*, 58(2): 486–515.

Dale, Daniel. 2020. Fact check: A guide to 9 conspiracy theories Trump is currently Pushing. *CNN*. [online]. 2 September. www.cnn.com/2020/09/02/politics/fact-check-trump-conspiracy-theories-biden-covid-thugs-plane/index.html

Daniels, David D. 2020. The Black Church has been getting "souls to the polls" for more than 60 years. *The Conversation*. [online]. 30 October. theconversation.com/the-black-church-has-been-getting-souls-to-the-polls-for-more-than-60-years-145996

Dawsey, Josh, Michael Scherer, and Annie Linskey. 2020. Campaign of contrasts: Trump's raucous crowds vs. Biden's distanced gatherings. *Washington Post*. [online]. 9 September. www.washingtonpost.com/politics/campaign-of-contrasts-trumps-raucous-crowds-vs-bidens-distanced-gatherings/2020/09/08/8633e69a-f1dc-11ea-b796-2dd09962649c_story.html

Deason, Grace, and Kris Dunn. 2022. Authoritarianism and perceived threat from the novel coronavirus. *International Journal of Psychology*, 57(3): 341–351.

Delli Carpini, Michael X., and Scott Keeter. 1996. *What Americans know about politics and why it matters*. New Haven, CT: Yale University Press.

De Zavala, Agnieszka Golec, Aleksandra Cislak, and Elzbieta Wesolowska. 2010. Political conservatism, need for cognitive closure, and intergroup hostility. *Political Psychology*, 31(4): 521–541.

Dodson, Kyle. 2015. Gendered activism: A cross-national view on gender differences in protest activity. *Social Currents*, 2(4): 377–392

Doherty, David, and E. Scott Adler. 2014. The persuasive effects of partisan campaign mailers. *Political Research Quarterly*, 67(3): 562–573

Douglas, Karen M. 2021. COVID-19 conspiracy theories. *Group Processes & Intergroup Relations*, 24(2): 270–275.

Douglas, Karen M., Joseph E. Uscinski, Robbie M. Sutton, Aleksandra Cichocka, Turkay Nefes, Chee Siang Ang, and Farzin Deravi. 2019. Understanding conspiracy theories. *Political Psychology*, 40(Supplement 1): 3–35.

Drakulich, Kevin, and Megan Denver. 2022. The partisans and the persuadables: Public views of Black Lives Matter and the 2020 protests. *Perspectives on Politics*, 20(4): 1191–1208.

Drakulich, Kevin, Kevin H. Wozniak, John Hagan, and Devon Johnson. 2020. Race and policing in the 2016 presidential election: Black Lives Matter, the police, and dog whistle politics. *Criminology*, 58(2): 370–402.

Druckman, James N. 2003. The power of television images: The first Kennedy-Nixon debate revisited. *The Journal of Politics*, 65(2): 559–571.

Druckman, James N. 2004. Priming the vote: Campaign effects in a US Senate election. *Political Psychology*, 25(4): 577–594

Druckman, James N., Matthew S. Levendusky, and Audrey McLain. 2018. No need to watch: How the effects of partisan media can spread via interpersonal discussions. *American Journal of Political Science*, 62 (1): 99–112.

Druckman, James N., and Mary C. McGrath. 2019. The evidence for motivated reasoning in climate change preference formation. *Nature Climate Change*, 9(2): 111–119.

Du Bois, W. E. B. [1903] 1986. The souls of Black folk. In Nathan Huggins (ed.) *Writings*. New York: Library of America, 357–547.

Dunlap, David S. 2015. 1973: Meet Donald Trump. *The New York Times*. [online]. 30 July. www.nytimes.com/times-insider/2015/07/30/1973-meet-donald-trump/

Dyck, Joshua J., and James G. Gimpel. 2005. Distance, turnout, and the convenience of voting. *Social Science Quarterly*, 86(3): 531–548.

Edel, Charles. 2021. Dealing with authoritarian regimes is oldest challenge in American history. *The Hill*. [online]. 3 July. thehill.com/opinion/whitehouse/561471-dealing-with-authoritarian-regimes-is-the-oldest-challenge-in-american?rl=1

Edelson, Jack, Alexander Alduncin, Christopher Krewson, James A. Sieja, and Joseph E. Uscinski. 2017. The effect of conspiratorial thinking and motivated reasoning on belief in election fraud. *Political Research Quarterly*, 70(4): 933–946.

Emmrich, Stuart. 2020. Last night's presidential debate was a "Shitshow" and a "Train Wreck": Can we survive two more like this? *Vogue Magazine*. [online]. 9 September. www.vogue.com/article/presidential-debate-shitshow-donald-trump-joe-biden-chris-wallace

Enders, Adam M., Joseph E. Uscinski, Michelle I. Seelig, Casey A. Klofstad, Stefan Wuchty, John R. Funchion, Manohar N. Murthi, Kamal Premaratne, and Justin Stoler. 2021. The relationship between social media use and beliefs in conspiracy theories and misinformation. *Political Behavior*, 45: 1–21.

Engelhardt, Andrew M., Stanley Feldman, and Marc J. Hetherington. 2021. Advancing the measurement of authoritarianism. *Political Behavior*, (May): 1–24. doi.org/10.1007/s11109-021-09718-6

Enos, Ryan D., and Anthony Fowler. 2018. Aggregate effects of large-scale campaigns on voter turnout. *Political Science Research and Methods*, 6(4): 733–751.

Erikson, Robert S., and Christopher Wlezien. 2012. *The timeline of presidential elections: How campaigns do (and do not) matter*. Chicago: University of Chicago Press.

Fahs, Breanne, and Eric Swank. 2022. Friends or foes? U.S. Women's perceptions of racial justice and the Black Lives Matter protests during the COVID-19 pandemic. *Journal of Women, Politics & Policy*, 43(4): 446–462.

Fausset, Richard. 2021. Before Breonna Taylor and George Floyd, there was Ahmaud Arbery. *New York Times*. [online]. 28 February. www.nytimes.com/2021/02/28/us/ahmaud-arbery-anniversary.html

Federico, Christopher M., Emily L. Fisher, and Grace Deason. 2017. The authoritarian left withdraws from politics: Ideological asymmetry in the relationship between authoritarianism and political engagement. *The Journal of Politics*, 79(3): 1010–1023.

Feldman, Stanley. 2003. Enforcing social conformity: A theory of authoritarianism. *Political Psychology*, 24(1): 41–74

Feldman, Stanley, Leonie Huddy, Julie Wronski, and Patrick Lown. 2019. The interplay of empathy and individualism in support for social welfare policies. *Political Psychology*, 41(2): 343–362.

Feldman, Stanley, and Karen Stenner. 1997. Perceived threat and authoritarianism. *Political Psychology*, 18(4): 741–770.

Fessler, Pam. 2020. Trump's calls for poll watchers raise fears about voter intimidation. *NPR*. [online]. 30 September. www.npr.org/2020/09/30/918766323/trumps-calls-for-poll-watchers-raises-fears-about-voter-intimidation

Filindra, Alexandra, Noah J. Kaplan, and Beyza E. Buyuker. 2021. Racial resentment or sexism? White Americans' outgroup attitudes as predictors of gun ownership and NRA membership. *Sociological Inquiry*, 91(2): 253–286.

Finkel, Eli J., Christopher A. Bail, Mina Cikara, Peter H. Ditto, Shanto Iyengar, Samara Klar, Lilliana Mason et al. 2020. Political sectarianism in America. *Science*, 370(6516): 533–536.

Finkel, Steven E. 1995. *Causal analysis and panel data*. Thousand Oaks, CA: Sage Publications.

Finkel, Steven E., and John G. Geer. 1998. A spot check: Casting doubt on the demobilizing effect of attack advertising. *American Journal of Political Science*, 42(2): 573–595.

Fiorina, Morris P. 1981. *Retrospective voting in American national elections*. New Haven: Yale University Press.

Fiorina, Morris P., and Samuel J. Abrams. 2008. Political polarization in the American public. *Annual Review of Political Science*, 11: 563–588.

Fiorina, Morris, and Matthew Levendusky. 2006. Disconnected: The political class versus the people. In Pietro S. Nivola and David W. Brady (eds.) *Red and Blue Nation? Volume I: Characteristics and causes of America's polarized politics*. Washington, DC: Brookings Institution Press and Stanford, CA: Hoover Institution Press. 49–118.

Fowler, James H., Laura A. Baker, and Christopher T. Dawes. 2008. Genetic variation in political participation. *American Political Science Review*, 102(2): 233–248.

Franklin, Charles H. 1991. Eschewing obfuscation? Campaigns and the perception of US Senate incumbents. *American Political Science Review*, 85(4): 1193–1214.

Freelon, Deen, and David Karpf. 2015. Of big birds and bayonets: Hybrid *Twitter* interactivity in the 2012 presidential debates. *Information, Communication & Society*, 18(4): 390–406.

Freeston, Mark H., Josée Rhéaume, Hélène Letarte, Michel J. Dugas, and Robert Ladouceur. 1994. Why do people worry? *Personality and Individual Differences*, 17(6): 791–802.

French, David. 2020. It's clear that America is deeply polarized. No election can overcome that. *Time Magazine*. [online]. 4 November. time.com/5907318/polarization-2020-election/

Frey, William H. 2021. Turnout in 2020 election spiked among both Democratic and Republican voting groups, new census data shows. *Brookings Institute*. [online]. www.brookings.edu/research/turnout-in-2020-spiked-among-both-democratic-and-republican-voting-groups-new-census-data-shows/

Fridkin, Kim L., and Patrick J. Kenney. 2011. The role of candidate traits in campaigns. *The Journal of Politics*, 73(1): 61–73.

Fridkin, Kim L., and Patrick J. Kenney. 2019. *Taking aim at attack advertising: Understanding the impact of negative campaigning in US senate races*. New York: Oxford University Press.

Fridkin, Kim L., Patrick J. Kenney, Sarah Allen Gershon, Karen Shafer, and Gina Serignese Woodall. 2007. Capturing the power of a campaign event: The 2004 presidential debate in Tempe. *The Journal of Politics*, 69(3): 770–785.

Fridkin, Kim, Patrick Kenney, Amanda Wintersieck, and Jill Carle. 2017. The upside of the long campaign: How presidential elections engage the electorate. *American Politics Research*, 45(2): 186–223.

Fridkin, Kim L., Patrick J. Kenney, Sarah Allen Gershon, and Gina Serignese Woodall. 2008. Spinning debates: The impact of the news media's coverage of the final 2004 presidential debate. *The International Journal of Press/Politics*, 13(1): 29–51.

Fridkin, Kim, Amanda Wintersieck, Jillian Courey, and Joshua Thompson. 2017. Race and police brutality: The importance of media framing. *International Journal of Communication*, 11: 3394–3414.

Funk, Carolyn L. 1996. The impact of scandal on candidate evaluations: An experimental test of the role of candidate traits. *Political Behavior*, 18(1): 1–24.

Gadarian, Shana Kushner, Sara Wallace Goodman, and Thomas B. Pepinsky. 2022 *Pandemic politics*. Princeton, NJ: Princeton University Press.

Gamboa, Suzanne. 2015. Donald Trump announces presidential bid by trashing Mexico, Mexicans. *NBC News*. [online]. 16 June. www.nbcnews.com/news/latino/donald-trump-announces-presidential-bid-trashing-mexico-mexicans-n376521

GaSton, Sophia, and Joseph E. Uscinski. 2018. Out of the shadows: Conspiracy thinking on immigration. *Centre for Social & Political Risk, London: Henry Jackson Society*. [online]. henryjacksonsociety.org/wp-content/uploads/2018/12/Out-of-the-Shadows-Conspiracy-thinking-on-immigration.pdf

Gawronski, Bertram. 2012. Back to the future of dissonance theory: Cognitive consistency as a core motive. *Social Cognition*, 30(6): 652–668.

Gelman, Andrew, and Gary King. 1993. Why are American presidential election campaign polls so variable when votes are so predictable? *British Journal of Political Science*, 23(4): 409–451.

Gerber, Alan, and Donald Green. 1999. Misperceptions about perceptual bias. *Annual Review of Political Science*, 2(1): 189–210.

Gerber, Alan, Mitchell Hoffman, John Morgan, and Collin Raymond. 2020. One in a million: Field experiments on perceived closeness of the election and voter turnout. *American Economic Journal: Applied Economics*, 12(3): 287–325.

Gerber, Alan S., Gregory A. Huber, David Doherty, and Conor M. Dowling. 2011. The big five personality traits in the political arena. *Annual Review of Political Science*, 14: 265–287.

Gilens, Martin. 1995. Racial attitudes and opposition to welfare. *The Journal of Politics*, 57(4): 994–1014.

Glick, Peter. 2019. Gender, sexism, and the election: Did sexism help Trump more than it hurt Clinton? *Politics, Groups, and Identities*, 7(3): 713–723.

Glick, Peter, and Susan T. Fiske. 1996. The ambivalent sexism inventory: Differentiating hostile and benevolent sexism. *Journal of personality and social psychology*, 70(3): 491–512.

Glick, Peter, and Susan T. Fiske. 2001. An ambivalent alliance: Hostile and benevolent sexism as complementary justifications for gender inequality. *American psychologist*, 56(2): 109–118.

Glinitzer, Konstantin, Tobias Gummer, and Markus Wagner. 2021. Learning facts about migration: Politically motivated learning of polarizing information about refugees. *Political Psychology*, 42(6): 1053–1069.

Goertzel, Ted. 1994. Belief in conspiracy theories. *Political Psychology*, 15(4): 731–742.

Goldberg, Andreas C., Simon Lanz, and Pascal Sciarini. 2019. Mobilizing different types of voters: The influence of campaign intensity on turnout in direct democratic votes. *Electoral Studies*, 57(2019): 196–222.

Goldmacher, Shane. 2020. Six takeaways from the first presidential debate. *New York Times*. [online]. 30 September. www.nytimes.com/2020/09/30/us/politics/debate-takeaways.html

Goldstein, Susan B. 1999. Construction and validation of a conflict communication scale. *Journal of Applied Social Psychology*, 29(9): 1803–1832.

Gomez, Brad T., and J. Matthew Wilson. 2001. Political sophistication and economic voting in the American electorate: A theory of heterogeneous attribution. *American Journal of Political Science*, 45(4): 899–914.

Gomez, Justin. 2020. Trump vs. Biden on the issues: Racial justice. *ABC News*. [online]. 29 September. abcnews.go.com/Politics/trump-biden-issues-racial-justice/story?id=73145335

Grady, Constance. 2018. The waves of feminism, and why people keep fighting over them, explained. *Vox*. [online]. 20 July. www.vox.com/2018/3/20/16955588/feminism-waves-explained-first-second-third-fourth

Graham, David A. 2016. The myth of Gerald Ford's fatal "Soviet Domination" gaffe. *The Atlantic*. [online]. 2 August. www.theatlantic.com/politics/archive/2016/08/the-myth-of-gerald-fords-disastrous-soviet-domination-gaffe/493958/

Graham, David A. 2020. The last time Trump alleged massive fraud. *The Atlantic*. [online]. 12 November. www.theatlantic.com/ideas/archive/2020/11/kris-kobach-and-search-mythical-voter-fraud/617069/

Green, Donald P., and Alan S. Gerber. 2019. *Get out the vote: How to increase voter turnout*. Washington, DC: Brookings Institution Press.

Green, Donald P., and Michael Schwam-Bard. 2015. Mobilization, participation, and American democracy: A retrospective and postscript. *Party Politics*, 22(2): 158–164.

Green, Eva G. T., Christian Staerkle, and David O. Sears. Symbolic racism and Whites' attitudes towards punitive and preventive crime policies. *Law and Human Behavior*, 30(4): 435–454.

Gronke, Paul. 2015. Election administration and perceptions of fair elections. *Electoral Studies*, 38: 1–9.

Gwertzman, Bernard. 1976. Ford denies Moscow dominates East Europe. *The New York Times*. [online]. 7 October. www.nytimes.com/1976/10/07/archives/ford-denies-moscow-dominates-east-europe-carter-rebuts-him-ford.html

Haddad, Mohammed. 2021. How many people have been killed by police since George Floyd? *Aljazeera.com*. [online]. 25 May. www.aljazeera.com/news/2021/5/25/how-many-people-have-police-killed-since-george-floyd

Hair, Joseph F., and Luiz Paulo Fávero. 2019. Multilevel modeling for longitudinal data: Concepts and applications. *RAUSP Management Journal*, 54: 459–489.

Halberstam, Yosh, and Brian Knight. 2016. Homophily, group size, and the diffusion of political information in social networks: Evidence from Twitter. *Journal of Public Economics*, 143: 73–88.

Hannity, Sean. 2020. Biden refuses to answer if he would try to pack The Supreme Court. *Hannity [Fox News] (USA)*. 29 September. Available from NewsBank: Access World News: infoweb-newsbank.com.ezproxy1.lib.asu.edu/apps/news/document-view?p=AWNB&docref=news/17DD6C108 72E3608

Harlow, Summer, Danielle K. Kilgo, Ramón Salaverría, and Víctor García-Perdomo. 2020. Is the whole world watching? Building a typology of protest coverage on social media from around the world. *Journalism Studies*, 21(11): 1590–1608.

Hartocollis, Anemona, and Yamiche Alcindor. 2017. Women's march highlights as huge crowds protest Trump: 'We're Not Going Away'. *The New York Times*. [online]. 21 January. www.nytimes.com/2017/01/21/us/womens-march.html

Hartman, Todd K., Thomas V. A. Stocks, Ryan McKay, Jilly Gibson-Miller, Liat Levita, Anton P. Martinez, Liam Mason, Orla McBride, Jamie Murphy, Mark Shevlin, Kate M. Bennett, Philip Hyland, Thanos Karatzias, Frederique Vallieres, and Richard P. Bentall. 2021. The authoritarian dynamic during the COVID-19 pandemic: Effects on nationalism and anti-immigrant sentiment. *Social Psychological and Personality Science*, 12(7): 1274–1285.

Haspel, Moshe, and H. Gibbs Knotts. 2005. Location, location, location: Precinct placement and the costs of voting, *The Journal of Politics*, 67(2): 560–573.

Hayes, Andrew F. 2022. *Introduction to mediation, moderation, and conditional process analysis: A regression-based approach* (3rd ed.). New York: The Guilford Press.

Hayes, Chris. 2020. *All in with Chris Hayes [MSNBC] (USA)*. 17 September. Available from NewsBank: Access World News: infoweb-newsbank-com.ezproxy1.lib.asu.edu/apps/news/document-view?p=AWNB&docref=news/17D9786D43934880

Healy, Andrew, and Gabriel S. Lenz. 2014. Substituting the end for the whole: Why voters respond primarily to the election-year economy. *American Journal of Political Science*, 58(1): 31–47.

Healy, Andrew, and Neil Malhotra. 2013. Retrospective voting reconsidered. *Annual Review of Politics*, 16: 285–306.

Healy, Jack. 2021. These are the 5 people who died in the capitol riot. *New York Times*. [online]. 11 January. www.nytimes.com/2021/01/11/us/who-died-in-capitol-building-attack.html

Healy, Patrick, and Jonathan Martin. 2016. Donald Trump won't say if he'll accept result of election. *New York Times*. [online]. 19 October. www.nytimes.com/2016/10/20/us/politics/presidential-debate.html

Henry, Patrick J., and David O. Sears. 2002. The symbolic racism 2000 scale. *Political Psychology*, 23(2): 253–283.

Herron, Michael C., and Daniel A. Smith. 2012. Souls to the polls: Early voting in Florida in the shadow of House Bill 1355. *Election Law Journal*, 11(3): 331–347.

Hetherington, Marc J. 2008. Turned off or Turned on? How polarization affects political engagement. In Pietro S. Nivola and David W. Brady (eds.) *Red and Blue Nation? Volume I: Characteristics and causes of America's polarized politics*. Washington, DC: Brookings Institution Press and Stanford, CA: Hoover Institution Press, 1–33.

Hetherington, Marc J., and Michael Nelson. 2003. Anatomy of a rally effect: George W. Bush and the war on terrorism. *PS: Political Science & Politics*, 36(1): 37–42.

Hetherington, Marc, and Elizabeth Suhay. 2011. Authoritarianism, threat, and Americans' support for the war on terror. *American Journal of Political Science*, 55(3): 546–560.

Hibbs, Douglas A. 2000. Bread and peace voting in US presidential elections. *Public Choice*, 104(1): 149–180.

Highton, Benjamin. 2017. Voter identification laws and turnout in the United States. *Annual Review of Political Science*, 20(May): 149–167.

Hillygus, D. Sunshine. 2005. The missing link: Exploring the relationship between higher education and political engagement. *Political Behavior*, 27(1): 25–47.

Hillygus, D. Sunshine. 2010. Campaign effects on vote choice. In Jan Leighley (ed.) *The Oxford handbook of American elections and political behavior*. Oxford: Oxford University Press, 326–345.

Hillygus, D. Sunshine, and Simon Jackman. 2003. Voter decision making in election 2000: Campaign effects, partisan activation, and the Clinton legacy. *American Journal of Political Science*, 47(4): 583–596.

Hillygus, D. Sunshine, and Todd Shields. 2009. *The persuadable voter: Wedge issues in presidential campaigns*. Princeton, NJ: Princeton University Press.

Hinckley, Story. 2020. Amid a pandemic, Republicans become the new door-knocking warriors. *Christian Science Monitor*. [online]. 14 October. www.csmonitor.com/USA/Politics/2020/1014/Amid-a-pandemic-Republicans-become-the-new-door-knocking-warriors

Hochschild, Arlie. 2020. Is Donald Trump a bully or bold protector? That depends on whom you ask. *The Guardian*. [online]. 11 October. www.theguardian.com/commentisfree/2020/oct/11/is-donald-trump-a-bully-or-bold-protector-that-depends-on-whom-you-ask

Holan, Angie Drobnic. 2019. In context: Donald Trump's 'very fine people on both sides' remarks. *PolitiFact*. [online]. 26 April. www.politifact.com/article/2019/apr/26/context-trumps-very-fine-people-both-sides-remarks/

Holbrook, Thomas. 1996. *Do campaigns matter?* Thousand Oaks, CA: Sage.

Holbrook, Thomas. 1999. Political learning from presidential debates. *Political Behavior*, 21(1): 67–89.

Hollander, Barry A. 2018. Partisanship, individual differences, and news media exposure as predictors of conspiracy beliefs. *Journalism & Mass Communication Quarterly*, 95(3): 691–713.

Holt, Lester. 2020. Trump contradicts CDC director on COVID vaccine timeline. *NBC Nightly News*. 17 September. Available from NewsBank: Access World News: infoweb-newsbank-com.ezproxy1.lib.asu.edu/apps/news/document-view?p=AWNB&docref=news/17DD176CD51C9E08

Huber, Gregory A., and Kevin Arceneaux. 2007. Identifying the persuasive effects of presidential advertising. *American Journal of Political Science*, 51(4): 957–977

Huddy, Leonie., Stanley Feldman, and Payel Sen. 2023. Complexities in the measurement of explicit racial attitudes. In Jon A. Krosnick, Tobias H. Stark, and Amanda L. Scott (eds.) *The Cambridge handbook of implicit bias and racism*. Cambridge: Cambridge University Press. www.cambridge.org/core/books/cambridge-handbook-of-implicit-bias-and-racism/DE430B0B0E51DEA222DC78896656A982#fndtn-metrics

Imhoff, Roland. 2015. Beyond (right-wing) authoritarianism. In Michal Bilewicz, Aleksandra Cichocka, and Wiktor Soral (eds.) *The psychology of conspiracy*. New York: Taylor & Francis, 122–142.

Imhoff, Roland, and Martin Bruder. 2014. Speaking (un–) truth to power: Conspiracy mentality as a generalised political attitude. *European Journal of Personality*, 28(1): 25–43.

Imhoff, Roland, and Pia Lamberty. 2020. A bioweapon or a hoax? The link between distinct conspiracy beliefs about the Coronavirus disease (COVID-19) outbreak and pandemic behavior. *Social Psychological and Personality Science*, 11(8): 1110–1118.

Iyengar, Shanto, and Donald R. Kinder. 1987. *News that matters: Television and American opinion*. Chicago: University of Chicago Press.

Iyengar, Shanto, and Masha Krupenkin. 2018. The strengthening of partisan affect. *Political Psychology*, 39: 201–218

Iyengar, Shanto, and Adam F. Simon. 2000. New perspectives and evidence on political communication and campaign effects. *Annual Review of Psychology*, 51: 149–169.

Iyengar, Shanto, Gaurav Sood, and Yphtach Lelkes. 2012. Affect, not ideology: A social identity perspective on polarization. *Public Opinion Quarterly*, 76(3): 405–431.

Jackman, Tom. 2021. Police union says 140 officers injured in Capitol riot. *Washington Post*. [online]. 27 January. www.washingtonpost.com/local/public-safety/police-union-says-140-officers-injured-in-capitol-riot/2021/01/27/60743642-60e2-11eb-9430-e7c77b5b0297_story.html

Jackson, Jon. 2021. 4 capitol police officers have died by suicide since the January 6 insurrection. *Newsweek*. [online]. 2 August. www.newsweek.com/3-capitol-police-officers-have-died-suicide-since-january-6-insurrection-1615452

Jacobs, Lawrence R., and Robert Y. Shapiro. 1994. Issues, candidate image, and priming: The use of private polls in Kennedy's 1960 presidential campaign. *American Political Science Review*, 88(3): 527–540.

Jacobson, Gary C. 2015. How do campaigns matter? *Annual Review of Political Science*, 18: 31–47.
Jarman, Jeffrey W. 2005. Political affiliation and presidential debates: A real-time analysis of the effect of the arguments used in the presidential debates. *American Behavioral Scientist*, 49(2): 229–242.
Jefferson, Hakeem, Fabian G. Neuner, and Josh Pasek. 2021. Seeing blue in Black and White: Race and perceptions of officer-involved shootings. *Perspectives on Politics*, 19(4): 1165–1183.
Jennings, Freddie J., Benjamin R. Warner, Mitchell S. McKinney, Cassandra C. Kearney, Michelle E. Funk, and Josh C. Bramlett. 2020. Learning from presidential debates: Who learns the most and why? *Communication Studies*, 71(5): 896–910.
Johnston, Richard, Michael G. Hagen, and Kathleen Hall Jamieson. 2004. *The 2000 presidential election and the foundations of party politics*. New York, Cambridge: Cambridge University Press.
Jones, Jeffrey. 2013. Honesty ratings of police, clergy differ most by party. *Gallup*. [online]. www.gallup.com/poll/166487/honesty-ratings-police-clergy-differ-party.aspx
Jones, David R., and Monika L. McDermott. 2022. Partisanship and the politics of COVID vaccine hesitancy. *Polity*, 54(3): 408–434.
Jost, John T., Delia S. Baldassarri, and James N. Druckman. 2022. Cognitive-motivational mechanisms of political polarization in social-communicative contexts. *Nature Reviews Psychology*, 1(10): 1–17
Jost, John T., Chadly Stern, Nicholas O. Rule, and Joanna Sterling. 2017. The politics of fear: Is there an ideological asymmetry in existential motivation? *Social Cognition*, 35(4): 324–353.
Kahn, Kim Fridkin, and Patrick J. Kenney. 1999. Do negative campaigns mobilize or suppress turnout? Clarifying the relationship between negativity and participation. *American Political Science Review*, 93(4): 877–889.
Kalla, Joshua L., and David E. Broockman. 2018. The minimal persuasive effects of campaign contact in general elections: Evidence from 49 field experiments. *American Political Science Review*, 112(1): 148–166
Kam, Cindy D., and Allison M. N. Archer. 2021. Mobilizing and demobilizing: Modern sexism and turnout in the# MeToo era. *Public Opinion Quarterly*, 85(1): 172–182.
Kam, Cindy D., and Donald R. Kinder. 2007. Terror and ethnocentrism: Foundations of American support for the war on terrorism. *The Journal of Politics*, 69(2): 320–338.
Kapur, Sahil. 2020. Trump has signaled he won't accept an election lost. Many of his voters agree. *NBC News*. [online]. 29 October. www.nbcnews.com/politics/2020-election/trump-has-signaled-he-won-t-accept-election-loss-many-n1245304
Karol, David, and Edward Miguel. 2007. The electoral cost of war: Iraq casualties and the 2004 US presidential election. *The Journal of Politics*, 69(3): 633–648.
Kelsey, Adam. 2016. Donald Trump's 2012 election tweetstorm resurfaces as popular and electoral vote appear divided. *ABC News*. [online]. 9 November. abcnews

.go.com/Politics/donald-trumps-2012-election-tweetstorm-resurfaces-popular-electoral/story?id=43431536
Keneally, Meghan. 2020. List of Trump's accusers and their allegations of sexual misconduct. *ABC News*. [online]. 18 September. abcnews.go.com/Politics/list-trumps-accusers-allegations-sexual-misconduct/story?id=51956410
Kenski, Kate, Bruce W. Hardy, and Kathleen Hall Jamieson. 2010. *The Obama victory: How media, money, and message shaped the 2008 election*. New York: Oxford University Press.
Kessler, Glenn, and Joe Fox. 2021. The false claims that Trump keeps repeating. *Washington Post*. [online]. 20 January. www.washingtonpost.com/graphics/politics/fact-checker-most-repeated-disinformation/
Kessler, Glenn, and Slavador Rizzo. 2020. President Trump's false claims of vote fraud: A chronology. *Washington Post*. [online]. 5 November. www.washingtonpost.com/politics/2020/11/05/president-trumps-false-claims-vote-fraud-chronology/
Key, Valdimer Orlando. 1966. *The responsible electorate*. Cambridge, MA: Harvard University Press.
Kiewiet, D. Roderick. 1983. *Macroeconomic and micropolitics: The electoral effects of economic issues*. Chicago: University of Chicago Press.
Kilgo, Danielle, and Rachel Mourão. 2019. Media effects and marginalized ideas: Relationships among media consumption and support for Black Lives Matter. *International Journal of Communication*, 13: 4287–4305.
Kim, Yongkwang. 2019. How conspiracy theories can stimulate political engagement. *Journal of Elections, Public Opinion and Parties*. www.tandfonline.com/doi/full/10.1080/17457289.2019.1651321
Kinder, Donald R. 1986. Presidential character revisited. In Richard R. Lau and David O. Sears (eds.) *Political cognition*. Hillsdale, NJ: Lawrence Erlbaum, 233–255.
Kinder, Donald R., and Cindy D. Kam. 2010. *Us against them: Ethnocentric foundations of American opinion*. Chicago: University of Chicago Press.
Kinder, Donald R., and D. Roderick Kiewiet. 1981. Sociotropic politics: The American case. *British Journal of Political Science*, 11(2): 129–161
Kinder, Donald R., and Lynn M. Sanders. 1996. *Divided by color: Racial politics and democratic ideals*. Chicago: University of Chicago Press.
Knight, Dacre. 2021. COVID-19 pandemic origins: Bioweapons and the history of laboratory leaks. *Southern medical journal*, 114(8): 465–467.
Knuckey, Jonathan, and Komysha Hassan. 2020. Authoritarianism and support for Trump in the 2016 presidential election. *The Social Science Journal*, 59(1): 47–60. doi.org/10.1016/j.soscij.2019.06.008.
Koerner, Ascan F., and Mary Anne Fitzpatrick. 1997. Family type and conflict: The impact of conversation orientation and conformity orientation on conflict in the family. *Communication Studies*, 48(1): 59–75.
Kolata, Gina, and Roni Caryn Rubin. 2020. "Don't Be Afraid of Covid," Trump says, undermining public health messages. *New York Times*. [online]. 8 October. www.nytimes.com/2020/10/05/health/trump-covid-public-health.html
Kranish, Michael, and Matt Viser. 2020. After the Anita Hill hearings in 1991, Joe Biden began a long quest to redeem himself with women. *Washington*

*Post.* [online]. 2 August. www.washingtonpost.com/politics/after-the-anita-hill-hearings-in-1991-joe-biden-began-a-long-quest-to-redeem-himself-with-women/2020/07/31/ee939b8a-9576-11ea-82b4-c8db161ff6e5_story.html

Kühne, Rinaldo, Christian Schemer, Jörg Matthes, and Werner Wirth. 2011. Affective priming in political campaigns: How campaign-induced emotions prime political opinions. *International Journal of Public Opinion Research*, 23(4): 485–507.

Kumar, V. Vineeth, and Geetika Tankha. 2022. The relationship between personality traits and COVID-19 anxiety: A mediating model. *Behavioral Sciences*, 12: 24.

Lamberty, Pia K., Jens H. Hellmann, and Aileen Oeberst. 2018. The winner knew it all? Conspiracy beliefs and hindsight perspective after the 2016 US general election. *Personality and Individual Differences*, 123(1): 236–240.

Lane, Robert E. 1955. Political personality and electoral choice. *American Political Science Review*, 49(1): 173–190.

Lang, Marissa. 2020. Federal officials stockpiled munitions, sought 'heat ray' device before clearing Lafayette Square, whistleblower says. *Washington Post*. [online]. 17 September. www.washingtonpost.com/local/dc-protest-lafayette-square/2020/09/16/ca0174e4-f788-11ea-89e3-4b9efa36dc64_story.html

Lanoue, David J., and Peter R. Schrott. 1989. Voters' reactions to televised presidential debates: Measurement of the source and magnitude of opinion change. *Political Psychology*, 10(2): 275–285.

Larsen, Knud S., and Ed Long. 1988. Attitudes toward sex-roles: Traditional or egalitarian? *Sex Roles*, 19(1–2): 1–12.

Lau, Richard R. 1982. Negativity in political perception. *Political Behavior*, 4(4): 353–378.

Lau, Richard R., and Gerald M. Pomper. 2004. *Negative campaigning: An analysis of US Senate elections*. Lanham, MD: Rowman & Littlefield.

Laustsen, Lasse, and Alexander Bor. 2017. The relative weight of character traits in political candidate evaluations: Warmth is more important than competence, leadership and integrity. *Electoral Studies*, 49: 96–107.

Lavine, Howard, Milton Lodge, and Kate Freitas. 2005. Threat, authoritarianism, and selective exposure to information. *Political Psychology*, 26(2): 219–24.

Lazarsfeld, Paul F., Bernard Berelson, and Hazel Gaudet. 1948. *The people's choice: How the voter makes up his mind in a presidential campaign*. New York: Columbia University Press.

Leighley, Jan, and Jonathan Nagler. 2013. *Who votes now? Demographics, issues, inequality, and turnout in the United States*. Princeton, NJ: Princeton University Press.

Lemire, Jonathan, Jill Colvin, and Alan Suderman. 2020. Amid protests, Trump talks of war – and reelection. *AP News*. [online]. 1 June. apnews.com/article/virus-outbreak-donald-trump-ap-top-news-politics-violence-b3817623ef861818803b5676d43741ea

Leonhardt, David, and Ian Prasad Philbrick. 2021. One year later on the anniversary of George Floyd's murder, we examine its legacy so far. *The New York Times*. [online]. 25 May. www.nytimes.com/2021/05/25/briefing/george-floyd-legacy-anniversary.html

Leonnig, Carol D., Shane Harris, and Josh Dawsey. 2019. Trump's calls with foreign leaders have long worried aides, leaving some 'genuinely horrified.'

*Washington Post.* [online]. 4 October. www.washingtonpost.com/politics/trumps-calls-with-foreign-leaders-have-long-worried-aides-leaving-some-genuinely-horrified/2019/10/04/537cc7a8-e602-11e9-a331-2df12d56a80b_story.html

Levendusky, Matthew. 2013. Partisan media exposure and attitudes toward the opposition. *Political Communication*, 30(4): 565–581.

Levendusky, Matthew, Josh Pasek, R. Lance Holbert, Andrew Renninger, Yotam Ophir, Dror Walter, Bruce Hardy, Kate Kenski, Ken Winneg, Daniel Romer, and Kathleen Hall Jamieson. 2023. *Democracy amid crises: Polarization, pandemic, protests, and persuasion.* New York: Oxford University Press.

Levy, Morris. 2021. Winning cures everything? Beliefs about voter fraud, voter confidence, and the 2016 election. *Electoral Studies*, 74: 1–8.

Lewis, Tanya. 2020. Nine COVID-19 myths that just won't go away. *Scientific American.* [online]. 18 August. www.scientificamerican.com/article/nine-covid-19-myths-that-just-wont-go-away/

Lewis-Beck, Michael S. 1988. *Economics and elections: The major western democracies.* Ann Arbor: University of Michigan Press.

Lewis-Beck, Michael S., and Tom W. Rice. 1992. *Forecasting elections.* Washington, DC: Congressional Quarterly Press.

Liptak, Kevin, Kaitlan Collins, Betsy Klein, Jim Acosta, and Paul LeBlanc. 2020. President Donald Trump and first lady Melania Trump test positive for COVID-19. *CNN.* [online]. 2 October. www.cnn.com/2020/10/01/politics/hope-hicks-positive-coronavirus/index.html

Lizotte, Mary-Kate. 2020. *Gender differences in public opinion.* Philadelphia: Temple University Press.

Lohse, Gerald, Steven Bellman, and Eric J. Johnson. 2000. Consumer buying behavior on the Internet: Findings from panel data. *Journal of Interactive Marketing*, 14(1): 15–29.

Lopez, German. 2020. The reviews are in: The first presidential debate was a disaster. *Vox.* [online]. 30 September. www.vox.com/2020/9/30/21495046/presidential-debate-trump-biden-reviews-who-won-disaster

Lyman, Brian. 2020. Fact check: Historians do teach that first Black members of Congress were Republicans. *USA Today.* [online]. 18 June. www.usatoday.com/story/news/factcheck/2020/06/18/fact-check-democrats-republicans-and-complicated-history-race/3208378001/

Lynch, Timothy J. 2020. Republicans have used a 'law and order' message to win elections before. This is why Trump could do it again. *The Conversation.* theconversation.com/republicans-have-used-a-law-and-order-message-to-win-elections-before-this-is-why-trump-could-do-it-again-145306

Ma, Yanni, Graham Dixon, and Jay D. Hmielowski. 2019. Psychological reactance from reading basic facts on climate change: The role of prior views and political identification. *Environmental Communication*, 13(1): 71–86.

Maio, Gregory R., and Victoria M. Esses. 2001. The need for affect: Individual differences in the motivation to approach or avoid emotions. *Journal of Personality*, 69(4): 583–614.

Makse, Todd, and Anand E. Sokhey. 2010. Revisiting the divisive primary hypothesis: 2008 and the Clinton – Obama nomination battle. *American Politics Research*, 38(2): 233–265.

Malhotra, Neil, Melissa R. Michelson, Todd Rogers, and Ali Adam Valenzuela. 2011. Text messages as mobilization tools: The conditional effect of habitual voting and election salience. *American Politics Research*, 39(4): 664–681.

Mann, Christopher B. 2021. Can conversing with a computer increase turnout? Mobilization using chatbot communication. *Journal of Experimental Political Science*, 8(1): 51–62.

Markus, Gregory B., and Philip E. Converse. 1979. A dynamic simultaneous equation model of electoral choice. *The American Political Science Review*, 73(4): 1055–1070.

Martin, Adam. 2020. Daily U.S. coronavirus cases second-highest on election day. *Wall Street Journal*. [online]. 5 November. www.wsj.com/livecoverage/covid-2020-11-04

Martin, Jonathan, and Alexander Burns. 2020. With cross talk, lies and mockery, Trump tramples decorum in debate with Biden. *New York Times*. [online]. 29 September. www.nytimes.com/2020/09/29/us/politics/trump-biden-debate.html

Mason, Melanie. 2020. The presidential cover-up, or how Trump went from shunning to wearing a mask. *Los Angeles Times*. [online]. 14 July. www.latimes.com/politics/story/2020-07-14/trump-coronavirus-mask-evolution

Matthews, J. Scott. 2019. Issue priming revisited: Susceptible voters and detectable effects. *British Journal of Political Science*, 49(2): 513–531.

Mattila, Mikko, Hanna Wass, Peter Söderlund, Sami Fredriksson, Päivi Fadjukoff, and Katja Kokko. 2011. Personality and turnout: Results from the Finnish longitudinal studies. *Scandinavian Political Studies*, 34(4): 287–306.

Mazzoni, Mary. 2021. Women CEOs are breaking records in the Fortune 500. *Triple Pundit*. [online]. 7 June. www.triplepundit.com/story/2021/women-ceos-fortune-500/723736

McCarthy, Justin. 2020. Confidence in accuracy of U.S. election matches record low. *Gallup*. [online]. 30 October. news.gallup.com/poll/321665/confidence-accuracy-election-matches-record-low.aspx

McDonald, Michael P. 2020. November general election turnout rates. *United States Elections Project*. www.electproject.org/2020g

McGowen, Ernest B., and Kristin N. Wylie. 2020. Racialized differences in perceptions of and emotional responses to police killings of unarmed African Americans. *Politics, Groups, and Identities*, 8(2): 396–406.

McKinney, Mitchell S., & Diana B. Carlin. 2004. Political campaign debates. In Lynda L. Kaid (ed.) *Handbook of political communication research*. Mahwah, NJ: Lawrence Erlbaum, 203–234.

McKinney, Mitchell S., Leslie A. Rill, and Esther Thorson. 2016. Civic engagement through presidential debates: Young citizens' political attitudes in the 2012 election. *American Behavioral Scientist*, 58(6): 755–775.

McKinney, Mitchell S., and Benjamin R. Warner. 2013. Do presidential debates matter? Examining a decade of campaign debate effects. *Argumentation and Advocacy*, 49(4): 238–258.

Miller, Joanne M., Kyle L. Saunders, and Christina E. Farhart. 2016. Conspiracy endorsement as motivated reasoning: The moderating roles of political knowledge and trust. *American Journal of Political Science*, 60(4): 824–844.

Miller, Warren E., and J. Merrill Shanks. 1996. *The New American voter*. Cambridge, MA: Harvard University Press.

Miller, Jon D., Logan T. Woods, and Jason Kalmbach. 2022. The impact of the Covid-19 pandemic in a polarized political system: Lessons from the 2020 election. *Electoral Studies*, 80: 1–10.

Mitchell, Glenn E., and Christopher Wlezien. 1995. The impact of legal constraints on voter registration, turnout, and the composition of the American electorate. *Political Behavior*, 17(2): 179–202.

Mondak, Jeffery J., Matthew V. Hibbing, Damarys Canache, Mitchell A. Seligson, and Mary R. Anderson. 2010. Personality and civic engagement: An integrative framework for the study of trait effects on political behavior. *American Political Science Review*, 104(1): 85–110.

Montanaro, Domenico. 2020. Trump derails 1st presidential debate with Biden, and 5 other takeaways. *NPR*. [online]. 30 September. www.npr.org/2020/09/30/918500976/trump-derails-first-presidential-debate-with-biden-and-5-other-takeaways

Morris, Robert C., and Ryan Jerome LeCount. 2020. The value of social control: Racial resentment, punitiveness, and White support for spending on law enforcement. *Sociological Perspectives*, 63(5): 697–718.

Mullinix, Kevin J., Toby Bolsen, and Robert J. Norris. 2021. The feedback effects of controversial police use of force. *Political Behavior*, 43(2021): 881–898.

Mutz, Diana C. 2002. The consequences of cross-cutting networks for political participation. *American Journal of Political Science*, 46(4): 838–855.

Mutz, Diana C., and Byron Reeves. 2005. The new videomalaise: Effects of televised incivility on political trust. *American Political Science Review*, 99(1): 1–15.

Myrdal, Gunnar. 1944. *An American dilemma: The Negro problem and modern democracy*. New York: Random House.

Nannestad, Peter, and Martin Paldam. 1997. The grievance asymmetry revisited: A micro study of economic voting in Denmark, 1986–92. *European Journal of Political Economy*, 13(1): 81–99.

Nelson, Libby. 2016. Donald Trump's history of misogyny, sexism, and harassment: A comprehensive review. *Vox*. [online]. 12 October. www.vox.com/2016/10/8/13110734/donald-trump-leaked-audio-recording-billy-bush-sexism

Niño, Michael D., and Brittany N. Hearne. 2022. Dimensions of acculturation and biological dysregulation among Latina/os: The role of ethnic background, gender, and immigrant generation. *Ethnicity & Health*, 27(4): 963–979.

Norrander, Barbara. 2008. The history of gender gaps. In Lois Duke Whittaker (ed.) *Voting the gender gap*. Champaign, IL: University of Illinois Press, 9–32.

Norris, Pippa, Holly Ann Garnett, and Max Grömping. 2020. The paranoid style of American elections: Explaining perceptions of electoral integrity in an age of populism. *Journal of Elections, Public Opinion and Parties*, 30(1): 105–125.

NPR. 2020. What's changed since polls were wrong about 2016's presidential election. *NPR*. [online]. 28 October. www.npr.org/2020/10/28/928556186/whats-changed-since-polls-were-wrong-about-2016s-presidential-election

Oliver, J. Eric, and Thomas J. Wood. 2014. Conspiracy theories and the paranoid style(s) of mass opinion. *American Journal of Political Science*, 58(4): 952–966.

Panagopoulos, Costas. 2012. Campaign context and preference dynamics in US presidential elections. *Journal of Elections, Public Opinion and Parties*, 22(2): 123–137.

Papaioannou, Kostas, Myrto Pantazi, Jan-Willem van Prooijen. 2023. Is democracy under threat? Why belief in conspiracy theories predicts autocratic attitudes. *European Journal of Social Psychology*, 53(5): 846–856. doi.org/10.1002/ejsp.2939

Parker, Kim, Nikki Graff, and Ruth Igielnik (2019). Generation Z looks a lot like millennials on key social and political issues. *PEW Research*. [online]. www.pewresearch.org/social-trends/2019/01/17/generation-z-looks-a-lot-like-millennials-on-key-social-and-political-issues/

Paz, Christina. 2020. All the President's lies about the coronavirus an unfinished compendium of Trump's overwhelming dishonesty during a national emergency. *The Atlantic*. [online]. 2 November. www.theatlantic.com/politics/archive/2020/11/trumps-lies-about-coronavirus/608647/

Peeples, Lynne. 2020. Face masks: What the data say. *Nature*, 586(7828): 186–189.

Peterson, David A. M. 2009. Campaign learning and vote determinants. *American Journal of Political Science*, 53(2): 445–460.

Peterson, Erik, Sharad Goel, and Shanto Iyengar. 2019. Partisan selective exposure in online news consumption: Evidence from the 2016 presidential campaign. *Political Science Research and Methods*, 9(2): 1–17.

Pettypiece, Shannon. 2022. Biden signs police reform executive order on anniversary of George Floyd's death. *NBC News*. [online]. 25 May. www.nbcnews.com/politics/white-house/biden-signs-police-reform-executive-order-anniversary-george-floyds-de-rcna30548

Pomper, Gerald M. 2005. The presidential election: The ills of American politics after 9/11. In Michael Nelson (ed.) *The elections of 2004*. Washington: CQ Press, 42–68.

Popkin, Samuel L. 2012. *The candidate: What it takes to win – and hold – the White House*. New York: Oxford University Press.

Pratto, Felicia, Jim Sidanius, Lisa M. Stallworth, and Bertram F. Malle. 1994. Social dominance orientation: A personality variable predicting social and political attitudes. *Journal of Personality and Social Psychology*, 67(4): 741-

Prichard, Eric C., and Stephen D. Christman. 2020. Authoritarianism, conspiracy beliefs, gender and COVID-19: Links between individual differences and concern about COVID-19, mask wearing behaviors, and the tendency to blame China for the virus. *Frontiers in Psychology*, 11: 1–7

Prior, Markus. 2007. *Post-broadcast democracy: How media choice increases inequality in political involvement and polarizes elections*. New York: Cambridge University Press.

Prior, Markus. 2012. Who watches presidential debates? Measurement problems in campaign effects research. *Public Opinion Quarterly*, 76(2): 350–363.

Ratliff, Kate A., Liz Redford, John Conway, and Colin Tucker Smith. 2019. Engendering support: Hostile sexism predicts voting for Donald Trump over

Hillary Clinton in the 2016 US presidential election. *Group Processes & Intergroup Relations*, 22(4): 578–593.

Redlawsk, David P. 2002. Hot cognition or cool consideration? Testing the effects of motivated reasoning on political decision making. *Journal of Politics*, 64(4): 1021–1044.

Reuters. 2020. U.S. saw Summer of Black Lives Matter protests demanding change. *Reuters*. [online]. 7 December. www.reuters.com/article/global-poy-blm/u-s-saw-summer-of-black-lives-matter-protests-demanding-change-idUSKBN28H1K1

Riccardi, Nicholas. 2020. Here's the reality behind Trump's claims about mail voting. *AP News*. [online]. 30 September. apnews.com/article/virus-outbreak-joe-biden-election-2020-donald-trump-elections-3e8170c3348ce3719d4bc7182146b582

Richey, Sean. 2017. A birther and a truther: The influence of the authoritarian personality on conspiracy beliefs. *Politics & Policy*, 45(3): 465–485.

Rizzo, Salvador. 2020. Trump's fusillade of falsehoods on mail voting. *Washington Post*. [online]. 11 September. www.washingtonpost.com/politics/2020/09/11/trumps-fusillade-falsehoods-mail-voting/

Rogowski, Jon. 2014. Electoral choice, ideological conflict, and political participation. *American Journal of Political Science*, 58(2): 479–494.

Rosenstone, Steven J. 1983. *Forecasting presidential elections*. New Haven: Yale University Press.

Rosenstone, Steven J., and John Mark Hansen. 1993. *Mobilization, participation, and democracy in America*. New York: Macmillan Publishing Company.

Rosenstone, Steven J., and Raymond E. Wolfinger. 1978. The effect of registration laws on voter turnout. *The American Political Science Review*, 72(1): 22–45.

Schaffner, Brian F. 2005. Priming gender: Campaigning on women's issues in US Senate elections. *American Journal of Political Science*, 49(4): 803–817.

Schaffner, Brian F., Matthew MacWilliams, and Tatishe Nteta. 2018. Understanding White polarization in the 2016 vote for president: The sobering role of racism and sexism. *Political Science Quarterly*, 133(1): 9–34.

Schattschneider, Elmer Eric. (1960). *The semi-sovereign people: A realist's view of democracy in America*. New York: Holt, Reinhart, and Winston.

Scherer, Zachary. 2021. Majority of voters used nontraditional methods to cast ballots in 2020. *Census*. [online]. 29 April. www.census.gov/library/stories/2021/04/what-methods-did-people-use-to-vote-in-2020-election.html

Schraufnagel, Scot, Michael J. Pomante, and Quan Li. 2020. Cost of voting in the American States: 2020. *Election Law Journal: Rules, Politics, and Policy*. www.liebertpub.com/doi/10.1089/elj.2020.0666

Schrott, Peter R., and David J. Lanoue. 2013. The power and limitations of televised presidential debates: Assessing the real impact of candidate performance on public opinion and vote choice. *Electoral Studies*, 32(4): 684–692.

Schwartz, Brian. 2020. Joe Biden pledges to pick a woman to be his running mate. *CNBC*. [online]. 15 March. www.cnbc.com/2020/03/15/democratic-debate-joe-biden-pledges-to-pick-a-woman-as-his-running-mate.html

Semetko, Holli A., and Patti M. Valkenburg. 2000. Framing European politics: A content analysis of press and television news. *Journal of Communication*, 50(2): 93–109.

Shaverdian, Narek, Debra N. Yeboa, Liz Gardner, Paul M. Harari, Kaiping Liao, Susan McCloskey, Richard Tuli, Neha Vapiwala, and Reshma Jagsi. 2019. Nationwide survey of patients' perspectives regarding their radiation and multidisciplinary cancer treatment experiences. *Journal of Oncology Practice*, 15(12): e1010–e1017.

Shaw, Daron R. 1999. A study of presidential campaign event effects from 1952 to 1992. *The Journal of Politics*, 61(2): 387–422.

Shaw, Daron R., Lindsay Dun, and Sarah Heise. 2022. Mobilizing peripheral partisan voters: A field experimental analysis from three California congressional election campaigns. *American Politics Research*, 50(5): 587–602.

Shino, Enrijeta, and Daniel Smith. 2020. Political knowledge and convenience voting. *Journal of Elections, Public Opinion and Parties*, 32(2) (September): 1–21. www.tandfonline.com/doi/full/10.1080/17457289.2020.1814308

Shino, Enrijeta, and Daniel A. Smith. 2021. Pandemic politics: COVID-19, health concerns, and vote choice in the 2020 general election. *Journal of Elections, Public Opinion and Parties*, 31(sup1): 191–205.

Segers, Grace. 2020. Trump says he wears masks "when needed" and mocks Biden's masks. *CBS News*. [online]. 30 September. www.cbsnews.com/news/trump-says-he-wears-masks-when-needed-and-mocks-bidens-masks/

Seipel, Arnie. 2016. Trump makes unfounded claim that 'Millions' voted illegally for Clinton. *NPR*. [online]. 27 November. www.npr.org/2016/11/27/503506026/trump-makes-unfounded-claim-that-millions-voted-illegally-for-clinton

Sides, John, Chris Tausanovitch, and Lynn Vavreck. 2022. *The bitter end: The 2020 presidential campaign and the challenge to American democracy*. Princeton, NJ: Princeton University Press.

Sides, John, and Lynn Vavreck. 2014. *The Gamble: Choice and chance in the 2012 presidential election*. Princeton, NJ: Princeton University Press.

Silva, Daniela. 2020. Trump's call for supporters to watch polls 'very carefully' raises concerns of voter intimidation. *NBC News*. [online]. 30 September www.nbcnews.com/news/us-news/trump-s-call-supporters-watch-polls-very-carefully-raises-concerns-n1241613

Sinclair, Betsy, Steven S. Smith, and Patrick D. Tucker. 2018. "It's largely a rigged system": Voter confidence and the winner effect in 2016. *Political Research Quarterly*, 71(4): 854–868.

Singer, Matthew. 2011. When do voters actually think "It's the Economy"? Evidence from the 2008 presidential campaign. *Electoral Studies*, 30(4): 621–632.

Smith, David Norman. 2019. Authoritarianism reimagined: The riddle of Trump's base. *The Sociological Quarterly*, 60(2): 210–223.

Smith, Terrance. 2020. Trump has longstanding history of calling elections 'rigged' if he doesn't like the results. *ABC News*. [online]. 11 November. abcnews.go.com/Politics/trump-longstanding-history-calling-elections-rigged-doesnt-results/story?id=74126926

Sniderman, Paul M., and Thomas Leonard Piazza. 1993. *The scar of race.* Cambridge, MA: Harvard University Press.

Socia, Kelly M., Melissa S. Morabito, Brenda J. Bond, and Elias S. Nader. 2021. Public perceptions of police agency fairness and the willingness to call police. *The American Review of Public Administration,* 51(5): 360–373.

Solt, Frederick. 2012. The social origins of authoritarianism. *Political Research Quarterly,* 65(4): 703–713.

Southwell, Priscilla L. 2007. Vote-by-mail: Voter preferences and self-reported voting behavior in the state of Oregon. *American Review of Politics,* 28: 139–46.

Spence, Janet T., and Eugene D. Hahn. 1997. The attitudes toward women scale and attitude change in college students. *Psychology of Women Quarterly,* 21(1): 17–34.

Steeper, Frederick T. 1978. Public response to Gerald Ford's Statement in Eastern Europe in the second debate. In George F. Bishop, Robert G. Meadow, and Marilyn Jackson-Beeck (eds.) *The presidential debates: Media, electoral and policy perspectives.* New York: Praeger, 81–101.

Stempel, Carl, Thomas Hargrove, and Guido H. Stempel III. 2007. Media use, social structure, and belief in 9/11 conspiracy theories. *Journalism & Mass Communication Quarterly,* 84(2): 353–372.

Stenner, Karen. 2005. *The authoritarian dynamic.* New York: Cambridge University Press.

Stepp, Kyla K., and Jeremiah J. Castle. 2021. Research note: Authoritarianism, racial resentment, and attitudes on the Colin Kaepernick protests. *The Social Science Journal,* 1–11. www-tandfonline-com.ezproxy1.lib.asu.edu/action/showCitFormats?doi=10.1080%2F03623319.2021.1884781

Strickler, Ryan, and Edward Lawson. 2022. Racial conservatism, self-monitoring, and perceptions of police violence. *Politics, Groups, and Identities,* 10(2): 254–275.

Stroud, Natalie Jomini. 2011. *Niche news: The politics of news choice.* New York: Oxford University Press.

Sullivan, Andy. 2020. "This clown" – "Nothing smart about you": Un-presidential insults fly in first Trump-Biden debate. *Reuters.* [online]. 29 September. www.reuters.com/article/us-usa-election-debate-insults/this-clown-nothing-smart-about-you-un-presidential-insults-fly-in-first-trump-biden-debate-idUSKBN26LoR8

Summers, Juana. 2020. Trump calls Harris a 'Monster,' reviving a pattern of attacking women of color. *NPR.* [online]. 9 October. www.npr.org/2020/10/09/921884531/trump-calls-harris-a-monster-reviving-a-pattern-of-attacking-women-of-color

Sutton Robbie M., and Karen M. Douglas. 2014. Examining the monological nature of conspiracy theories. In Jan-Willem van Prooijen and Paul A. M. van Lange (eds.) *Power politics paranoia: Why people are suspicious their lead.* Cambridge: Cambridge University Press, 254–272.

Sweren-Becker, Eliza, Anne Glatz, and Elisabeth Campbell. 2020. Voting during COVID-19. *The Brennan Center for Justice.* [online]. 20 November. www.brennancenter.org/our-work/research-reports/voting-during-covid-19

Sydnor, Emily. 2019. *Disrespectful democracy: The psychology of political incivility.* New York: Columbia University Press.

Taylor, Steven. 2022. The psychology of pandemics. *Annual Review of Clinical Psychology*, 18: 581–609.

Taylor, Derrick Bryson. 2021. George Floyd protests: A timeline. *The New York Times*. [online]. 28 March. www.nytimes.com/article/george-floyd-protests-timeline.html

Tesler, Michael. 2013. The return of old-fashioned racism to White Americans' partisan preferences in the early Obama era. *The Journal of Politics*, 75(1): 110–123.

Testa, Paul F., Matthew V. Hibbing, and Melinda Ritchie. 2014. Orientations toward conflict and the conditional effects of political disagreement. *The Journal of Politics*, 76(3): 770–785.

Thomas, Deja, and Juliana Menasce Horowitz. 2020. Support for Black Lives Matter has decreased since June but remains strong among Black Americans. *Pew Research Center*. [online]. 16 September. www.pewresearch.org/fact-tank/2020/09/16/support-for-black-lives-matter-has-decreased-since-june-but-remains-strong-among-black-americans/

Troisi, Alfonso, Roberta Croce Nanni, Alessandra Riconi, Valeria Carola, and David Di Cave. 2021. Fear of COVID-19 among healthcare workers: The role of neuroticism and fearful attachment. *Journal of Clinical Medicine*, 10(19): 1–8.

Tuch, Steven A., and Ronald Weitzer. 1997. Trends: Racial differences in attitudes toward the police. *The Public Opinion Quarterly*, 61(4): 642–663.

Tufte, Edward. 1978. *Political control of the economy*. Princeton, NJ: Princeton University Press.

Twyman, Joe. 2008. Getting it right: YouGov and online survey research in Britain. *Journal of Elections, Public Opinion and Parties*, 18(4): 343–354.

Ulbig, Stacy G., and Carolyn L. Funk. 1999. Conflict avoidance and political participation. *Political Behavior*, 21(3): 265–282.

Uscinski, Joseph E., Adam M. Enders, Michelle I. Seelig, Casey A. Klofstad, John R. Funchion, Caleb Everett, Stefan Wuchty, Kamal Premaratne, and Manohar N. Murthi. 2021. American politics in two dimensions: Partisan and ideological identities versus anti-establishment orientations. *American Journal of Political Science*, 65(4): 877–895.

Uscinski, Joseph E., Casey Klofstad, and Matthew D. Atkinson. 2016. What drives conspiratorial beliefs? The role of informational cues and predispositions. *Political Research Quarterly*, 69(1): 57–71.

Uscinski, Joseph E., and Santiago Olivella. 2017. The conditional effect of conspiracy thinking on attitudes toward climate change. *Research & Politics*, 4(4): 1–9.

Uscinski, Joseph E., and Joseph M. Parent. 2014 *American conspiracy theories*. New York: Oxford University Press.

Valentino, Nicholas A., Vincent L. Hutchings, and Ismail K. White. 2002. Cues that matter: How political ads prime racial attitudes during campaigns. *American Political Science Review*, 96(1): 75–90.

Valentino, Nicholas A., Vincent L. Hutchings, and Dmitri Williams. 2004. The impact of political advertising on knowledge, internet information seeking, and candidate preference. *Journal of Communication*, 54(2): 337–354.

Van Prooijen, Jan-Willem, and Karen M. Douglas. 2018. Belief in conspiracy theories: Basic principles of an emerging research domain. *European Journal of Social Psychology*, 48(7): 897–908.

Vavreck, Lynn. 2009. *The message matters: The economy and presidential campaigns*. Princeton, NJ: Princeton University Press.
Vavreck, Lynn, and Douglas Rivers. 2008. The 2006 cooperative congressional election study. *Journal of Elections, Public Opinion and Parties*, 18(4): 355–366.
Verba, Sidney, Kay Lehman Schlozman, and Henry E. Brady. 1995. *Voice and equality: Civic voluntarism in American politics*. Cambridge: Harvard University Press.
Vonnahme, Greg, and Beth Miller. 2013. Candidate cues and voter confidence in American elections. *Journal of Elections, Public Opinion & Parties*, 23(2): 223–239.
Voth, Ben. 2017. The presidential debates 2016. In Robert E. Denton, (ed.) *The 2016 US presidential campaign*. London: Palgrave Macmillan, 77–98.
Walter, Annemarie S., and Hugo Drochon. 2020. Conspiracy thinking in Europe and America: A comparative study. *Political Studies*, 70: 1–20. journals.sagepub.com/doi/10.1177/00323217209726016
Wang, Haiyan, and Jan-Willem van Prooijen. 2022. Stolen elections: How conspiracy beliefs during the 2020 American presidential elections changed over time. *Applied Cognitive Psychology*, 37: 277–289.
Warner, Benjamin R., and Mitchell S. McKinney. 2013. To unite and divide: The polarizing effect of presidential debates. *Communication Studies*, 64(5): 508–527.
Weider-Hatfield, Deborah, and John D. Hatfield. 1995. Relationships among conflict management styles, levels of conflict, and reactions to work. *The Journal of Social Psychology*, 135(6): 687–698.
Weinschenk, Aaron, and Costas Panagopoulos. 2016. Convention effects: Examining the impact of national presidential nominating conventions on information, preferences, and behavioral intentions. *Journal of Elections, Public Opinion and Parties*, 26(4): 511–531.
Wolak, Jennifer. 2020. Conflict avoidance and gender gaps in political engagement. *Political Behavior*. doi.org/10.1007/s11109-020-09614-5
Wolfinger, Raymond E., and Steven J. Rosenstone. 1980. *Who votes?* New Haven: Yale University Press.
Womick, Jake, Tobias Rothmund, Flavio Azevedo, Laura A. King, and John T. Jost. 2019. Group-based dominance and authoritarian aggression predict support for Donald Trump in the 2016 US presidential election. *Social Psychological and Personality Science*, 10(5): 643–652.
Yawn, Mike, and Bob Beatty. 2000. Debate-induced opinion change: What matters? *American Politics Quarterly*, 28(2): 270–285.
Yen, Hope, Swenson, Ali, and Amanda Seitz. 2020. AP FACT CHECK: Trump's claims of vote rigging are all wrong. *AP News*. [online]. 3 December. apnews.com/article/election-2020-ap-fact-check-joe-biden-donald-trump-technology-49a24edd6d10888dbad61689c24b05a5
Zaller, John. R. 1992. *The nature and origins of mass opinion*. Cambridge: Cambridge University Press.

# Index

Abrams, Stacey, 208–209
access to voting. *See* voting access
advertising, campaign effects
    through, 6–7
  digital advertising, 5–6
  on social media, 5–6
age
  election integrity confidence influenced
    by, 132
  support for racial justice influenced
    by, 102
Alter, Charlotte, 37
ambivalent sexism, 200–201
American First Action, 155
American National Election Study
    (ANES), 206
Arbery, Ahmaud, 101
authoritarianism
  assessments of candidate performance
    and, 47, 51–52
  COVID-19 pandemic and, 77–78, 81
  global contexts for, 19
  as psychological disposition, 18–20
    measures of, 20
  racial justice movements and, 100
  right-wing, 77–78
  of Trump, 19
  in U.S. political history, 18–19
    in 1952 presidential election, 19–20
    in 2016 presidential election, 19–20
  voter turnout influenced by, 166
avoidance. *See* conflict avoidance
Axelrod, David, 44

Baker, Peter, 21–22
Ball, Molly, 37
Barr, William, 93
Barrett, Amy Coney (Justice), 65, 73–74
Bash, Dana, 44
benevolent sexism, 17
Berman, John, 98–99
Biden, Joe, 15. *See also* COVID-19
    pandemic, during 2020 presidential
    election; electoral campaigns;
    presidential debates; 2020
    presidential election
  campaigning during COVID-19
    pandemic, 66–68
    digital operations, 67
    mask use, 67
    voter activation centers, 67
  conspiracy thinking about, 23
  election integrity confidence under,
    133–139
    electoral consequences for, 139–143
    partisan news sources as influence
      on, 136–138
    thermometer models for ratings of,
      139–143
    variables for, 133–134
  electoral campaign of
    during COVID-19 pandemic, 66–68
    evaluation as candidate influenced
      by, 148–159, 162
    after September debate, 151–152
  executive order for, 120
  Harris, K., and, 17, 98, 114

Biden, Joe (cont.)
　hostile sexism and, 17
　police support by public and, 117
　September 2020 presidential debate
　　and, 37
　　assessment of debate performance,
　　　42–54
　　as debate winner, 40–42
　　support of racial justice protests, 98
　　electoral consequences for,
　　　114–118
　Violence against Women Act and, 17
birtherism conspiracy theories, 14
*The Bitter End* (Sides, Tausanovitch and
　Vavreck), 3
Black Lives Matter movement
　defund the police movement as part of,
　　120–121
　public support of, 94–95
　　changes in, 120
　racial resentment as influence on, 14
　Trump criticism of, 97
Black voters, turnout in 2020 presidential
　election, 183
Blake, Jacob, 98–99
Blitzer, Wolf, 44
Bowser, Muriel, 93
Brooks, Rayshard, 101
Brown, Michael, 14
Bruni, Frank, 10
Bush, George H. W., 7–8
Bush, George W., 40, 210

campaign effects
　through advertising, 6–7
　　digital advertising, 5–6
　　on social media, 5–6
　closeness of electoral race and, 9
　fundamentals of, 6–7
　　advertising, 6–7
　　campaign events, 6
　　door-to-door canvassing, 8
　　political issues, 7–8
　for future campaigns, 200–202
　historical study of, 4–5
　　*The People's Choice*, 4–5
　hypodermic needle theory of, 5
　literature on, 4–10
　minimal effects, 5–6
　through negative messaging, 9
　persuasive effects, 5
　political polarization, 9

campaign messaging, during 2020
　presidential election, 193–196.
　*See also* voter participation
　and turnout
　about mail-in voting, 164–165
　access to voting and, 164–165
　citizen-centered theory of campaigns
　　and, 165, 190–191
　theoretical approach to, 164–166
　voter turnout influenced by, 180–183
　　on campaign issues, 180–181
　　convenience voting and, 183–190
　　demographic characteristics of
　　　citizens, 182–183
　　political characteristics of citizens,
　　　182, 182
　　psychological predispositions
　　　and, 181
campaign theory. *See* citizen-centered
　theory of campaigns
Carlson, Tucker, 75, 98
Carter, Jimmy, 39–40
Carville, James, 7–8
Chauvin, Derek, 92, 119–120
Cheney, Dick, 40
Cheney, Liz, 145
Christie, Chris, 65
citizen-centered theory of campaigns,
　10–26, 196. *See also* campaign
　messaging
　access to information, 10
　campaign messaging and, 165, 190–191
　COVID-19 pandemic and, 74
　political partisanship and, 10–12
　　prior information and, 11
　　psychological predispositions, 10–12
　psychological predispositions, 13
　　authoritarianism, 18–20
　　Big Five personality traits and, 12
　　conflict avoidance, 21–22
　　conspiracy thinking, 22–26
　　hostile sexism, 16–18
　　political partisanship and, 10–12
　　racial resentment, 14–16
　　September 2020 presidential debate
　　　assessment influenced by, 46,
　　　49–50
　　vote choice and, 12
　September 2020 presidential debate and,
　　38, 52
　　psychological predispositions and, 46,
　　　49–50

## Index

Clinton, Bill, 7–8
Clinton, Hillary, 97. *See also* 2016 presidential election
  conspiracy thinking about, 23
  in 2016 presidential debates, 122–123
CNN News, 44
Commission on Presidential Debates (CPD), September 2020 presidential debate and, 38, 62
conflict avoidance
  approach/avoidance component in, 22
  Conflict Communication Scale, 22
  during COVID-19 pandemic, 78–79, 81
  as psychological predisposition, 21–22
  measures of, 22
  racial justice protests and, 100–101, 107–108
  September 2020 presidential debate assessment and, 49
  tolerance toward, 21
  voter turnout influenced by, 170
Conflict Communication Scale, 22
conspiracy thinking
  about COVID-19 pandemic, 23
  about voter fraud, 24
  on assassination of Kennedy, J. F., 23
  during COVID-19 pandemic, 76–77, 81
  election integrity confidence influenced by, 127, 132
  support for Trump and, 133–134, 137–138
  Fox News and, 24
  historical trajectory of, 23
  measures of, 25–26
    for psychological predispositions, 26
  media influences on, 24
  participation in conventional politics, 24
  as psychological disposition, 22–26
  QAnon, 23
  racial justice protests and, 100, 107–108
  September 2020 presidential debate assessment and, 47, 51–52
  Trump and, 23
    election integrity claims by, 133–134
  in U.S. political contexts, 23, 24
  voter turnout influenced by, 24, 170–171
convenience voting
  campaign messaging as influence on, 183–190
  voter turnout and, 179–190

Conway, Kellyanne, 65
Cooper, Anderson, 98–99
Cooper, John, 75
COVID-19 pandemic, during 2020 presidential election, 1–2, 90–91
  Biden campaign during, 66–68
    digital operations, 67
    mask use, 67
    public trust in handling pandemic, 84, 89–90
    voter activation centers, 67
  as campaign issue, 152–154
    voter preference changes influenced by, 160
  case count, 63
  as election issue, 63, 72
    changes in citizens' views, 71–74
    citizen-centered theory of campaign and, 74
    Trump diagnosis as influence on, 73–74
  methodological approach to, 69–71
    demographic characteristics in, 79
    political characteristics of respondents, 75–79
  mortality rates on election day, 63
  in news stories, 75–76
    on Fox News, 75
  political partisanship differences and, 67, 72–73
    among Democrats, 72
    among Republicans, 72
  priming voters and, 70
    after Trump diagnosis, 83–90
  psychological predispositions and, 76–79
    to authoritarianism, 77–78, 81
    to conflict avoidance, 78–79, 81
    conspiracy thinking, 76–77, 81
    to racism, 78, 81–82
    to sexism, 78, 81–82
  public worries about, 79–83, 88
    authoritarianism and, 81
    Biden and, 84, 89–90
    conflict avoidance and, 81
    conspiracy thinking and, 81
    by gender, 82
    models for, 79, 84
    by race, 82
    racism as influence on, 81–82
    sexism as factor in, 81–82
    Trump and, 85–87, 89

COVID-19 pandemic, during 2020 (cont.)
  retrospective voting and, 70
  superspreader events, 65, 73–74
  Trump campaign during, 66–68
    contraction of/hospitalization for viral infection, 1–2, 62, 68–69, 73–74, 83–90, 194
    declaration as national emergency, 64–65
    lack of mask use during, 66
    political partisanship and, 67
    public trust in handling pandemic, 85–87, 89
    rejection of mask mandates, 72–73
    Republican National Committee coordination with, 66
    social distancing guidelines, 64–65
COVID-19 pandemic, in U.S.
  Centers for Disease Control confirmation of, 63–64
  conspiracy thinking about, 23
  early cases during, 63–64
  global economic impact of, 2
  gross domestic product during, 2
  history of, 63–65
  mortality rates, 2, 63
  in *New York Times*, 68–69
  social distancing guidelines, 64–65
  unemployment rates during, 2
  voter turnout influenced by, 168–169, 186
  World Health Organization and, 63–64
CPD. *See* Commission on Presidential Debates (CPD); September 2020 presidential debate and
Cruz, Ted, 122

Dahl, Robert, 209–210
debates. *See* presidential debates; September presidential debate
Declaration of Independence, U.S., 18
defund the police movement, 120–121
democracy. *See* representative democracy
Democratic party
  confidence in election integrity, 124
  racial justice protests and, 97–99
  response to COVID-19 pandemic, 72
Dickerson, John, 38
digital advertising, campaign effects and, 5–6
Dillon, Jen O'Malley, 67
Duterte, Rodrigo, 19

Edel, Charles, 18
election integrity, public beliefs in
  age as factor in, 132
  assessment of, 143–146
  under Biden, 133–139
    electoral consequences for, 139–143
    partisan news sources as influence on, 136–138
    thermometer models for ratings of, 139–143
    variables for, 133–135
  as campaign issue, 150, 154
  confidence levels among voters, 129–132
    among Biden supporters, 129–130
    among Trump supporters, 129–130
    variable measures for, 130, 131
    "winner's effect" and, 129–130
  conspiracy thinking and, 127, 132
    support for Trump and, 133–134, 137–138
  determinants of confidence in, 125–132
    assessment of, 125–129
    demographic factors in, 128–129
    psychological predispositions as, 128, 132, 137–138
    trust in government as, 127–128
    "winner's effect," 125–126
  education level as factor in, 132
  electoral consequences of, 139–143
    thermometer models for candidate ratings, 139–143
  news sources as influence on, 127, 136
    authoritarianism as predisposition and, 138–139
    among Biden supporters, 136–138
    among Trump supporters, 136–138
  partisan differences in, 124, 126
  voter turnout influenced by, 169
  "winner's effect"
    confidence levels among voters influenced by, 129–130
    as determinant of confidence, 125–126
electoral campaigns, during 2020 presidential election. *See also* campaign effects; citizen-centered theory of campaigns
  for Biden
    during COVID-19 pandemic, 66–68
    evaluation as candidate, 148–159, 162
    after September debate, 151–152

campaign issues as element of
  candidate evaluation influenced by,
    149–150
  COVID-19 pandemic, 152–154
  electoral integrity claims, 150, 154
  state of economy, 150
  support for social justice protests,
    155–156
candidate evaluation influenced by,
  148–159, 162–163
  by assessment of political rival,
    150–151
  campaign issues as factor in, 149–150
  changes in, 157–159
  multilevel modeling for, 158
  in November thermometer measures,
    151–159
  political partisanship and, 156, 159,
    161–162
  psychological predispositions as
    influence on, 150, 151, 156–157
  after September debate, 149, 151–152,
    157–159
COVID-19 pandemic and
  as campaign issues, 152–154
  voter preference changes influenced
    by, 160
postmortem of, 147–148
  in news media, 147, 148
psychological predispositions and
  candidate evaluation influenced by,
    150, 151, 156–157
  voter preference changes influenced
    by, 159
representative democracy and, 3
theoretical approach to, 147–148
for Trump
  advisor concerns about electoral
    integrity claims, 147–148
  evaluation as candidate, 148–159,
    162–163
voter preference changes and, 159–162
  COVID-19 pandemic as influence
    on, 160
  multilevel logic modeling and, 160, 161
  psychological predispositions and, 159
electoral fraud, claims of. *See also* election
    integrity; voter fraud
  by Trump, 3, 24, 122–125, 133
  through mail-in voting, 123
  Stop the Steal movement, 144
  for 2012 presidential election, 122

for 2016 presidential election,
    122–124
  for 2012 presidential campaign, 122
Emmrich, Stuart, 37
Esper, Mark, 93

Fair Housing Act, U.S. (1968), 14
Fauci, Anthony, 65, 75–76
Fleisher, Ari, 45
Floyd, George, murder of, 92, 99, 101. *See
    also* Black Lives Matter movement
  legislation as result of, 120
  racial unrest as response to, 2–3
  social justice protests in response to,
    92–97
    Black Lives Matter movement and,
      93–97
    long-term implications of, 119–121
    public support of, 94–95
    Trump's response to, 92–93
    systematic racism as factor in, 120
Ford, Gerald, 39–40
*Fox & Friends First*, 38
Fox News, 38
  conspiracy thinking and, 24
  COVID-19 pandemic coverage, 75
  2020 presidential debate and, 44–45
Frankel, Max, 39–40
fraud. *See* voter fraud

Garner, Eric, 14, 99
GDP. *See* gross domestic product (GDP)
gender. *See also* women
  public worries about COVID-19
    pandemic by, 82
  racial justice protests by, 103
Goldmacher, Shane, 61
Google Transparency Project, 155
Gore, Al, 210
gross domestic product (GDP), during
    COVID-19 pandemic, 2
Guthrie, Savannah, 37–38

Haberman, Maggie, 21–22
Haley, Nikki, 201
Hanks, Tom, 64
Hannity, Sean, 38, 44–45
Harris, DeAndre, 14
Harris, Kamala, 17, 18, 98, 114, 201
Hasen, Rick, 145
Hayes, Andrew, 50
Hayes, Chris, 75–76

Hewitt, Don, 39
Heyer, Heather, 14
Hill, Anita, 17
Holt, Lester, 38, 76
hostile sexism
  Biden and, 17
  elements of, 17–18
  history of, 16–17
  measures of, 18
  as psychological predisposition, 16–18
  Trump and, 17, 18
hypodermic needle theory, of campaign effects, 5

implicit association tests, of racism, 15

January 6th Capitol attacks, 144–145, 208
Johnson, Dion, 101
justice. See racial justice

Kennedy, John F.
  assassination conspiracies about, 23
  1960 presidential election and, 39
Kerry, John, 40
Key, V. O., 70
Kim Jong Un, 19
King, Martin Luther, Jr. assassination of, 2, 14, 93
Kueng, J. Alexander, 119–120

Lane, Thomas, 119–120
Latino voters, voter turnout for 2020 presidential election, 183
Lazarsfeld, Paul, 4–5
Lee, Mike, 65
Limbaugh, Rush, 76–77
Los Angeles Times, 114

mail-in voting ballots
  campaign messaging about, 164–165
  electoral fraud claims and, 123
mask use, during COVID-19 pandemic, by Biden, 67
McCain, John, 69
McCarthy, Joseph, 18
#MeToo Movement, 16
messaging. See campaign messaging
Meyer, Ron, 38
Milley, Mark, 93
Montanaro, Domenico, 37
mortality rates, for COVID-19 pandemic, on election day, 2, 63

negative messaging, against opposing candidates, 9
*New York Times*, 10, 21–22, 39–40, 61
  Trump COVID-19 diagnosis and hospitalization in, 68–69
news media. See also Fox News; *New York Times*; specific news media
  COVID-19 pandemic coverage, 75–76
  election integrity influenced by, 127, 136
  authoritarianism predispositions and, 138–139
  Biden support and, 136–138
  among Biden supporters, 136–138
  Trump support and, 136–138
  among Trump supporters, 136–138
  postmortem of 2020 electoral campaigns, 147, 148
  racial justice protest coverage
    political partisanship and, 98–99
    support of police and, 112–113
  September 2020 presidential debate coverage in, 43–46
1940 presidential election, in U.S., 4
1952 presidential election, in U.S., 19–20
1992 presidential election, in U.S., 7–8
1960 presidential election, debate during, 39
1976 presidential election, debate during, 39–40
Nixon, Richard, 39, 97

Obama, Barack, 69, 122
  birtherism claims against, 14
  conspiracy thinking about, 23
October presidential debate, during 2020 election, virtual options for, 62
O'Donnell, Rosie, 17
Oswald, Lee Harvey, 23

Papathanasiou, Gus, 208
partisanship, political
  candidate evaluation influenced by, 156, 159, 161–162
  citizen-centered theory of campaigns and, 10–12
  prior information for voters and, 11
  psychological predispositions and, 10–12
  COVID-19 pandemic and, 67, 72–73
    among Democrats, 72
    among Republicans, 72
  election integrity influenced by, 124, 126

racial justice protests influenced by, 97–99
  citizens' support for racial justice protests and, 108
  news coverage as influence on, 98–99
  September 2020 presidential debate and assessments of candidate performance and, 43, 45–46, 49
  assessments on "winner" of debate, 41–42
  September 2020 presidential debate assessment influenced by, 43, 45–46, 49
  voter turnout influenced by, 166–167
*The People's Choice* study, 4–5
polarization, political. *See also* partisanship
  campaign effects and, 9
  voter turnout influenced by, 172–173
police brutality. *See also* Floyd, George, murder of
  racial justice protests against
  methodological approach to, 95–97
  public support for, 96
police forces, support of
  defund the police movement and, 120–121
  racial justice movements and, 108–113
  Biden ratings influenced by, 117
  changes in, 112–113
  measurement indices for public support, 108–112
  news coverage as influence on, 112–113
  psychological predispositions and, 109, 113
  by race, 102
  Trump ratings and, 117
  during 2020 presidential election, 96
political partisanship. *See* partisanship
political polarization. *See* partisanship; polarization
presidential debates. *See also* October presidential debate; September presidential debate
  during 1960 presidential election, 39
  during 1976 presidential election, 39–40
  during 2004 presidential election, 40
  voter impact from, 40
priming voters, 70
  after Trump diagnosis for COVID, 83–90
Progressive Movement, 16

psychological predispositions. *See also* authoritarianism; citizen-centered theory of campaigns; conflict avoidance; conspiracy thinking; racial resentment
  assessment of, 196–200
  candidate evaluations influenced by, 150, 151, 156–157
  during COVID-19 pandemic, 76–79
  to authoritarianism, 77–78, 81
  to conflict avoidance, 78–79, 81
  to conspiracy thinking, 76–77, 81
  racism and, 78, 81–82
  to sexism, 78, 81–82
  for election integrity confidence, 128, 132, 137–138
  for police support, 109, 113
  for racial justice protests, 99–101, 106–108
  voter participation and turnout influenced by, 169–171, 178–179, 181
  conflict avoidance, 170
  conspiracy thinking and, 170–171
  voter preference changes influenced by, 159
public trust, in U.S. government, 207–208
  confidence in election integrity and, 127–128
Putin, Vladimir, 19

QAnon, 23

race. *See also* racial stereotyping; racial unrest; racism
  police support influenced by, 102
  public worries about COVID-19 pandemic by, 82
racial justice, racial relations and, public response to. *See also* Black Lives Matter movement; Floyd, George, murder of; police forces
  by age, 102
  assessment and contextualization of, 103–108
  authoritarianism and, 100
  Biden support of, 98
  Biden support of, electoral consequences for, 114–118
  citizens' support for racial justice protests, 103–108
  changes in, 107–108

racial justice, racial relations (cont.)
  demographic factors for, 108
  measurement of, 103–106
  political partisanship and, 108
  psychological predispositions and, 106–108
  variables for, 104
 conflict avoidance and, 100–101, 107–108
 conspiracy thinking and, 100, 107–108
 Democrat responses to, 97–99
 electoral consequences of, 113–118
  for Biden, 114–118
  thermometer ratings, 115–117
  for Trump, 114–118
 by gender, 103
 long-term implications of, 119–121
 methodological approach to, 95–97
 as most important national issue, 94–95
 partisan responses to, 97–99
  citizens' support for racial justice protests and, 108
  news coverage as influence on, 98–99
 police brutality and
  methodological approach to, 95–97
  public support for protests against, 96
 racial resentment and, 99–100
 Republican responses to, 97–99
 Trump criticism of, 97
 Trump criticism of, electoral consequences of, 114–118
 during 2020 presidential election, 97–103
  demographic characteristics, 101–103
  partisan differences in, 97–99
  political characteristics, 97–99
  psychological dispositions as factor in, 99–101
  public support for police, 96
racial resentment
 Black Lives Matter movement influenced by, 14
 election integrity confidence influenced by, 134, 137–138
 history of, 14
 as measure of racism, 15, 16
 as psychological disposition, 14–16
  for voting preferences, 15–16
 racial justice protests and, 99–100
 September 2020 presidential debate assessment influenced by, 51
 Trump response to, 14–15

racial stereotyping, September 2020 presidential debate assessment influenced by, 46–47
racial unrest, Floyd murder and, 2–3
racism. *See also* racial resentment
 during COVID-19 pandemic, 78, 81–82
 explicit measures, 15
 implicit association tests of, 15
 racial resentment as measure of, 15, 16
 systematic, 120
 threat measures, 15
 of Trump, 15
 voter turnout influenced by, 166
representative democracy, 209–210
 electoral campaigns as element of, 3
Republican National Committee (RNC), 66
Republican Party
 confidence in election integrity, 124
 coordination with Trump campaign during COVID-19 pandemic, 66
 racial justice protests and, 97–99
 response to COVID-19 pandemic, 72
resentment. *See* racial resentment
retrospective voting, during COVID-19 pandemic, 70
right-wing authoritarianism (RWA), 77–78
RNC. *See* Republican National Committee
Romney, Mitt, 122
Roosevelt, Franklin D., 4
RWA. *See* right-wing authoritarianism (RWA)

Schattschneider, E. E., 21
Schieffer, Bob, 40
Second Wave Feminist Movement, 16
*The Semi-Sovereign People* (Schattschneider), 21
September presidential debate, during 2020 election
 assessments of candidate performance, 42–54, 61–62
 authoritarian thinking as factor in, 47, 51–52
 conflict avoidance issues and, 49
 conspiracy thinking as factor in, 47, 51–52
 determinants of ratings for, 43–47
 in news media, 43–46
 performance ratings, 47–52
 political partisanship as factor in, 43, 45–46, 49

psychological predispositions as
influence on, 46, 49–50
racial resentment as influence on, 51
racial stereotyping as influence on,
46–47
sexist stereotyping as influence on,
46–47
assessments on "winner" of debate
Biden as winner, 40–42
judgments in, 52–54
political partisanship as influence on,
41–42
through polls and surveys, 40–41
regression predictions for, 1, 53
Biden and, 37
assessment of debate performance,
42–54
as debate winner, 40–42
candidate evaluations influenced by,
149, 151–152, 157–159
citizen-centered theory of campaigns
and, 38, 52
Commission on Presidential Debates,
38, 62
electoral consequences of, 54–56
negative critiques of, 37–38
October evaluations of candidates
influenced by, 56–61
changes in, 60–61
regression analysis of, 60
political partisanship and
assessments of candidate performance
by, 43, 45–46, 49
assessments on "winner" of debate
and, 41–42
Trump and, 3
assessment of debate performance,
42–54, 61–62
falsehoods by, 37
voter participation influenced by, 168
sexism. *See also* hostile sexism
ambivalent, 200–201
benevolent, 17
COVID-19 pandemic and, 78, 81–82
election integrity confidence influenced
by, 134
September 2020 presidential debate
assessment influenced by, 46–47
voter turnout influenced by, 166
social justice movements. *See also* Black
Lives Matter movement; racial
justice

as campaign issue during 2020
presidential election, 155–156
social media, campaign advertising
on, 5–6
Soros, George, conspiracy thinking
about, 23
Stephanopoulos, George, 37–38
Stop the Steal movement, 144
January 6th Capitol attacks, 144–145
superspreader events, during COVID-19
pandemic, 65, 73–74
systematic racism, Floyd murder as, 120

Tapper, Jake, 44
Taylor, Breonna, 101
Thao, Tuo, 119–120
thinking. *See* conspiracy thinking
Thomas, Clarence, 17
Tillis, Thom, 65
*Time Magazine*, 37
Todd, Chuck, 37–38
Trump, Donald, 202–204. *See also*
COVID-19 pandemic, during 2020
presidential election; electoral
campaigns; 2016 presidential
election; 2020 presidential election
American First Action, 155
authoritarianism of, 19
during 2016 presidential election,
19–20
birtherism claims by, 14
on Black Lives Matter movement, 97
claims of electoral fraud by, 3, 24,
122–125
conspiracy thinking about, 23
election integrity and, 133–134
criticism of racial justice movements, 97
electoral consequences of, 114–118
on election integrity, 133–139, 205–207
conspiracy thinking as predisposition
and, 133–134
electoral consequences for, 139–143
partisan news sources as influence on,
136–138
racial resentment as predisposition
and, 134, 137–138
sexism predispositions and, 134
thermometer models for ratings of,
139–143
variables for, 133–135
electoral campaign during 2020
presidential election

Trump, Donald (cont.)
  advisor concerns about electoral integrity claims, 147–148
  evaluation as candidate, 148–159, 162–163
  hostile sexism of, 17
    towards Harris, K., 18
  January 6th Capitol attacks, 144–145
  launch of election campaign, 15
  police support by public and, 117
  on racial resentment, 14–15
  racism of, 15
  refusal to accept electoral results, 3, 145–146
  September 2020 presidential debate and, 3
    assessment of debate performance, 42–54, 61–62
    falsehoods during, 37
  Stop the Steal movement, 144
  in 2016 presidential debates, 122–123
2000 presidential election, 205, 210
2004 presidential election, debate during, 40
2012 presidential election, in U.S., 122
2016 presidential election, in U.S.
  authoritarianism and, 19–20
  presidential debates during, 122–123
  Trump's claims of electoral fraud, 122–124
2020 presidential election, in U.S. *See also* COVID-19 pandemic, during 2020 presidential election; September presidential debate
  costs of, 1
  methodological approach to, 26–33
    with Dynata, 27
    panel design, 26–29
    samples in, 26–29
    survey questionnaire, 29–30
  methodological approaches to, 4–10
  postmortem analysis of, 202–204
  racial justice protests during, 97–103
    demographic characteristics, 101–103
    partisan differences in, 97–99
    political characteristics, 97–99
    psychological dispositions as factor in, 99–101
    public support for police, 96
  sociocultural context for, 2–3
  voter participation and turnout for, 1, 175–180
    for Black voters, 183
    campaign issues and events as influence on, 176–178
    confidence in election integrity as factor for, 169
    convenience voting and, 179–190
    COVID-19 pandemic as influence on, 168–169, 186
    dependent variables for, 175, 176
    for Latino voters, 183
    multilevel logistic model predictions for, 177
    political knowledge as factor in, 182
    psychological predispositions as influence on, 178–179
    public views on social justice protests, 169
    September debate as influence on, 168

unemployment rates, during COVID-19 pandemic, 2
United States (U.S.). *See also* COVID-19 pandemic, in U.S.; COVID-19 pandemic, during 2020 presidential election; *specific presidential elections*
  authoritarianism in, 18–19
    in 1952 presidential election, 19–20
    in 2016 presidential election, 19–20
  conspiracy thinking in, 23, 24
  Declaration of Independence, 18
  Fair Housing Act, 14
  presidential elections in, 204–210
    peaceful transfers of power after, 204–205
  public trust in government, 207–208
    confidence in election integrity and, 127–128
  Violence Against Women Act, 17

Violence Against Women Act, U.S. (1994), 17
*Vogue*, 37
voter activation centers, 67
voter fraud
  conspiracy thinking about, 24
  mail-in voting and, 123
  Trump's early claims of, 3, 24
voter participation and turnout. *See also* 2020 presidential election
  authoritarianism as influence on, 166
  campaign characteristics as factor in, 171–175

campaign issues, 180–181
negativity of campaign, 171–172
political polarization and, 172–173
campaign messaging as influence on, 180–183
convenience voting and, 183–190
demographic characteristics of citizens, 182–183
political characteristics of citizens, 182, 182
psychological predispositions and, 181
conspiracy thinking as influence on, 24
demographic characteristics as influence on, 167–168
early research on, 166–168
partisan attachment and, 166–167
political characteristics as influence on, 165–168, 173
in presidential elections from 1920–2020, 165
priming voters, 70
after Trump diagnosis for COVID, 83–90
psychological predispositions as factor in, 169–171, 178–179, 181
conflict avoidance, 170
conspiracy thinking and, 170–171
racism as influence on, 166
retrospective voting, 70
sexism as influence on, 166
voting access
campaign messaging and, 164–165
voter turnout influenced by, 174
registration requirements, 174
state by state variations in, 174–175

Wallace, Chris, 37
Warren, Earl (Chief Justice), 23
*Washington Post*, 123, 147, 148
Willkie, Wendell, 4
Wilson, Rita, 64
"winner's effect"
confidence levels among voters influenced by, 129–130
as determinant of confidence, 125–126
Woman's Suffrage Movement, 16
women. *See also* hostile sexism
#MeToo Movement, 16
Second Wave Feminist Movement, 16
Woman's Suffrage Movement, 16
Woodward, Bob, 64

Printed in the United States
by Baker & Taylor Publisher Services